Population and Revenue in the Towns of Palestine in the Sixteenth Century

Amnon Cohen and Bernard Lewis

Population and Revenue in the Towns of Palestine

in the Sixteenth Century

PRINCETON UNIVERSITY PRESS
Princeton, New Jersey

Published by Princeton University Press
Princeton, New Jersey
In the United Kingdom: Princeton University Press
Guildford, Surrey

Library of Congress Cataloging in Publication Data
will be found on the last printed page of this book

Publication of this book has been aided by grants
from the Paul Mellon Fund of Princeton University Press
and the Near Eastern Studies Department
of Princeton University

Printed in the United States of America
by Princeton University Press
Princeton, New Yersey

CONTENTS

List of Maps, Plates, and Tables	vi
Note on Transcription	viii
Preface	x

PART I · POPULATION AND REVENUE

1 · The *Taḥrīr* registers of Palestine	3
2 · Population	19
3 · Taxes and Revenues	42

PART II · THE TOWNS

4 · Jerusalem	81
5 · Hebron	107
6 · Gaza	117
7 · Ramle	135
8 · Nabulus	145
9 · Safed	155

Conclusion	
Bibliography	173
Appendix	183
Index	189
Plates	201

LIST OF MAPS, PLATES, AND TABLES

MAPS

1. Palestine 79
2. Jerusalem. Based on V. Guérin, Plan de Jérusalem, 1889 80
3. Hebron. Based on Hebron city map, municipality of Hebron, with reference to survey of Palestine, Jaffa, 1938 106
4. Gaza. Based on Militärgeographische Angaben über Palästina und Transjordanien (Berlin, 1941) 118
5. Ramle. Based on survey of Palestine, 1947 136
6. Nabulus. Based on J.-A. Jaussen, Naplouse et son district (Paris, 1927), Plate 9 146
7. Safed. Based on survey of Palestine, Jaffa, 1938 154

PLATES

1–4. Jerusalem. Register 516, fols. 14–17, showing Christian and Jewish quarters, and part of the enumeration of revenue. 201

5–6. Jerusalem. Register 289, pp. 44–6, showing the enumeration of revenues. 205

7–9. Jerusalem. Register 346 showing *Ḫāṣṣ* of Governor and new *Ḫāṣṣ*. 207

10. Hebron. Register 515 (end of quarters—enumeration of revenues). 210

11. Gaza. Register 546, fols. 10a and 48b. Beginning of enumeration of *Ḫāṣṣ* of Sultan and of Governor. 211

12. Ramle. Register 546, fols. 121b and 128b showing *Ḫāṣṣ* of Sultan and of Governor. 212

13. Nabulus. Register 549, fols. 9b and 67b, showing *Ḫāṣṣ* of Sultan and of Governor. 213

14. Safed. Register 300, synoptic survey of the Sanjak. 214

15. Safed. Register 300, pp. 41–2. Enumeration of revenues. 215

CONTENTS

LIST OF MAPS, PLATES, AND TABLES

MAPS

PLATES

TABLES OF CITIES

1. Quarters and Population of Jerusalem 92
2. Quarters and Population of Hebron 111
3. Quarters and Population of Gaza 127
4. Quarters and Population of Ramle 140
5. Quarters and Population of Nabulus 149
6. Quarters and Population of Safed 161

NOTE ON TRANSCRIPTION

THIS study, dealing with an Arabic-speaking area under Turkish administration, and based on both Turkish and Arabic sources, involves special problems of transcription. Both Arabic and Ottoman Turkish are written in the Arabic script, and Turkish also uses a large number of Arabic loanwords. Many of these are however pronounced and sometimes used differently in the two languages (rather as "revolution," common to English and French, is differently pronounced and understood). In the Arabic script these differences do not appear; in transcription they cannot be avoided.

In transcribing Turkish and Arabic names and terms in the following pages, we have used two different systems, based on those commonly used by Turkish and Arabic scholars. Broadly speaking, we have used the Turkish transcription for Turkish books, records, etc., and for the technical terms of Turkish administration; Arabic for Arabic books, classical Islamic terms (e.g., *shaykh, sharīʿa, kharāj, jizya, bayt al-māl, mujāwir, mukhallafāt*), and place names. Many Ottoman terms are a mixture of Turkish, Persian, and Arabic words and grammatical forms. In these we have followed the dominant, usually the Turkish, pattern. Where a word or name has already passed into English usage (e.g., kadi, sanjak, waqf, or the names of the six towns discussed in this book) we have used the accepted form.

The main differences between the two systems are as follows:

Turkish	Arabic
c	j
e	a
ğ	gh
ḫ	kh
ḳ	ḳ or q (here ḳ only)
s̱	th
ş	sh
v	w
ẕ	dh
ż	ḍ

In addition, Turkish uses some letters unknown to Arabic. The most important are:

ç	ch as in *church*
ı	i something between *i* as in *will* and *u* as in *radium*

In the siyāḳat script used in Ottoman finance registers, diacritical dots are commonly omitted; the reading of names and terms is therefore often difficult without previous knowledge, and sometimes conjectural even then. In the enumeration of the city quarters beginning page 81 below and in a few other places, we have as far as possible reproduced the original text in Arabic script, and given our own reading in transcription.

PREFACE

THIS book has a long and somewhat disturbed history. It begins in 1949 when I was given permission to work in the Prime Minister's Archives (*Başbakanlık Arşivi*) in Istanbul, and elected to study the registers of land, population, and revenue relating to the countries of the Fertile Crescent during the first century of Ottoman rule. My intention was not to attempt a general history of the area in this period but rather to make a series of studies in detail at selected points—soundings in the registers, dealing with limited topics and related to specific areas. I decided to begin with Palestine, which offered the richest documentation from outside sources and also, at that time, some advantages of access. For these reasons it seemed the most promising starting point for what was then a venture into virtually unknown territory. After a preliminary study on "the Ottoman archives as a source for the history of the Arab lands," published in the *Journal of the Royal Asiatic Society* in October 1951, I began to prepare a series of articles, the first of which was published in the *Bulletin of the School of Oriental and African Studies* in 1954, under the title "Studies in the Ottoman Archives—I." This presented a picture of Palestine in the early Ottoman period and was intended as an introduction to the material as a whole. My plan at that time was to follow it with a documented analysis of the quarters, population, and taxation of the six towns in Palestine, and then after that to do further studies on selected rural and urban areas in Syria and Iraq. The second of the articles, dealing with Jerusalem, was already written, and a Hebrew version was published in the Israeli periodical *Jerusalem* in 1956; transcripts and drafts on the other cities of Palestine were in various stages of preparation.

At this point my work was interrupted by the news that a further supply of registers, relating to the same period and area, was to be found in the archives of the Survey and Cadastral office in Ankara (*Tapu ve Kadastro Müdürlüğü*). My studies hitherto had been based exclusively on registers in the archives in Istanbul. The material in Ankara was of the same type and although, as it later emerged, it was not very considerable in quantity, it nevertheless promised important additional material, particularly on the later years of the period. For some time it was impossible to obtain the necessary permission and facilities to consult these registers, and in the circumstances I could not proceed. To work with incomplete documentation is difficult, but possible. To work in the knowledge that further relevant information is extant but not yet accessible is quite another matter. There seemed every reason to hope that in a not too distant future the registers in Ankara, like those in Istanbul, would be made accessible to scholarly research; until that time there was no choice but to set this task aside, and to turn to other matters.

In due course the archives at the Survey and Cadastral Office in Ankara were indeed partially opened to scholarship, and some measure of access was permitted. By that time however I was otherwise engaged, and was not able to resume my long interrupted studies.

A fortunate encounter with Dr. Amnon Cohen of the Hebrew University in Jerusalem provided a solution to the problem. Dr. Cohen had published an important monograph on Palestine in the eighteenth century, as well as a number of articles on other aspects of Palestinian history in the Ottoman period. In response to my invitation, he agreed to join with me in completing the study of the relevant documents and the preparation of the resulting book. The reading of the Ankara registers, as well as of some additional material which subsequently came to light in Istanbul and Jerusalem, is entirely due to Dr. Cohen, to whom I am also indebted for a great deal of local, topographical, and other knowledge which would have been beyond my own resources. What follows consists of my own original drafts, amended and amplified by Dr. Cohen, and new matter written by him; the final text was seen and revised by both authors.

There remains the pleasant task of expressing my thanks to the various institutions that have helped in the preparation of this work—first to the directors and the administration of the Prime Minister's Archives in Istanbul and of the Survey and Cadastral Office in Ankara; then to the trustees of Mishkenot Shaananim in Jerusalem, who by inviting me to stay there in 1973–1974 as their guest, provided me with the leisure and opportunity to carry out an important part of this work; finally to the School of Oriental and African Studies in the University of London, to Princeton University, and to the Institute for Advanced Study in Princeton, all of which have contributed in various ways toward making this book possible. A special word of thanks is due to Mr. Ehud Toledano, for his help in preparing the typescript for the press.

Princeton, 18 August 1975 BERNARD LEWIS

For an Israeli (then Palestinian) born student of the Middle East it is natural, perhaps, to be attracted by the history of his own country. Having spent some time and much energy on research of Ottoman Palestine in later periods further accentuated my interest and created yet another stimulus for an attempt to figure out the formative years of that rule during the sixteenth century.

Professor B. Lewis's suggestion that we combine my interest with his knowledge in an attempt to study and analyze the Ottoman *taḥrīr* registers was first mentioned to me during the International Congress of Orientalists in Canberra, Australia. I regarded it not only as a compliment but also as a challenge, which in spite of my doubts I could not decline. In retrospect, the academic year of 1972–3 which I spent in London turned out to be not only most pleasant but also very instructive from many respects. For this I would like first and foremost, to thank Professor B. Lewis for the guidance and inspiration he offered me throughout our joint enterprise. My stay in Great Britain was facilitated by the hospitality and kindness of the School of Oriental and African Studies of the University of London. The British Council was generous in financing another part of that year in London. To both institutions I am most grateful. Last but not least may I thank Carta, Jerusalem, for drawing the town-sketches, and the Hebrew University of Jerusalem for its own contribution to the creation and the completion of this work.

Jerusalem, 8 October 1975 — Amnon Cohen

PART I

POPULATION AND REVENUE

• 1 •

THE *TAḤRIR* REGISTERS OF PALESTINE

THE Ottoman *taḥrīr* was the latest form of an institution which can be traced back to classical Islamic times and beyond, to the bureaucracies of the ancient Middle Eastern empires. The term denoted the work of commissions sent to survey tax-paying population, lands, crops and revenues in the towns and villages for fiscal purposes. The data collected in this way was then recorded (*taḥrīr*—writing down, recording in writing) in registers. In early Islamic times this was known as the *ḳānūn*, and fragments of such registers have survived among the Egyptian papyri. There are frequent references to them in the Arabic sources of the Mamluk period, and also in those of the Seljuq and Mongol régimes, though few examples, and those fragmentary, are known.[1] The Ottoman state is the only one of the classical Islamic empires which survived into modern times—the only one, therefore, whose records, when no longer required for practical administrative purposes, were not scattered and destroyed like those of earlier, vanished Empires, but preserved, thanks to the enlightened care of a generation of scholars and officials who realized their value.

The commission which carried out the *taḥrīr* was called *taḥrīr heyeti*, and produced registers (*defter*), known as *Tapu*[2] *defterleri*. The series as a whole was sometimes called the Imperial Register—*Defter-i Ḫāḳānī*.[3] These registers are of three main kinds:[4] (a) *Defter-i Mufaṣṣal* ("detailed register"), which are the most interesting and valuable; (b) *Defter-i Icmāl* ("synoptic inventory") which give a summary based on the *mufaṣṣal*, omitting details like names of

[1] Lewis, "Daftar," *EI*², vol. II, pp. 79–81.

[2] "*tāpū*", an abbreviation of "*tāpū senedi*"—land certificate accepting the conditions of service. Originally "an act of homage" it is used to designate both the title-deed and the fee payable for it, for the holding of a landed estate (Ménage, *Bulletin of the School of Oriental and African Studies (BSOAS)*, vol. XXXVI (1973), p. 658; Redhouse, *A Turkish and English Lexicon*, s.v; Fekete, *Die Siyāqat-Schrift*, p. 218, n. 14.

[3] Barkan, s.v., *EI*², vol. II, pp. 81–3; I. H. Uzunçarşılı, *Merkez ve bahriye teşkilatı*, pp. 95–110; Fekete, *Die Siyāqat-Schrift*, pp. 75–84.

[4] Lewis, *Journal of the Royal Asiatic Society (JRAS)* (1951), pp. 146–9.

taxpayers/inhabitants and giving the taxes only in lump-sums for each territorial unit; (c) *Defter-i der dest* ("register of [matters] in hand") and *Defter-i Rūznāmçe* ("daybook"), respectively records of incoming information and deeds of grant (*berāt*) copies as they occurred.

As far as we know the usual procedure was to make these in two copies.[5] One was kept in the central registry (*Tapu, Defterḫāne*); the other copy went to the province, to be kept together with the *sijill* registers in the *sharīʿa* court. The only sample of these that has come to light in Palestine is a *mufaṣṣal taḥrīr* dated 997/1588–9, of the sanjak of Jerusalem. Identical with the copy left in the capital, it was kept intact (and because of its length was not copied like other official documents) at the *sharīʿa* court of Jerusalem.[6]

Most of the surviving registers for sixteenth-century Palestine are in Istanbul, a few of them damaged, the rest intact.[7] In the course of the classification of the *Maliyeden müdevver* (i.e., transferred from the Archives of the Ministry of Finance) series in the *Başbakanlık* archives in Istanbul, during the last few years, some additional defters have come to light. There may have been others which existed and are now lost. Some registers, mainly dating back to the second half of the century, are in the Cadastral Office in Ankara.[8] This study is based mainly on *mufaṣṣal* registers, with some complementary information from the available *icmāls*, most of them in Istanbul. Of the registers kept in Ankara we were able to use only nos. 515–516 (Jerusalem), 545 (Gaza) and 549 (Nabulus).

There is conflicting evidence with regard to the frequency with which *taḥrīrs* should have been, or actually were, carried out in the Ottoman Empire. Luṭfī Pasha, who under Süleymān the Magnificent reached the post of Grand Vizier, and who previously served

[5] Cf. Fekete, *Belleten*, vol. XI (1947), p. 302.

[6] *Sijill* registers of the *sharīʿa* court in Jerusalem, vol. LXX. It should, however, be noted, that although dated 997 A.H. it was actually identical with the *tahrir* of 970 A.H. This is the only available copy which, to our knowledge, actually remained in a local court in this area. It is clear from its phrasing that this was only a copy, while the original was kept in Istanbul: ṣuret-i defter-i cedīd-i mufaṣṣal-ı livā-i Küds-i Şerīf budur ki naḳl olundu taḥrīren fī evāsıṭ-i Rebīʿ ül-āḫır sene 977.

[7] A descriptive list of these registers is found in B. Lewis, *JRAS* (1951), pp. 154 ff.

[8] For Palestine: *mufaṣṣal* registers as listed below, pp. 13–14. Volumes of other categories are as follows: Jerusalem: waqf no 514 (539) for 970/1562–3; *der dest* nos. 518–519. Safed: *mufaṣṣal* no. 541 (72) for 955/1548–9; *icmāl* no. 542 (312) (n.d.); Gaza: *icmāl* no. 547 (337) (n.d.); Nabulus: waqf no. 548 (546) for 1005/1596–7; *icmāl* no. 550 (320) (n.d.); Lejjūn: *mufaṣṣal* no. 535 (181) for 1005/1596–7; ʿAjlūn: *mufaṣṣal* no. 532 (185) for 1005/1596–7; *icmāls* nos. 533–4 (269–352) (n.d.).

in many provinces, including Syria, was very specific about it: "A *taḥrīr* should be carried out [once] in [every] thirty years."[9] The same figure[10] is repeated in the following century by another high-ranking official, Sarı Meḥmed Paṣha.[11] It is on this evidence, apparently, that Barkan speaks of "les recensements de la population et de l'impôt, recensements qui étaient faits tous les 30 ou 40 ans, suivant une ancienne tradition administrative."[12] An undated firman cited by Barkan adds formal support to the above-mentioned quotations from authoritative but informal "advice for rulers": "The *taḥrīr* of the Empire is a very necessary thing. [The carrying out of a] *taḥrīr* of the Empire once every thirty years is a *ḳānūn*. It should be regarded as binding in this matter."[13] On the other hand, Muṣṭafā Nūrī, in *Netāʾic ül-vuḳūʿāt* stresses the importance of carrying out a *taḥrīr* after the conquest of a province,[14] but adds that it was "usually" accomplished once every century, and was in any case discontinued after the time of Selīm II.[15] There is even a version reducing the interval between the *taḥrīrs* to an impossible one year.[16] Barkan[17] not only found a *taḥrīr* made in Murād III's time, i.e. after the death of Selīm II, but seems to have traced the reason for this administrative-fiscal initiative back to the inauguration of every new Sultan as part and parcel of the issue of new (or reaffirmed) official decrees and nominations. *Taḥrīrs* were still made at a comparatively late date for newly acquired provinces, e.g. seven registers compiled during the reigns of Aḥmed III (1115–43/1703–30), and Maḥmūd I (1143–68/1730–54) of the new provinces added to the empire as a result of the Ottoman intervention in Persian affairs at that time.[18]

Kaldy Nagy seems to disagree with Barkan's assumption, noting that only once did he find in the Hungarian provinces that

---

[9] Luṭfī Paṣa, *Āṣaf-nāme*, p. 41: otuz yılda bir taḥrīr olunup. For Luṭfī's biography see p. IX.
[10] Cf. Makrīzī, *Khiṭaṭ*, who mentions every thirty years in Egypt ("Daftar," *EI*²).
[11] Wright, *Ottoman Statecraft*, p. 74 text, p. 119 (translation).
[12] Barkan, *Journal of Economic and Social History of the Orient (JESHO)*, vol. I (1958), p. 11.
[13] "Tahrīr-i memleket gayet lâzimdir. Otuz yılda bir kere tahrīr-i memleket kanundur. Bu hususa tekayyüd lâzimidir" (Barkan, *İstanbul Üniversitesi, İktisat Fakültesi Mecmuası [IFM]*, vol. II (1941), p. 12, n. 14).
[14] (Vol. I, p. 143) "fetḥ-i memālik vāḳiʿ oldukça erāżīsi taḥrīr ettirilip."
[15] Muṣṭafā Nūrī, *Netāʾic ül-vuḳūʿāt*, vol. I, p. 145.
[16] Ahmet Rasim, cited in Tunçer, *Toprak hukuku*, p. 77.
[17] Barkan, *IFM*, vol. II (1941), pp. 14–17.
[18] Lewis, in *Mélanges Massé* (Teheran, 1963), pp. 259–63.

a new register was compiled on the accession of a new sovereign.[19] On this occasion the new *taḥrīr* was ordered by the Ottoman authorities only nine years after the previous one, a much shorter interval than that indicated by Luṭfī or the undated firman. The view that a *taḥrīr* is determined by a specific cause rather than a fixed time-limit, is partly shared by Inalcık. A *taḥrīr* was made, he says,[20] either upon the conquest of a new province of the Empire or upon the advent of a new Sultan or when substantial changes with regard to income occurred (the introduction of revenues previously extraneous to the register, fiscal reforms or unforeseen changes). In this respect Inalcık reflects Barkan's interpretation of the *taḥrīrs* as attempts made by the central administration to bring its existing information up to date, and in particular to increase its potential income by reappraising the yields of a given area in the light of its development. It was "in any case for the advantage of the State"[21] that frequent *taḥrīrs* were carried out in the heyday of the Empire. This explanation seems more plausible than Luṭfī's arbitrary assertion: "The dead and the sick being omitted there should be a re-registration and a comparison with the old register; the [number of] *reʿāyā* should not be smaller than [it was in] the old register."[22] This oversimplified presentation can hardly be substantiated by the evidence in our registers. Although the copy of the previous register was given to the *taḥrīr*-takers,[23] it did not serve, as far as we can deduce from our registers, as anything more than an important reference book. The firmans authorizing the *taḥrīr* are very explicit on this matter. In the Sanjak of Gaza, for instance, the *taḥrīr* was to be very carefully compiled as a "revised (*tecdīd*) version of the old registers" after those responsible have "meticulously investigated[24] . . . the yields of that province" in accordance with both the *Sharīʿa* and the *Ḳānūn*. Similar terminology is used in the firman concerning the *taḥrīr* of the Sanjak of Safed.[25]

[19] Kaldy-Nagy, *Acta Orientalia academiae scientiarum Hungaricae*, vol. XXI (1968), pp. 186–7.

[20] Inalcık, *Defter-i sancak-i Arvanid*, p. xviii.

[21] Barkan, *IFM*, vol. II (1941), p. 4.

[22] "Mürde ve marīżi çıkıp tekrār yazılmak gerek ve eski defter ile taṭbīk olunup reʿāyā eski defterden noḳṣān üzere olmamak gerek" (*Āṣaf-nāme*, p. 41).

[23] Cf. Kaldy-Nagy, *Acta Orientalia*, vol. XXI (1968), p. 193. For further details see Gökbilgin, *Edirne ve Paşa livası*, p. 103 passim.

[24] Register 304, p. 23, kemā hū ḥaḳḳuhu taḥḳīḳ ve tedkīk olunmağın, dated 1 Rajab 964.

[25] Register 300, p. 6. A *ḳānūn* of Süleymān the Magnificent indicates it very clearly: "efrād-i nāsdan bir ferd ve ebvâb-i mahsulâttan bir habbe cüzʾi ve külli harici-ez-defter nesne kalmayub" (Barkan, *IFM*, vol. II [1941], p. 21). For a similar description

What, in fact, can the historian hope to learn from these registers? Their value obviously lies in two fields, the demographic and the economic, in both of which they provide considerable quantities of detail, statistics and information extending over a significant period of time. Their value, however, in both respects, has been very differently assessed by modern scholars. For Barkan they offer "en un mot, tout ce qu'il faut à un historien économiste."[26] For Kaldy Nagy, on the other hand, they "register the taxes and tithes which, as we believe, were not yet actually collected at the time of the census" and exhibit "the estimated income" as opposed to an account of the actual receipts.[27] Cook's assessment of their value for historical demography is even more negative: "the demographic interest of this material is severely limited. It is in general totally uninformative as to the age and sex structure of the population. It does, however, purport to list the overwhelming majority of the adult male population, and to indicate which of them were heads of households. By comparing such lists for given areas at different times it is possible to derive crude indices of changes in population size."[28]

Our own study of the defters relating to sixteenth-century Palestine lead us to adopt an intermediate position in both respects. Certainly they cannot be regarded as an "ideal form" as was once suggested.[29] The figures given for the individual taxes represent global estimates of what is expected rather than statements of the amounts actually collected, and are moreover stated in a money of account. Often the global figure represents the purchase price agreed with a tax-farmer, and even with taxes directly collected by government commissioners the figure is notional rather than practical.[30] In addition there are numerous technical deficiencies, such as faulty spelling of names (places and quarters as well as people), inconsistent terminology and usage (Arabic and Turkish forms interchanging, different names given for apparently the same taxes, variations in the grouping of revenues with a single total figure for several taxes) inaccurate

see Muṣṭafā Nūrī, *Netā'ic ül-Vuḳū'āt*, vol. I, p. 143; Uzunçarşılı, *Merkez ve bahriye teşkilatı*, pp. 97, 102.

[26] Barkan, *JESHO*, vol. I (1958), p. 12. Tunçer, *Toprak hukuku*, p. 76 uses even higher superlatives.

[27] Kaldy-Nagy, *Acta Orientalia*, vol. XXI (1968), p. 183; vol. XIII (1961), p. 32.

[28] Cook, *Population Pressure*, pp. 8–9.

[29] Tunçer, *Toprak hukuku*, p. 76.

[30] On the difference between the sums pledged and those actually collected in the eighteenth century see: Cohen, *Palestine in the eighteenth Century*, pp. 197–9.

transliteration, incomplete statistics, mistakes of arithmetic, and sometimes a time-lag behind the pace of events.[31]

Nevertheless, despite these defects, the registers remain a most interesting and valuable source for certain aspects of the history of Palestine during almost the whole of the first century of Ottoman rule. The value of this information can be seen all the more clearly when we contrast it with what is available for earlier and even for later centuries. On the matters with which they deal, there is no period in the history of Palestine on which we have better information, until the time when historical study is facilitated, if that is the right word, by the bureaucratic activities of the modern state. It is sufficient to contrast the registers with the fragmentary and contradictory scraps of information gathered from European consular reports and travellers' accounts to see how valuable they are.

On the economic side some of the information in the registers is factual in that the figures given are related to amounts actually collected and remitted.[32] Even when the figures are notional they are of value, and represent the latest development of a long bureaucratic tradition. Already in classical Islam, both in theoretical and documentary evidence, a distinction appears between *aṣl* and *istikhrāj*, the first representing the initial assessment and estimate, the second the amount actually collected.[33] The figures, therefore, represent a genuine stage in the process of financial administration and not random fantasy. The fact that we have a sequence of registers over a period of time, and some outside evidence to serve as control, enables us to use these figures to document the processes of development and change. They tell us little of events or individuals, for the movements they reflect are at a deeper level, and at a slower rhythm. Through them we can achieve some insight into the social and economic patterns of the time, the structure and movement of society and administration, the evolution of groups and institutions. More

[31] To quote two examples: the earthquake in Jaffa in 1546 is said by European travellers to have caused considerable damage in Palestine. This is not reflected in the defters (Lewis, *Necati Lugal Armağanı* (1969), p. 443). Similarly, the expulsion of the Frankish monks from their convent on Mount Zion in the years 1551–2 is not referred to in the relevant register and entry as one would have expected (cf. below, p. 87, n. 36). Cf. "The surveys do not state the case for a bad year, a year of war or famine," McGowan, *Archivum Ottomanicum*, vol. I (1969), p. 147.

[32] The *taḥrir* registers are thus basically different from the *mühimme defterleri* in that they contain what in modern parlance is called statistical matter—statements and tabulations of data on the existing situation in various fields of administration. For the differences between these two sources see: Heyd, *Ottoman Documents*, pp. xv–xvii; Halasi Kun, in *Türk Dili ve Tarihi hakkında Araştırmalar* (1952), pp. 82 ff.

[33] Bosworth, *JESHO*, vol. XII (1969), pp. 123–4; "Daftar," *EI*[2], vol. II, pp. 79–81.

particularly we can draw both detailed information and more general conclusions on topics like numbers and distribution of population, taxation, land-tenure, religious minorities, towns, villages, and nomads. Any given register provides a general as well as detailed, though static, picture of these and other aspects at a given moment; the series of registers for the districts of Palestine, though sometimes incomplete, covers virtually the whole country and almost the whole century.

The same considerations apply to the demographic as to the economic data. For the eighteenth and most of the nineteenth century, not to speak of earlier times, the evidence available to us makes it impossible to answer (except by guesswork) even such simple and obvious questions as the number of inhabitants and their religious and ethnic distribution. While the registers cannot answer the modern demographer's questions on such matters as family size and age and sex structure, they nevertheless give useful indications on the composition and distribution of population, on the rise and fall of numbers, within regions and within identified groups, and also on the movements of nomadic groups from one place to another. These data are more difficult to extrapolate than age and sex structure, and the information provided is correspondingly more valuable. Even estimates and still more assessments are usually done with some reference to reality, and their recurrence or modification is always meaningful. When compared with each other and tabulated for the whole century they provide an indication of the major fiscal and demographic trends of development in this period.

A word may be pertinent at this stage with regard to the term Palestine. This term had already ceased to have any political or administrative significance before the arrival of the crusaders; it was revived with the establishment of the British Mandate, when it was officially adopted as the name of the country. It has, therefore, no precise geographical connotation but is here used to cover the western or cisjordanian part of the state set up under British Mandate, after the partition of Ottoman Syria. Under the late Mamluks this area was divided into the *niyābas* of Safed and Gaza, both under the authority of the Mamluk viceroy in Damascus. After the Ottoman conquest the country was divided into the four sanjaks (in Arabic, *liwāʾ*) of Jerusalem, Gaza, Nabulus and Safed, the last-named including part of what is now southern Lebanon. In the earliest Ottoman period the central area around Jenīn constituted a separate entity known as the *iḳṭāʿ* of Ṭurābāy and enjoying a special status. Later this was abolished and this area incorporated in the ordinary Ottoman system most of it in the Sanjaḳ of Lejjun.

The fifteen[34] *mufaṣṣals* used in this work fall into six groups corresponding to six separate surveys conducted in the sixteenth century in Palestine. The dates of these surveys, with the sanjaks covered in the registers consulted are:

1. 932/1525–6	Jerusalem, Gaza, Safed
2. *ca.* 945/1538–9	Jerusalem, Gaza, Safed, Nabulus
3. 955/1548–9	Gaza, Nabulus
4. 961–4/1553–7	Jerusalem, Gaza, Safed
5. 970–*ca.* 975/1562–7	Jerusalem, Safed
6. 1005/1596–7	Jerusalem, Gaza, Nabulus

Unfortunately, the series is far from complete and even some of the available volumes are defective and lack important sections. The surviving registers from the first years of Ottoman rule in Syria suggest that *taḥrīrs* were carried out at very frequent intervals.[35] The distribution of registers as tabulated above could mean that each date represents a year in which a general *taḥrīr* was conducted in the province of Damascus, including the four sanjaks with which we are concerned. If this is so, then *taḥrīrs* were carried out at far greater frequency than either prescribed by Luṭfī or suggested by Barkan and Inalcık, and the evidence relating to the *taḥrīrs* for Palestine imposes some qualification of the explanations cited above. They were not undertaken immediately after the occupation, but rather about seven years later, no doubt because of the unstable conditions prevailing in the early years. It may well be that *taḥrīrs* were commissioned by newly invested Sultans, and in point of fact we have examples of *taḥrīrs* dating from the reign of Süleymān, Selīm II, Meḥmed III; in the last two cases the *taḥrīrs* available were carried out a short time after their accession. But this was by no means the only occasion, nor was the ten year interval of Hungary[36] applicable to our case: sometimes, as shown by the above table, the interval was substantially shorter. It seems that the pace of events, economic development (due, no doubt, to such factors as greater security, better administration, Jewish immigration, and the advantages of incorporation in a large and thriving empire) was the main reason which dictated the frequency of *taḥrīrs,* though one should not exclude the possibility that reshuffles in

[34] The ten registers listed in Lewis, *JRAS* (October 1951), pp. 154–5, plus register 17738 *Maliyeden müdevver* in Istanbul, and four registers from Ankara (see p. 12).

[35] For a detailed list of registers in Istanbul see Lewis, in *JRAS* (1951), pp. 149–55.

[36] Kaldy-Nagy, *Acta Orientalia,* vol. XXI (1968), pp. 186–7.

the administration in Istanbul (and perhaps even Damascus) also had a bearing on it. The *taḥrīrs* did not stop with Selīm II,[37] nor does the quality of their findings, editing or compilation deteriorate after the time of Süleymān. From the evidence available with regard to sixteenth-century Palestine we cannot substantiate the claim[38] that technically a correlation existed between the actual conditions in the country and the final form of the records left behind. Whereas this assertion seems right with regard to the first half of the century, during the heyday of the Empire, no significant deterioration in the standard of the *defters* can be traced when the economy and administration were declining. There seems, however, to have been a certain slowing-down in the pace and frequency in which *taḥrirs* were conducted in the last twenty years of the century; this might have basically been a result of the general deterioration of administration and economy, and thus of both the need and the skill to carry out *taḥrīrs* as previously.

The *mufaṣṣal* registers commonly begin with the *ḳānūnnāme* setting forth in detail the fiscal practice and regulations of the province.[39] The earliest of these, usually drafted soon after the conquest of the province, is normally a codification of existing procedure. The later ones show some of the changes introduced by the Ottomans (e.g., the *ḳānūnnāme* of Gaza reproduced in Register 546 dated 1005/1596–7 mentions an increase in the rate of *Jizya* levied as compared with the older version, register 304, dated 964/1556–7).[40] Some of the *defters* also have introductions, tables of contents, and systematized summaries of the data they contain. In some cases, the *ḳānūnnāme* is preceded by a long firman ordering its compilation and mentioning specifically the names of those entrusted with this task. In the registers dating from the end of the century this is replaced by a few lines indicating the sultan on whose orders it was carried out, the year in which the register was handed over to the *defterḫāne* and the names of both the high-

[37] As claimed by Muṣṭafā Nūrī, *Netā'ic ül-vuḳū'āt*, vol. I, p. 145. Nor is Barkan's reference to Murād III as the last Sultan to have had *taḥrīrs* conducted, in *IFM*, Vol. II (1941), p. 13) convincing. Our *taḥrīrs* of 1005/1596–7 were explicitly ordered by Meḥmed III (Register 515, p. 1).

[38] Barkan, *IFM*, vol. II (1941), pp. 5–6.

[39] Cf. Fekete, *Belleten*, vol. XI (1947), pp. 308–10.

[40] "[On the *jizya* paid] according to the old *kānūn* an addition (*ziyāde*) of five aspers [levied from] each Christian and ten aspers [levied from] every Jew [was ordered] upon the accession (*Cülūs-ı Hümāyūn*) of the Sultan." On the question of the rate of calculation of the *jizya* in Ottoman silver currency see below, p. 71.

ranking official commissioned for this task and the scribe who actually did the writing. It appears that both at the beginning and at the end of the period, the same officials were in charge of some of the sanjaks of Palestine.

After the introductory matter comes the chief town of the sanjak followed by the districts (*nāḥiye*) which are divided into villages. Two sanjaks, Jerusalem and Gaza, are divided into two districts, each headed by a town from which it takes its name (in addition to the two already mentioned, Hebron and Ramle, respectively). Thus the major administrative centres in Palestine in the sixteenth century are the only six towns: Jerusalem, Hebron, Gaza, Ramle, Nabulus, and Safed. All other places in Palestine are classed as villages, though some of them (see p. 19) reach a considerable size. Some of the famous towns of ancient and modern times, on the other hand, really are no more than villages—as Acre, Jaffa, Bethlehem, Tyre (at this time part of the sanjaks of Safed), Nazareth. These six towns of Palestine form the subject of this study.

The following is a list of the *mufaṣṣal* registers[41] from which statistical information on the towns was obtained. Their whereabouts are indicated by I for Istanbul and A for Ankara.

Jerusalem and Hebron:	427 (932 H.)	I
	1015 (945 H.)	I
	289 (961 H.)	I
	342 (970 H.)	I
	346 (970 H.)	I
	516 (970 H.)	A
	515 (1005 H.)	A
Gaza and Ramle:	427 (932 H.)	I
	1015 (945 H.)	I
	265 (955 H.)	I
	304 (964 H.)	I
	546 (1005 H.)	A
Nabulus:	1038 (*ca.* 945 H.)	I
	258 (955 H.)	I
	549 (1005 H.)	A
Safed:	427 (932 H.)	I
	1038 (*ca.* 945 H.)	I
	300 (963 H.)	I
	17738 (*ca.* 975 H.)	I

[41] With the sole exception of 346, which is an *Icmāl* register.

The town (*kaṣaba, şehir, madīna*)[42] is referred to as *nefs-i* followed by its name. When compared with the other formulae used in the same registers (*ḳarye-i, mezraʿa-i* etc.) this may be slightly misleading, as the latter words have the precise denotation of "village" and "uninhabited village". That, probably, is why *nefs* is sometimes regarded as a special category "meaning, usually, a city."[43] Gökbilgin[44] is much more precise in taking the whole as a compound term *(nefs-i şehir ve ḳaşaba)*. *Nefs*, of course, is the Arabic word *nafs*, meaning "the same," "itself." It is true that in our texts it appears together with "town," but this does not give it any new connotation. *Nefs-i x*, meaning "x itself" or "x proper," is the Ottoman way of distinguishing "x [the town] itself" from "x the district," both bearing the same name. This is the situation in Palestine. In other provinces *nefs* is said to have been used to designate a town which does not have anything in common with the name of the larger administrative unit to which it belonged.[45] It is old Islamic practice to use the same name for a province or even a country and for its capital city. Thus, Miṣr means Egypt or Cairo, S̲h̲ām means Syria or Damascus, etc. Most provinces and districts are known by the name of the town which was their administrative center. The administrative centers of *nāḥiyes*, other than those of the provincial capitals, are usually no more than villages. In such cases the *nāḥiye* is usually named after the chief village, which is itself designated *nefs-i*. Hebron and Ramla, the only towns which are not the administrative centers of sanjaks, are designated *nefs-i*.

The population of the town is the first category recorded, each quarter (*maḥalle*) appearing under a separate heading, probably regarded as a distinct unit.[46] (In different defters the quarters in the cities and the villages in the provinces are listed in different sequence, probably indicating different routes taken by the *taḥrīr* commissions.) Below the heading are listed the inhabitants of the

[42] *şehir* and *ḳaşaba* are both technical terms of Ottoman administration. The first denotes a town as such, the second is used more specifically of the administrative centre of a district. The word *madīna* does not form part of the Ottoman technical vocabulary, and in these registers is used only of Hebron, see below, p. 112, n 19. In Hungary, as noted by Fekete, the term *şehir* was applied to a place where a kadı was established (*Belleten*, vol. XI [1947], p. 310). In Palestine this term was used also when a deputy-judge (*nāʾib*) functioned.

[43] N. Göyünc (*Mardin Sancağı*, p. 56, n. 5), who even wonders if *nefs* does not imply "the place where the kadi is."

[44] Gökbilgin, *Edirne ve Paşa livası*, p. 11.

[45] In Rumelia, as demonstrated by Gökbilgin, *Belleten*, vol. XX (1956), pp 253–61.

[46] When a table of contents appears at the beginning of the register, the quarters are listed separately, like the villages.

quarter, householders or bachelors, in lines of five to seven names each. At the end of each list the total of the inhabitants of that quarter is usually given, with a breakdown of their different categories.

A word may be said about the accuracy of the population figures. There is sometimes a discrepancy between the figure given for the inhabitants of a *maḥalle* and the number of names appearing in the corresponding list. These discrepancies, due to carelessness or to other unexplained factors, are usually small, and do not much affect the general statistical picture. The same is true of the very few instances where a total is given for a whole town, independently of the figures given for the individual quarters or communities. There are, however, some instances where a line of names or several lines escaped the eye of the scribe when he copied the register, so that the total appears larger than its components put together. The opposite case, in which the names listed add up to a slightly higher figure than the given total, also occurs. When transcribing the registers we have given both versions, adding the results arrived at by our calculations in square brackets. In the tabulation, however, we have usually referred to the higher figure available.

The quarters were usually ethnically and religiously homogeneous. However, there are instances when more than one element is specifically referred to in a given quarter. Christians and Jews, and sometimes other elements (e.g., Mamluk Jundīs, Kurds, Turcomans) are indicated, as are also persons exempt from taxation (*muʿāf*). Christians and Jews are also frequently subdivided into their various communities (Orthodox, Coptic, Armenian, Latin, etc., and Sefardic, Ashkenazi, Oriental, Samaritan,[47] etc.). The basic classification of the population, for fiscal purposes, is into three classes:

1. Tax-paying households (*ḫāne*). A married man with his family, constituting a fiscal unit. Only the name of the householder appears in the lists, and there is no way to state positively the number of persons in each household. Varying considerably from one case to another, the average family seems to have been slightly larger than it is in the modern times. The coefficient used by different scholars in this respect tends to oscillate between five and seven.[48] We

[47] Though opposed to and by rabbinical Judaism, they basically adhere to the law of Moses, but reject the prophets. Even the fact that they were the first to accuse the Jews of tampering with the Holy Scripture did not stop the Ottoman government from regarding them, for taxation purposes, as Jews.

[48] The former being Barkan's estimate (*Türkiyat Mecmuası*, vol. X [1953], p. 11 and *JESHO*, vol. I [1958], p. 21); the latter being F. Sümer's (in *Islam Ansi-*

have used a conjectural coefficient of six for a *ḫāne*[49] in our calculations. No subdivision can be traced in this category, though a few individuals are designated by their status or functions or those of their fathers, e.g. *nāʾib ḳalʿa, ibn nāʾib ḳalʿa.*

2. Tax-paying bachelors (*mücerred*), that is male adults who have reached the age of puberty (at about fifteen years of age).[50] In the lists the names of bachelors are marked with a small *mīm.* They are usually interspersed in each list, where they tend to appear side by side with their married kin.

3. Households or individuals exempt from tax (*muʿāf*). These fall into two main groups:

a. Muslim religious personages—Imam, *Khaṭīb,* Muezzin, Sharīf, *ḥājji, sayyid, muʿallim, müderris, muḥaṣṣil,* as well as residents in *zāwiyas.* Non-Muslim clerics were not exempted by the State, and are, therefore, not indicated.[51]

Certain other categories are explicitly designated in the lists of names. These include minor religious functionaries serving in the mosques, such as the doorkeeper (*bawwāb*) and the sweeper (*farrāsh*), responsible for cleaning the floors and laying the mats. The term *ḫādim,* which also occurs in this context, poses a problem. Its literal meaning is "servant" or "attendant"; its common Ottoman connotation at this time is "eunuch." Eunuchs are known to have been imported specially for service in mosques, and the word could well have either meaning. As against this, a *sijill* of Jerusalem dated 1003/1594–5 speaks of "one of the *sayyids,* the *ḫādims* of the mosque" (aḥad al-sāda al-khuddām bi'l-Masjid al-Aḳṣā). Such persons, descendants of the prophet, and hereditary custodians of the mosque, would certainly not have been eunuchs and would

klopedisi, vol. VI, p. 461, as quoted in Göyünç, *Mardin Sancağı,* p. 86. See also McGowan, *Archivum Ottomanicum,* vol. I (1969), pp. 138–96, and particularly pp. 157–62. See also Russel, *JESHO,* vol. III (1960), pp. 265–6.

49 We refer to this term as one family only, though this was not always the case. In Karaman in the sixteenth century it sometimes (when *ʿavāriż-ḫāne* was discussed) comprised of as many as three poor families (Beldiceanu and Beldiceanu-Steinherr, *JESHO,* Vol. XI, [1968] p. 62). See also Barkan's reference to the difference between *ḫāne* understood to be a family in the *taḥrir* registers, and "a fiscal unit" in the *jizya* registers (Barkan, *Belgeler,* vol. I (1964), pp. 5–7).

50 Cook (*Population Pressure,* pp. 64–5), who cites many examples to that effect as well as a specific reference which leads him to believe that this term "was also applicable to the man who ceased to be married." On the age of puberty see "Bāligh," *EI*², vol. I, p. 993.

51 Christian monks in Jerusalem, however, appear to be exempted in some registers though not in others. On the exemption of monks in the Ottoman Empire see Lemerle and Wittek, *Archives d'histoire du droit oriental,* vol. III (1948), pp. 468–9.

probably have held some more exalted post than that of mosque servants.

b. Disabled persons—the blind, mad and crippled. In accordance with the Ḥanafi law, exemption on this ground is granted to Christians and Jews, as well as Muslims.[52]

In addition, exemption from taxes was enjoyed by two other classes in Palestine: retired members of the Mamluk *Jund al-Ḥalḳa*; and peasants on lands that are waqfs in favour of the *Ḥarameyn Şarīfeyn* and of Jerusalem and Hebron.[53]

The inhabitants are normally referred to without any family names, the usual form being a first name followed by the name of his father ("X the son of (*veled*) Y"). Their place of origin is sometimes recorded (al-Maghribī, al-Shāmī, al-Miṣrī, al-Khalīlī etc.) There are indications that members of the same family continued to live next to each other even after their marriage. The *taḥrīr* (either carried out from house to house or in a given place, to which all the *reʿāyā* were obliged to come[54]) very often lists consecutive households, the heads of which are sons to the same father (thus referred to as "his brother", "his son", etc.).

Another classification maintained throughout the defters is that of religion. There were three religions in Palestine: Muslims, Christians and Jews, of which the last two paid certain additional taxes.[55] Their separate registration was, therefore, necessary for fiscal purposes, and the registers enable us to determine the numbers and location of Jews and Christians not only in terms of the country as a whole but also in their specific locations within the cities. The minority communities were primarily town-dwellers. Jews are to be found in all but Ramle, Christians in all but Safed; small groups of Samaritans appear in Nabulus and Gaza. A special case is that of monasteries which are situated either within the towns or in their surroundings, their occupants being regarded as inhabitants of the city (this occurs chiefly in Jerusalem).

With one possible exception Muslims as such form a single fiscal category, and are not normally distinguished by ethnic origin or linguistic nationality (though at times one can identify them by

[52] Ibrāhim b. Muḥammad al-Halabī, *Multaḳā al-Abḥur*, p. 126; D'Ohsson, *Tableau général*, vol. V (1824), p. 23 (cf. Marghīnānī, vol. II, p. 137, *al-Wıḳāya* p. 246, Ḳudūrī, *Mukhtaṣar*, p. 131, quoted by E. Strauss [Ashtōr], *Tōledōth ha-Yehūdīm*, vol. II, p. 263, n. 3).

[53] The term *Ḥarameyn Şerifeyn*, "the two Noble Shrines," refers to Mecca and Medına, and there is indeed a separate series in the Ottoman archives, the *Ḥarameyn Muḥāsebesi* and *Ḥarameyn Muḳāṭaʿası*, dealing with waqfs established in their favour.

[54] Kaldy-Nagy, *Acta Orientalia*, vol. XXI (1968), p. 190.

[55] On the special case of some exceptional Muslim categories see below, p. 18

their names). Only two categories receive separate mention:

a. Nomads and semi-nomads, still organized in tribes. In most cases, quite naturally, these are not to be found in towns. There are, however, various ways in which nomadic tribes are mentioned in this context in sixteenth-century Palestine. One is as individuals. In Hebron, for instance, there are members of the Ṭurābāy[56] tribes who were very powerful in Northern Palestine at that period, and, as appears from these records, had off-shoots reaching as far south as Hebron. In the same town, a strong sense of identity was preserved with the bedouin hinterland or past, to the extent of having some of its quarters still designated as either Ḳaysī or Yamanī.[57] In most other cities (with the exception of Ramle) relations with the bedouins seem to have assumed a permanent, established character. Special taxes were levied from them in return for the right to pasture in the neighbourhood of the town. In Nabulus it was called "tax on the bedouins" (*resm-i ʿurbān*), levied at the rate of 31,000 aspers for the Imperial Domain (*ḫāṣṣ-i ṣāhī*)[58] in 1538–9. In Safed it was called "duty on winter-pasturage" (*ḳıshlaḳ*),[59] probably from the nearby bedouins, at the rate of 4,000 aspers both in 1555–6 and in *ca.* 1567. While this belonged to the Imperial Domain, the governor of Safed received as appanage (*ḫāṣṣ-i mīr-i livāʾ*) the proceeds of the same tax from the bedouins of the *Biḳāʿ*, amounting to 10,000 aspers at these dates. The most noteworthy in this respect was Gaza, which seems to have had close and formalized links. The appanage given to the Sanjak-Bey includes:

TABLE 1

Bedouins of	*1525–6*	*ca. 1538–9*	*1548–9*	*1556–7*	*1596–7*
Banī ʿAṭiyya	5,000 Imperial Domain (ID)	15,000	15,000	15,000	15,000
Banī ʿAṭāʾ	5,000	12,000	15,000	15,000	15,000
Banī Haytham and Malāliḥa		8,000	6,000	6,000	6,000
Banī Sawālima		12,500	15,000	15,000	15,000
Jürüm	20,000	25,000	5,000	5,000	5,000

[56] Heyd, *Ottoman Documents*, pp. 45–6.

[57] An old distinction, allegedly dating back to pre-Islamic times, between Arab tribes of northern (Ḳays) and those of southern origin (Yaman). With the spread of Islam the feud between them was brought over to many parts of the Middle East, *inter alia* Palestine, where it continued to be regarded as a focal point of many local differences. See below, p. 107, n. 3. See also Baer and Hoexter, "Ḳays" in *EI²*. For eighteenth century Palestine see Cohen, *Palestine in the Eighteenth Century*, pp. 8–11. For nineteenth century Palestine see Hoexter, *Asian and African Studies*, vol. X (1974).

[58] See below, p. 42.

[59] On this, as well as other taxes levied see Çağatay, *Ankara Universitesi Dil ve Tarih Coğrafya Fakultesi Dergisi*, vol. V (1947), pp. 483–511. See below, p. 66

One cannot even guess at the numbers of these bedouins, but each confederation stood for either just under or, rarely, over ten tribes. While the decrease of income from some of them may indicate that from the late forties they had in part moved away to other grounds, by the same token the relations of some of them with the town (or its governor) must have developed considerably during the first two decades under review. A special case was that of certain nomadic Kurds in the vicinity of Nabulus who paid a tax called *resm-i ricāliye* (960 aspers per year). This may mean that they held suspect religious beliefs.[60] The *resm-i ricāliye,* levied only in *ca.* 1538–9, was discontinued later, perhaps because they either moved away or were sedentarized. Two small groups of Döger Turcomans are recorded in Jerusalem, as residing in the Bāb al-ʿAmūd and Banī Zayd quarters.[61]

b. Jundīs.[62] This was a component of the Mamluk army, both in Egypt and in Syria, though with some variation of usage between the two. They were recruited from the sons of the Mamluks, *awlād al-nās,* who were assigned *iḳṭāʿs* for their support. The Syrian element, far stronger than its counterpart in Egypt, notably during the years of decline, outlived the Mamluk regime, at least, in some cities of Palestine. These, already mentioned as exempt from taxes, are described as "former members of the *Jund al-Ḥalḳa* in the time of the Circassians (i.e., the Mamluk Sultanate), now retired." They resided mainly in the towns. Throughout the sixteenth century they are still recorded as a separate element in most of the quarters of Safed as well as in Gaza. The largest group was in Gaza, the second in Safed—the capitals of the two *niyābas* into which Palestine was divided in Mamluk times. In addition smaller groups resided in Jerusalem, Ramle, and a few villages.

[60] Cf. extremist Shiʿites such as Nuṣayris and Ismailis in Northern and Central Syria, who paid a special tax called *dirham al-rijāl.* Sauvaget, *Bulletin d'études orientales,* tom. XII (1948), p. 44; Barkan, *Kanunlar,* p. 216.

[61] See p. 83. On the Döger Turcomans who settled in parts of Syria and Palestine in the Mamluk and Ottoman periods see Sümer, *Türkiyat Mecmuası,* vol. X (1953), pp. 139 ff.; s.v. "Döger," *EI*², pp. 613–14.

[62] Cf. Ayalon, "Ḥalḳa," *EI*², vol. III, p. 99; Ayalon, *BSOAS,* vol. XV (1953), pp. 448–59; I. M. Lapidus, *Muslim Cities,* p. 116; Gaudefroy-Demombynes, *La Syrie,* pp xxxii–xxxiv, 139.

• 2 •

POPULATION

1. TRENDS AND DEVELOPMENTS

THE six cities of Palestine did not have large populations.[1] At the beginning of the century four of them had about 5,000–6,000 inhabitants, the remaining two even less. The most important of them in population, as well as in other respects, was Jerusalem, which remained so throughout the century, except for a short period recorded in 1538–9, when it fell behind Gaza. The smallest of them during the whole century was Ramle. It was not, in fact, much bigger in this respect than neighbouring villages like Lidd, Majdal or Dayr al-Dārūm, and in the later years of the century it became much smaller than some of them (notably Majdal, which in 1596–7 had twice the population).

As important as the cities of Palestine may have been in the local context, they are small by the standards of the Ottoman Empire as a whole. If we compare them, for example, with the sixteen main cities of the Empire at the beginning of the century, even the largest in Palestine will fall within the bottom 40%, comprising less than 1,000 households.[2] In this respect they compare rather unfavourably not only with Istanbul (or for that matter other important cities on the Mediterranean),[3] but with the other major cities of the Empire, or even of Syria, throughout the century. Thus, Barkan's demographic characterization of the most important cities of the Ottoman Empire as "agglomérations de peu d'importance"[4] applies even more strongly to the towns of Palestine. None of them even approach the figures for Aleppo and Damascus:[5]

[1] Inalcık notes the same feature in fifteenth-century Arvanid, where the population of the main cities mentioned usually varies between 100 and 200 households, he calls them as "town-villages" (*kasaba-köyler*) (Inalcık, *Defter-i sancak-i Arvanid*, p. xxvii)

[2] Barkan, *Recueils de la société Jean Bodin, La Ville* (1955), p. 295, Table 2.

[3] Barkan, *JESHO*, vol. I (1958), pp. 27, 28, n. 1.

[4] Barkan, *JESHO*, vol. I (1958), p. 27.

[5] Barkan, *ibid.*, p. 27, table no. 4. While the second figure in each pair indicates population, the first figure represents the number of households; quoted by Barkan, *Turkiyat Mecmuası*, vol. X (1953), p. 19. See also his article in *Recueils de la Société Jean Bodin*, p. 292, table I.

TABLE 2

	Prior to 1520	1520–30	1571–80	After 1580
Aleppo	11,224/67,344	10,342/56,881	8,242/45,331	8,430/46,365 (in 1586)
Damascus		10,423/57,326		7,778/42,779 (in 1595)

Even the combined figure for all six usually lagged behind either of these two. But the conparison may be carried a little further. One of the conclusions drawn by Barkan from table 4 is that Istanbul, Damascus, and Aleppo constitute an exception to a general rule. Whereas all the others indicate an increase in their population at the average rate of 90% during the sixteenth century, thereby behaving in a way similar to other cities of the Mediterranean (83,66%), Aleppo and Damascus show the very opposite trend ("dont la population n'avait cessé de décroître au XVI siècle").[6] The first comment to be made on this last statement is that while the figures on Aleppo provide ample justification for it, the same can hardly be said with regard to Damascus. All one can state concerning the latter is that its population as recorded at the turn of the century was about 25% lower than the figure recorded in the 1520's. It may well have been that the number of inhabitants in this town increased after 1530, and fell back in the later part of the century. Figures extracted by Bakhit from the *defters* for Damascus, while differing somewhat from Barkan's, show the same pattern of development even more clearly. Bakhit's figures are[7]:

TABLE 3

	Households	Bachelors
950/1543	8,277	471
955/1548	9,339	625
977/1569	8,621	622

It will be seen that the tendency indicated by these statistics from Damascus accords very well with the pattern which emerges from the *defters* for the cities of Palestine. Moreover, the figures provided by Barkan in the same article for the *whole* of the sanjak of Damascus indicate a substantial upsurge between 1521 and 1548, and a slow trend downward in the second half of the century.[8]

[6] Barkan, *JESHO*, vol. I (1958), p 27

[7] Bakhit, p. 57.

[8] Barkan, *ibid.*, p. 25 and *Türkıyat Mecmuası*, vol. X (1953), p. 19.

This may well indicate a development in Damascus parallel to those discerned in all the cities of Palestine. However, while this last conjecture remains to be documented and proved, it seems that the case for Palestine is clear, as we shall try to describe in some detail.

In four out of the six towns there is a possibility of assessing the rate of growth during the period 1525–38, making due allowance for improved registration and records. Setting aside Hebron, which in the registers shows a staggering growth in population of over 600%, the rate of increase is (roughly) 30% in Ramle, 50% in Jerusalem, 90% in Gaza. A similar rate is to be noted in the following decade or so: 15% in Hebron, 30% in Gaza, 40% in Ramle, 70% in Jerusalem. In the absence of information with regard to Safed, Nabulus is the first to show a reverse tendency, i.e., a decrease of 80%. In the following decade the pace of growth indicates contradictory trends. Whereas in Gaza and Hebron there is some insignificant growth, reaching 5% in the latter, Ramle witnessed an insignificant decrease, matched by 3% in Jerusalem. Outstanding in this period (1556—*ca.* 1566) is Safed, where the population grew at a rate of 25%. By the end of the century (information on Safed still missing) all the cities of Palestine were undergoing a steady, sometimes very substantial, process of population decline. By far the slowest pace is to be traced in Nabulus: 15% in almost half a century. During the last four decades both Ramle and Gaza decreased by half. Hebron diminished during thirty-five years by more than 30%, and the incomplete evidence left for Jerusalem indicates almost the same figure with regard to its Muslim inhabitants.

To sum up: the general trend in the population of the towns of Palestine in the sixteenth century was upward during the first half of the century, and with the exception of Safed downward during the second half. Even so, the total figure at the turn of the century was at least one third higher than the figure recorded after the Ottoman conquest. If we take the century as a whole, neither the six together nor any individual city fits into the so-called "Mediterranean pattern of growth." While certain towns (Jerusalem, Hebron) grew very considerably, others either witnessed a slow over-all growth (Gaza) or even a drop (Ramle). The net outcome is one of a growth-rate over the century which was about one third of the trend recorded by Barkan in his calculations for other cities. More instructive than this comparison between the beginning and end of the century would be an attempt to follow the changing curve a little more closely, thereby finding the very sharp and consistent rise during the first forty years of Ottoman rule, to be replaced by a not less conspicuously sharp fall in the following thirty years.[9] The last trend, both general and uninterrupted, seems to suggest that a comparison between the beginning and the end of the century is not necessarily very satisfactory, as its final point is not only arbitrary by definition, but it signifies only one spot on a declining curve. One is led to believe that if the figures were carried on to the seventeenth century, the difference would even be smaller. In any case, one should in the light of the statistical data from Palestine qualify Braudel's otherwise correct generalization: "Nous pouvons, sans risque excessif, étendre leur témoignage à la Méditerranée entière, la musulmane comme la chrétienne . . . un graphique du mouvement de la population . . . toutes les droites . . . signales des progressions nettes et constantes jusqu'aux dernières années du XVIe siècle."[10] This "long sixteenth century," which is characterized, as Braudel states, by an increase of the population of "*tous* les univers urbains" (author's italics) cannot be so categorically accepted, at least as far as Palestine of the same century is concerned.[11]

C. Issawi doubts the validity of the figures given for one element of the population of the Arab provinces, the Christian, as calculated by Barkan. Among other considerations he criticizes what appears to be "an annual rate of increase of 1.5% maintained over four centuries."[12] These comments may be applied in our case with even greater justification. How, then, could one try and reconcile these criticisms with the fact that the growth-rates indicated do not appear merely as a sporadic change in one certain case, but emerge from several parallel sets of figures, and at a far higher rate than those questioned by Issawi?

Issawi is speaking primarily of natural increase, and of a period of "over four centuries"; we are concerned with changes over much shorter periods, ranging from a few years to a few decades. These

[9] Barkan observes: "Sous certaines réserves, on peut admettre l'idée qu'il existe, tout au moins a cette époque, un rapport entre l'augmentation de la population des villes et l'accroissement de la population totale et que pour chacune de ces populations on peut accepter la même proportion" (*JESHO*, vol. I (1958), p. 27). In the light of our findings on the cities of Palestine, some caution on possible changes among the rural population seems appropriate.

[10] Braudel, *La méditerranée*, vol. I, p. 299.

[11] As well as some other examples, notably Aleppo and Damascus, to which this rule of thumb can not be applied. For some other examples of exceptions see Barkan, *Türkiyat Mecmuası*, vol. X (1953), p. 22 (Salonica).

[12] Issawi, *JESHO*, vol. I (1958), pp. 329–31. See also Russel, *JESHO*, vol. III (1960), pp. 266–9.

changes moreover are affected by numerous factors other than natural increase, the most important being improvements in the collection and recording of population data by the responsible officials, and movements of population, both internal, as between cities or between town and country, and international, through the arrival and settlement of newcomers from abroad.

The most conspicuous increase seems to have been the one recorded between 1525 and *ca.* 1539. As the *taḥrīr* of 1525 was the first one to be carried out in Palestine after the conquest, a certain allowance should be made for the inaccuracies and inefficiencies of the first years, the result of which was that the agents of the newly established government recorded an incomplete picture. This probably occurred not only in scattered villages, but also in the urban centers of administration.

But apart from presumed bureaucratic inadequacies, there are substantial reasons why the figures in the first *taḥrīr* may be regarded as unnaturally low.

One of them dates back to the last decades of the Mamluk period. After "a partial restoration of the fortunes of the [Mamlūk] empire . . . from about 1470, fresh and cumulative strains pushed Mamlūk Syria into the vortex of complete economic, political and social collapse."[13] The decline of international trade in the Mediterranean in the second half of the fifteenth century was precipitated by the consolidation of the Ottoman Empire in the eastern Mediterranean, and in time aggravated by the Portuguese discoveries and expansion in the Indian Ocean and around the Arabian Peninsula, which somewhat reduced the share of Egypt and Syria in the spice trade. Bedouin incursions also had a disruptive effect both on the sedentary population and on the overland trade between Syria and Egypt.

These were by no means the only expressions of aggression in public life in Syria. Inherent communal feuds frequently disturbed public order, as did Mamluk rebellions throughout Syria and Egypt. The exorbitant illegal taxation with which the Mamluks burdened the inhabitants, often coupled with devices like forced purchases (*ṭarḥ*), must have caused much distress to the local population, and especially to the town-dwellers.[14] The references of contemporary European travellers to the widespread decline on the eve of the Ottoman occupation are corroborated by a remark

[13] Lapidus, *Muslim cities*, pp. 32, 38.

[14] *Ibid.*, pp. 38–42. For details on forced purchases in Palestine (Nabulus, Jerusalem and Hebron), see pp. 57–58.

in the *taḥrīr* of Tripoli of 1519: "Three thousand villages had in the past been in the vilayet of Tripoli. Most of them became ruined as a result of the abundance of oppression and [other] unlawful innovations (*bidᶜat*). At present [only] eight hundred are inhabited, [while] the rest of it has become uninhabited (*mezraᶜa*)."[15]

It is in this context, indubitably aggravated by both the establishment of a new government and the presence of an occupying army, that the cities of Palestine should be seen. Although Hebron seems to have been the smallest in 1525, this fact may be ascribed to inaccuracies in the census, as it is impossible to assume so significant an increase (from about 800 to nearly 5,000 inhabitants) in the course of just over a decade. On the other hand, we can discern a similar quantitative (though not proportional) increase in Gaza in the same period. While this might also be ascribed to inaccuracy, it may be the result of a very substantial outflow of inhabitants to the neighboring hinterland. The difference between the figures for the Muslim and non-Muslim inhabitants is significant. The data concerning the religious minority groups indicate very little change between the first two *taḥrīrs*, presumably because they were very conspicuous in their quarters and had no reliable nearby refuge to which they could withdraw. It was the Muslim population which avoided officialdom by staying outside the city. One should bear in mind the bedouin tribes roaming freely in the vicinity of Gaza, as well as the very close links between Hebron and its immediate nomadic hinterland. It is among these tribesmen who had become so powerful in the immediately preceding period that their Muslim relatives or protégés preferred to find refuge until things got better. The Ottoman army did very little real fighting in Palestine, either on its way to Egypt or on its way back. It did however suffer a Mamluk attempt in Gaza to halt Selīm's advance, and the ensuing repression is thus described by Ibn Iyās: "He [Sinān Pasha] used the sword against the inhabitants of Gaza and [thus] kılled about one thousand people among them, men, children and even women."[16] These events, coupled with some continuing uncertainty as to the future, must have induced many of the townspeople to prefer the relative safety of the desert or the countryside. Hence a large part of the population directly affected by past

[15] "Vilâyet-i Trabulus'da bundan akdem üçbin miktari köy ve karye olup kesret-ı zulüm ve bıdᶜatten ekseri harap olup hâliyâ sekiz yüzü mamur bulunup bâkısi mezraᶜa olduğu" (Barkan, *Türkiyat Mecmuası*, vol. X (1953), p. 18).

[16] وقد لعب [سنان باشا] في اهل غزة بالسيف وقتل منهم نحو الف انسان
ما بين رجال وصغار وحتى نساء
(Muḥammad ibn Iyās, *Badāʾiᶜ al-zuhūr*, vol. V, p. 129).

experiences in Gaza, as well as that of Hebron with which it was closely related and linked, preferred not to return to the cities in the years immediately after the conquest.

In a less acute form, much of the same seems to have happened in all the other towns of Palestine. The keys of the main cities were sent to the new ruler as an act of submission even before he actually reached these places, but apart from the normal local apprehension and suspicion with regard to the newcomers, there are indications that in at least four towns the Ottoman army inflicted quite heavy blows on the inhabitants. In Ramle, a reliable account by a contemporary high Ottoman official says: "The inhabitants of Ramle became disobedient and deserved punishment; accordingly they were punished and there was looting and loss [of life]."[17] In Nabulus also there is an indication of what might have been widespread slaughter, in a reference to an official command not only to execute the former governor, but also "to kill the *aᶜvān* of Nabulus."[18] As for Safed, although there is no evidence of either specific orders to kill or of the actual killing of any part of the population, one may infer (especially in the light of the available description of what happened in Gaza under similar circumstances) what the Ottoman reaction was when rumors about an Ottoman defeat on the way to Egypt led to "extensive bloodshed in Safed."[19] Massacre obviously reduced numbers directly; it also did so indirectly, by causing fear and uncertainty, and thus delaying the return of absent citizens to the cities from which they had fled.

The high figures recorded in 1538–9, and again in 1548–9, indicate that after a decade or more of Ottoman rule, the tendency was reversed. The unprecedented growth-rate may be, to a certain and limited extent, a result of improved statistical techniques and a closer knowledge of the prevailing conditions on the part of the Ottomans. This is, however, only of a secondary importance. The main conclusions to be drawn from the figures recorded in these, as well as the subsequent *taḥrīrs*, are of an altogether new situation existing at least in the cities. The development went beyond a return to the situation which prevailed *prior* to the disruption of the late Mamluk and early Ottoman periods. The increasing security to both life and property, the absence of a rebellious and disorderly soldiery and a prospering economy culminated in a steady influx

[17] Ramle . . . ehālīsī ki nehc-i istikāmetten ḳadem-ı ṭāᶜatı ḫāric edip güşmāle müstahakk olmuşlardı istiḥkaklarına göre cezāları ve sezāları verılıp yağmā ve ḫasāret olundu (Celālzāde Musṭafā Çelebi, *Maʾāṣir-ı Selīm Ḫānī*, p. 191b).

[18] Ibn Tūlūn, *Mufākahat al-khıllān*, vol. II, p. 119.

[19] Ibn Ṭūlūn, *Mufākahat al-khillān*, vol. II, p. 41.

of inhabitants, largely but not exclusively Muslims, to the cities.

Very impressive rates of growth up to the middle of the century were replaced by a slowing-down in the next decade. The figures of 1556–62 are only very slightly higher than those recorded ten years earlier. The first signs of an eventual recession appear among the minorities, whose numbers start to decline, thus further off-setting the negligible increase among the Muslims. But these first signs notwithstanding, one can still generalize by saying that at least in terms of urban population the era of Süleymān the Magnificent was the golden age.

It is from that time onwards, i.e., from the 1560's, that the reverse tendency, that of recession, is clearly indicated. Once again, these developments should be viewed in the wider context of the general picture of Palestine. Although, as Barkan rightly notes, there were no massive urbanization processes at that period, it would seem that the pace of development in towns was faster than in the country-side.[20] This, however, is a problem which still awaits further research. But even with the scanty information available, we can observe parallel developments not only between Palestinian towns and their respective sanjaks, but on a wider scale even in the whole of Syria. Whereas the total Muslim population of the sanjaks of Damascus increased from 38,672 households in 1521 to 63,035 in 1548, the figure recorded in 1569 is 57,897.[21] The more interesting of the two is the second phase, in which a slight decrease can already be detected between 1548 and 1569, coinciding with a similar trend (referred to above) in the towns of Palestine. In other words, the decline of the population of the cities of Palestine noted during the last years of the reign of Süleymān was a part of a much wider development in the whole of Syria. It coincides with an economic crisis in Aleppo, and therefore, although not necessarily connected with the whole of the eastern Mediterranean, as stated by Braudel, its character cannot be referred to reasons termed as "personnelles," but rather as concerning at least Syria and Palestine.[22]

"Les villes naissent, progressent, déclinent suivant les pulsations mêmes de la vie économique."[23] In our context we may also add

[20] Cf. B. Lewis, *BSOAS*, vol. XVI (1954), p. 475, Table II.

[21] "Un phénomène de 'désertion des campagnes' au profit des grandes villes peut avoir eu lieu . . . Mais nous sommes au XVIe siècle et dans l'Empire Ottoman. L'attrait des grandes villes de l'époque de l'industrialisation massive est encore loin" (Barkan, *JESHO*, vol. I [1958], p. 25). The last figure in his earlier article, in *Türkiyat Mecmuası*, vol. X (1953), p. 19, is 57397

[22] Braudel, *La méditerranée*, vol. I, pp 489–90.

[23] *Ibid.*, p. 295.

political and administrative considerations. The decrease in population, slight at first then accelerating, must however be seen within the context of major developments affecting the whole of the Ottoman Empire, and indeed other countries. The import of American silver in large quantities was an important cause for the rise of prices in Spain and elsewhere. The inflationary pressures on the Ottoman economy further aggravated its situation, resulting in a decline in its local trade.[24] A most conspicuous outcome of all this was the disruption of the tax system.[25] Portuguese maritime activity in the Indian Ocean, though not immediately crucial, had an increasingly adverse effect on the traffic through the Middle Eastern trade routes throughout the century (though it was only at the beginning of the seventeenth century that these routes were circumvented).[26] However, it seems that the immediate, and perhaps even later effects of this were not as was at one time believed. Inalcık has shown[27] that in the first half of the sixteenth century spices were still reaching Egypt in considerable quantities. Our information[28] not only tallies with his findings, but even indicates similar trends in Syria both in the first and—to a lesser extent—in the second half of the century.

There are other indications of an accelerating economic decline between 1550 and 1570,[29] and this was aggravated by the growing administrative and political difficulties inside the central government. The local effects of these processes in Syria and Palestine can be discerned in the *tapu* registers and are explicitly described in the *mühimme* registers. The available official documents show increasing signs of decay in both the Janissary and the *Sipāhī* institutions in Syria. Absenteeism from their lands and disregard of commands from Istanbul led to low standards in the way the "feudal" element carried out its duties. Corruption, personal involvement in nonmilitary ventures, admission of local townspeople to their midst—all of these made the Janissaries less dangerous to their enemies in the field, more dangerous to the civil population

[24] Barkan, *Social Aspects of Economic Developments* (1964), pp. 21–24; idem, "The price revolution of the sixteenth century: a turning point in the economic history of the Near East," *International Journal of Middle Eastern Studies (IJMES)*, vol. VI (1975), pp. 3–28.

[25] Barkan, in *Social aspects* (1964), pp. 24–26. See also below, pp. 43–44.

[26] *Ibid.*, (1964), pp. 20–1.

[27] Inalcık, *The Cambridge History of Islam*, vol. I (1970), p. 332

[28] See below, pp. 63–64.

[29] Braudel, *La méditerranée*, vol. II, pp. 65–6.

among whom they lived.[30] Acts of oppression, extortion and fraud on behalf of the different administrative officials were widely reported.[31] Rebellious nomadic elements are reported as having again taken to the sword as early as 1552.[32] As a result of the last two factors the local population suffered severely, sometimes to the point of exhaustion.[33] Depreciation of the silver asper also contributed to the further distress of the inhabitants.[34] Rebellions in Syria, Egypt and Arabia, coupled with an upsurge in the Portuguese spice trade, led to an unprecedented diminution in this trade both in Egypt and in Syria, especially during the second half of the century.[35] Forced purchases were reintroduced at least in Safed, and given the general conditions one may assume that this was not an exception.[36] All these, and many similar developments add up to a very gloomy picture. How these gathering calamities affected the rural population is still to be established, though not difficult to imagine. With regard to the urban population, much closer to, thus more open to attack and mischief from the different agents of the state administration, the outcome is clear: a steady decline in population in the last forty years in all six cities of Palestine. Conditions in at least four of them (Jerusalem, Ramle, Hebron, and most conspicuously Nabulus) were further aggravated by the earthquake of 1546 and its aftermath.[37]

2. MINORITIES

A. JEWS

Safed appears to have been in some measure exempt from the developments which affected all the other cities of Palestine. The exemption is only partial, as can be seen from a more detailed examination of the population structure. The Muslim population of this city did, in fact, follow the very same pattern described above. In about a decade it diminished at the rate of 10%. The change in the demographic picture was due to the Jewish element,

[30] Heyd, *Ottoman Documents*, pp. 63–4

[31] *Ibid.*, pp. 45–7.

[32] *Ibid.*, pp. 45, 91–2, passim.

[33] *Ibid.*, p. 117.

[34] *Ibid.*, p. 120.

[35] Braudel, *La méditerranée*, vol. II, p. 357; vol. I, pp. 503–4, 507.

[36] Heyd, *Ottoman Documents*, pp. 133–4.

[37] Braslavski, *Studies*, pp. 227–31. The figure of casualties in Nabulus was apparently particularly high and was estimated at over 500. There is no reason to doubt that Safed, too, was affected.

which during the same years grew by about 30%. This was in line with former developments in this community in Safed: from almost a quarter of the population in 1525 it rose to about a half. Taken separately, the Jewish element quadrupled in this city in less than fifty years, keeping steadily to the same tendency of growth.

In contrast, the Jewish community in Nabulus declined. Following the general pattern of decrease throughout the century, but at a much faster pace, it contracted by half between 1538 and 1548, and by almost four fifths toward the end of the century. In Hebron the community seems to have suffered toward the middle of the century, only to regain some ground in the second half, when it remained unchanged at about half its initial strength. In Jerusalem and Gaza the Jewish population increased at the beginning of the sixteenth century, reaching its highest mark in the *taḥrīr* of 1548–9, which shows an increase of 70% and 30%, respectively. Later, as was the case in Palestine generally, it diminished very substantially in both cities, in Gaza falling even below its initial figure. As a result of some missing links it is difficult to draw many general conclusions, but if we assume for Nabulus and Hebron at the beginning of the Ottoman era the same figures as are recorded a decade later, and apply the same principle to Jerusalem at the end of the century, it would appear that the Jewish population in five of the main cities of Palestine (there were no Jews in Ramle) doubled in the course of the century, constituting 14% of the total in 1525, and about 20% in 1595.

The Jewish community of Safed was conspicuous in comparison both with the Muslims of the city and with the Jewish communities elsewhere. Throughout the century Safed had the highest[38] concentration of Jews in Palestine, and while in the first period after the Ottoman conquest the Jerusalem community was not much smaller, the gap between the two widened steadily as the years went by, confirming at least the numerical supremacy of the Jews of Safed among their co-religionists. A word on the relative importance of Safed *vis-à-vis* Jerusalem is pertinent here. Jewish immigration to Palestine grew steadily after the establishment of Ottoman rule. It affected various parts of the country, and more particularly the north, the district of Galilee. As between the cities, there was an increasing tendency to prefer Safed, the nonscriptural town, to

[38] A reference to their high standards of learning at the turn of the century can be traced in Sanderson's travels: "In this citie of Safett ar all the most learned and devout Jewes, and heare ar six coledges or scoles of learninge . . . and many adged goe purposelie to die ther" (Foster, *Travels of John Sanderson*, p. 97).

Jerusalem. Various factors may account for this. Conditions prevailing in Jerusalem at that time were unfavorable to the new arrivals, both as a result of the "ungenerous spirit" of communal administration, imposing heavy taxes on them, and of the apparently higher degree of hostility among the Muslim population.[39] Since Safed had never before this time had an important Jewish element, the community not only, as suggested by Schechter, "had no occasion to make regulations calculated to exploit the foreigner," but was virtually encouraging the immigrants by imposing lower taxes on them, and even exempting those among them who were Talmudists from taxation altogether.[40] No less important were economic considerations of a wider nature: the proximity of Safed to the ports of Sidon and Acre, as well as its relatively easier access to Damascus and its trade. These and others (see below, p. 60–1). proved to be basic considerations, especially for the flourishing wool industry in Safed. There were religious as well as material inducements. Safed was situated very close to the traditional tomb of Bar Yohay, and at a time when the general mood among Jews all over the world was one of expectation for the imminent coming of the Messiah, first to reveal himself, according to prophecies, in Galilee, the chief city of the north drew a preponderant part of Jewish immigrants to Palestine.

B. SAMARITANS

Samaritans are recorded in two cities, Nabulus and Gaza. In Gaza they were the smallest minority, and the only one that underwent a process of uninterrupted decrease, until at the end of the century they were less than one third of their original figure. By far the largest Samaritan community was in Nabulus, reaching the peak of its growth around the middle of the century, and finding itself reduced in the end of the century to two thirds of the figure given for 1538–9.

C. CHRISTIANS

Safed was without Christians throughout the century and so too was Hebron after its desertion by the last Christians in the early 1540's. In all the other cities they were a very important, if not the most important, minority. In Nabulus they owed their growing importance both to a numerical increase at the rate of 20% in sixty

[39] Schechter, in *Studies in Judaism*, vol. II (1908), p. 207. For many details on Jewish life in Jerusalem, see Cohen, *Ottoman Documents*.

[40] Y. Kena'ani, *Zion*, vol. VI (1934), pp. 178–80.

years and to the decrease in both the Jewish and the Samaritan communities. In Ramle, where they had no non-Muslim competitors,[41] they maintained a growth of 100% in the first half of the century, suffered a certain setback in the next decade, only to resume their former strength towards the end of the century. In Jerusalem, having overcome a certain weakening in the second decade of Ottoman rule, the Christians soon surpassed the Jewish community in 1553–4, and although they, too, started to decline in the 1560's, they still maintained their supremacy, 50% stronger than their initial position. By far the most important Christian center, demographically speaking, was Gaza: from the start the Christian community of Gaza kept its numerical superiority over all other minority communities, Christians or others, either in Gaza or in any other town, and throughout the century it increased without interruption. In 1556–7 it eventually reached its peak and thirty years later, having lost about 10%, it was still 25% of the whole population of the city, as it had been in the first *taḥrīr*.

D. CONCLUDING REMARKS

Not one of the six towns of Palestine in the sixteenth century was exclusively Muslim. Three of them—Jerusalem, Gaza and Nabulus—encompassed a very heterogeneous population. The Muslim element was predominant in all of them from the very beginning and although the minorities grew proportionally at an impressive pace, they still lagged far behind the Muslims. It is, perhaps, because of the same reason that the reverse tendency in the second half of the century was felt much less among the Christians than Muslims. Jerusalem had the most substantial minority population, to be followed very closely by Gaza. Exceptional in this respect was Safed, where the Jewish community grew rapidly, and almost equaled the Muslim majority in the late 1560's.

The *taḥrīr* registers offer few indications as to the reasons for increases or decreases in population. However, in two cases the origins of newcomers are indicated. The increase in Jews in Safed was largely due to an influx of immigrants from Europe. Between 1525 and 1555, the native Arabic-speaking Jewish community (*mustaʿriba*) gradually diminished and the immigrant communities increased rapidly. Although the places of origin varied, most of

[41] In Muslim society certain economic functions were usually concentrated in the hands of the various non-Muslim communities who therefore competed with one another, rather than with the Muslims.

the newcomers were either Portuguese or Spanish. The same tendency can still be discerned more than ten years later.

The second case is that of the Christians of the south. Whereas Hebron, which seems at first to have had a Christian minority, lost it in the forties, the number of Christians in the other three—i.e., Jerusalem, Ramle and Gaza—rose rapidly by immigration. Like the Jewish inhabitants of Safed, many of the Christians in these towns kept their original identity throughout the century. Thus one can fairly easily not only locate most of the Christians who disappeared from Hebron, but also trace back the origins of many others in Jerusalem, Ramle and Gaza. The records for these cities show a very substantial migration of Christians from the area lying south of Jerusalem.

It is impossible to tell whether this process started in the last years of the Mamluk period, or was a direct outcome of the Ottoman conquest. If the former, then it was accentuated under Ottoman rule. After the Ottoman conquest there was still a large community of Christians in Hebron, most of whom had left during the next ten years. The last Christians of Hebron disappear between *ca.* 1539 and 1553, but an almost identical number appears around the middle of the century in Gaza and Ramle, to be followed by another group which moved into Jerusalem ten years later. Similarly, the Christians from Shawbak and Bayt Jibrīn, already mentioned as being in Gaza in 932/1525–6, increased steadily in number until the 1550's. From references in the texts of the *defters,* it would seem that this increase was due in part at least to a further influx.[42] The neighborhood of Bethlehem seems to have provided Jerusalem with a substantial Christian element (from Bethlehem and Bayt Jāla) prior to 1553, as well as Gaza (from Taḳūʿ) fifteen years earlier. Similarly, the former inhabitants of the village of Bayt Rīmā, to the north of Jerusalem, were moving in increasing numbers to Gaza, as well as to Ramle (1556) and Jerusalem (1562). From these shreds of evidence it would seem that there was an influx into the cities, gathering momentum towards the middle of the century. From the registers it remains unclear, of course, whether these migrants were forced to leave their smaller villages, or attracted by the bigger towns. It seems that in Hebron, at least, the otherwise developing city could not offer its Christian inhabitants an adequate opportunity to share in the general benefits, so they were forced to look elsewhere. The same may well have happened at least in

[42] See below, p. 127.

the village of Bayt Rīmā, where very substantial numbers seem to have left. But the record for the large cities suggests that to the rural Christian population these offered greater protection and better economic prospects.

This trend is diametrically opposed to what has been noted in Hungary, where the period following the Ottoman conquest is characterized by a widespread decrease in the Christian element ("Le phénomène de la diminuation de la population hongroise est général pour tous les centres administratifs").[43] The important difference in Hungary was that Christians had only to cross the border in order to live under Christian rule. No such option was open to the Christians of Palestine.

3. JUNDIS

Three cities—Gaza, Safed and Jerusalem—had a significant *jundī* element among their inhabitants most of the century, whereas in a fourth one—Ramle—a negligible element is recorded only in 1556–7. At the beginning of the century they probably fled or disguised their real identity out of fear of reprisals by the Ottomans (and perhaps the local population also) for their close links with the former régime. In fact at least with regard to Gaza there is evidence that part of the *jund al-ḥalḳa* were suspected of having entertained a secret correspondence with Selīm. Although they later denied this allegation, the Mamluk ruler expelled them to Cairo, thus decreasing their number even prior to the Ottoman conquest.[44] The only place where they revealed their identity as early as 1525–6 was Safed, while in Gaza an earlier uprising of the inhabitants led to bloodshed by the occupying Ottoman army, no doubt driving away the very substantial *jundī* element. It was not until 1548–9 that *jundīs* are recorded for the first time in Jerusalem also.

From the available statistical data one can fairly certainly draw a further conclusion, i.e., that almost identically with the general trend among the population as a whole, the *jundīs* reached their highest mark in the early 1550's. At that time there were about three hundred of them in the whole of Palestine, in most cases having their own families and most probably leading ordinary lives. It is from that point onward that they started to dwindle as

[43] Perényi, in Todorov, *Studia Balcanica* (Sofia, 1970), p. 27. The author brings various statistics to that effect.

[44] Ibn Iyās, *Badāʾiʿ al-zuhūr*, vol. V, p. 17.

a separate entity. Even so, one is struck by the relatively slow pace of their disappearance. As late as the end of the century, i.e., eighty years after the Mamluk regime was uprooted, the *jundīs* were still very substantially represented at least in Gaza and Jerusalem. It may be noted here that although, quite naturally, they were concentrated in the southern part of Palestine, the *jundīs* were well represented in the north—Safed—as well. However, their largest number throughout the century was in Gaza, the nearest town to Egypt.

Apart from those who are listed as *jundīs,* it is obvious from personal names appearing in the lists of *tīmār* holders (e.g. Ināl, Durmu<u>sh</u>, etc., which are not Ottoman names) that some former Mamluks entered the Ottoman service as *Sipāhīs* and held *tīmārs.*

From the fact that *jundīs* are still listed eighty years after the end of the Mamluk Sultanate it is clear that although in the earlier registers they are described as "retired" (*müteḳāʿid*), this had, in fact, become a hereditary status recognized by the Ottomans.

4. QUARTERS

The names of several quarters indicate that at certain earlier stages their inhabitants were of a specific foreign or at least ethnically distinct origin. Such are the quarters of "the Egyptians" and "the Ba<u>sh</u>kirs" (Miṣriyyīn, Başḳardi)[45] in Ramle, "the Turcomans" in Ramle and Gaza, "the Kurds" (Akrād) in Safed, Gaza, and Hebron, "the North-Africans" (Ma<u>gh</u>āriba) in Jerusalem. On the last-named, the earliest register for Jerusalem has a note saying that there was a group of Ma<u>gh</u>ribī *mujāwirs* of the Ḥaram al-<u>Sh</u>arīf, residing in Jerusalem. Their quarter had been constituted a waqf by Saladin, whose action was confirmed by subsequent rulers. The Kurdish, Turcoman, and Ba<u>sh</u>kir quarters are no doubt a relic of the early Mamluk policy of settling warlike Kurds and Turcomans on the Palestine coastlands as a safeguard against a renewed attack from the West.[46] There is no evidence that these quarters still maintained their initial ethnic character. This may well have been true of the Ma<u>gh</u>āriba in Jerusalem, where certain

[45] The name already occurs in Mamluk times (Mujīr al-Dīn, *Al-Uns al-jalīl*, vol. II, p. 419; French translation in H. Sauvaire, *Histoire de Jérusalem*, p. 209). Ba<u>sh</u>kir elements served in the Mamluk army and some of them reached high posts in Syria (see Togan, "Ba<u>sh</u>d<u>j</u>irt" in *EI*², Vol. I, pp. 1075–7.

[46] Cf. Ayalon, *Islamic Culture*, vol. XXV (1951), pp. 89 ff.; A. N. Poliak, *Feudalism*, p. 9.

indications in the registers, as well as further information from the *sijill,* suggest that these were still to a large extent a separate element within the local population. Their separateness was no doubt accentuated and preserved by their adherence to the Mālikī school. Their status, however, seems to have been exceptional; this can be seen in the existence over the years of a Shaykh al-Maghāriba, which was not only an honorific title; in references to them as a *ṭāʾifa,* etc.

There are some reasons to believe that at least a part of those who lived in these quarters (other than the Maghāriba), were not differentiated from the rest of the population. First, the inhabitants of the Turcoman and Kurdish quarters tend to follow almost the same patterns of population changes to be noted among all the others. It is very unlikely that had they consisted exclusively or even mainly of a different element, these quarters would have followed precisely these lines, as there is no indication of a substantial influx of Kurds or Turcomans to the towns. Second, on one occasion, at least, when some Turcomans were regarded as such, they were referred to (in Jerusalem, *ca.* 1538–9) by a more specific tribal name (Döger). Third, Kurds were regarded as a specific element among the inhabitants. On one occasion (in Nabulus), Kurdish nomads were subject to a special poll-tax (probably also because of their being regarded religiously heretical to a certain degree).[47] But on other occasions, when living in towns, whether in the Akrād quarter or elsewhere, they were explicitly mentioned as a separate Muslim group, like the *jundīs*; not necessarily identical to the general Muslim *Sunnīs,* though this time they did not pay the above-mentioned tax. Fourth, the fact that *jundīs,* who were regarded as a distinct element, were divided among several quarters, indicates that the alleged homogeneity of these units was not too strictly maintained in the sixteenth century.

To sum up: these descendants of the different, mainly nomadic and non-Arabic-speaking elements were probably not regarded as distinct from the other inhabitants even though the quarters, and perhaps a certain part of those living there, still bore the old names. Thus, for instance, in the quarter called Kurdish in Gaza, there are, in different *taḥrīrs* up to the end of the century, inhabitants specifically designated as "the Kurd."[48] It seems certain that those of them who were originally nomadic were by the sixteenth century virtually sedentarized within the local population, and were not

[47] Cf. p. 18.
[48] See p. 37.

reinforced from their still nomadic kinsmen in other parts of Syria.[49]

Religious minorities seem to have followed the logical (and historical) pattern of concentrating in a certain area and thus more easily maintaining their special character. This was not necessarily the result of a sense of insecurity (although this must have been a major consideration), but an actual need to live within reach of their own places of worship. When their numbers were substantial, these communities had their own quarters (the Christian quarter in Jerusalem or the Jewish quarter in Hebron). Sometimes even subdivisions among communities were kept so distinct that "quarters" (which in point of fact could not have been any larger than several houses) were distinguished from one another by the common origin of their inhabitants (in Safed for Jews, most conspicuously, or in Gaza for Christians). Living in particular quarters was, naturally, the best way to ensure the homogeneity of the community, which was still however not always possible. But even in towns where they were divided among several quarters, these were always adjacent to one another. The members of the community would endeavor to live as close to one another as possible (Jews in Jerusalem were divided between Sharaf, Rīsha and Maslakh, which being situated between the first two was also called "the middle one"—al-Wusṭā; both Jews and Christians in Nabulus were concentrated in specific quarters, rather than scattered). Moreover, even ethnic minorities within Islam seem to have tried to live near the main centers of their own groups, though these had by this time lost most of their distinctive identity. Thus the probably newly settled Kurds in Safed preferred to live in the quarter of Ṣawāwīn, the nearest one to the "Kurds" (Akrād) quarter.

This last example may be related to another category, i.e., recently sedentarized bedouins who shared both religion and ethnic origin with the overwhelming majority, but still found it more expedient to live in one specific quarter to which they lent their name (Banī Zayd, Banī Ḥārith in Jerusalem, Miṣriyyin in Ramle (?), the different Ḳaysī and Yamanī quarters in Hebron). It may well be added that with regard to this category, both examples taken from Jerusalem and Hebron appear only in the first half of the century, thus indicating an eventual fading away of their special traits in the eyes of both the government and their neighbors.

In contrast to some other parts of the Ottoman Empire (e.g., Trabzon, where very often one comes across "quarter of the mosque x"),[50] only a few quarters in the towns of Palestine were

[49] Turcomans, for instance Cf. Sümer, vol. II (1950), pp. 512, 515.

[50] Gökbilgin, *Belleten*, vol. XXVI (1962), pp. 296–297.

named after a mosque (Ramle: al-Jāmiᶜ al-Abyaḍ; Safed: al-Jāmiᶜ al-Aḥmar; Hebron: S͟hayk͟h ᶜAlī; Jerusalem: al-S͟haraf). A substantial number of quarters drew their names (and perhaps some part of their population) from the main economic activity pursued by them, either with a reference to a central market or a common profession in the same quarter (Hebron: al-Ḳazzāzīn; Safed: Sūḳ; Nabulus: al-Ḳaysariyya; Gaza: Dār al-K͟huḍar, Dabbāg͟ha, Zaytūn (?); Ramle: Saḳḳāʾ).

Lapidus[51] speaks of a homogeneity of the inhabitants of the different quarters in the Mamluk time, based on religious, ethnic or occupational common denominators. One would not have expected this to vanish during the sixteenth century merely because of the new political rulers. However, with the exception of religious communities which maintained their close links on the common territorial basis of the quarter, there are indications that the main quarters of the cities of Palestine, unseparated as they were by any form of physical barrier, underwent a process of a demographic osmosis. Whatever homogeneity may have existed in Mamluk times, there seems little doubt that under Ottoman rule greater heterogeneity was introduced within the precincts of the various quarters. The accumulation of new elements in the Muslim quarters made the distinctions between these quarters less and less significant. The *taḥrīrs* show very clearly that the closely linked families and clans, fathers and sons, even members of the larger family circle, continued to live next to each other throughout the century in all the cities. But on the larger scale, that of the quarter (with the exception of those of the religious minorities), the growing number of newly established elements introduced a factor of variety. In quarters in all the cities one can trace various elements living side by side: Kurds, Egyptians, Mag͟hribīs. A quarter which, by its name, should at one time have been exclusively of one element, such as the Sajjāᶜiyya (originally: Sajjāᶜiyyat al-Akrād, "of the Kurds")[52] in Gaza, contains a decreasing number of persons designated explicitly as "Kurds," while, on the other hand, showing newly arrived "Egyptians." Formerly nomadic families like Ṭurābāy can be traced in different quarters of Hebron. Although Ottoman-Turkish elements (soldiers, functionaries) lived in the towns in their official capacity they did not settle in separate quarters, but

[51] For a detailed description of the Syrian towns the late Mamluk period see Lapidus, in Hourani, Stern, *The Islamic City*, pp. 196–9; Lapidus, *Muslim Cities*, pp. 85–7.

[52] See below, p 121.

fairly soon were to be found, especially in the second half of the century, intermarried with the local population and living among them.[53] There are many scattered references to this effect in the *sijill* of Jerusalem, and it is in this town that two sons of the *Nā᾽ib al-ḳalᶜa,* the officer in charge of the citadel, lived in two different quarters.

Frequently the *imām* and other religious functionaries head the list of the inhabitants of a given quarter, thus implying that religiously speaking each of these quarters was still regarded as one unit, possibly concentrating around one mosque. But it is perhaps more relevant that no functional titles (*S͟hayk͟h al-ḥāra* or *ᶜArīf al-ḥāra* of the late Mamluk period)[54] are mentioned in the *taḥrīr* registers. In one case only, sons of *S͟hayk͟h al-balad* are mentioned specifically (Gaza, Dār al-K͟huḍar, 1548–9), and even this exceptional reference is not repeated in the following *taḥrīr,* ten years later. Judging from our registers one can hardly avoid the conclusion that the newly established Ottoman administration in Palestine abolished either the function or the title of "head of the quarter," presumably as a result of the diminishing homogeneity of this unit, and replaced it with either the traditional heads of clans and families, or tax-collectors designated by the government. Had they been active or important in Palestine in the sixteenth century some reference would surely have been made to them in the *taḥrīrs.* Moreover, when a long and detailed list of the dignitaries (*Aᶜyān*) of the various quarters of Jerusalem in 1563 was drawn up, holders of different official titles like *ḳāḍī* or *miᶜmār bās͟hī* ("Head of the masons") were specifically mentioned as such, while no reference was made to *S͟hayk͟h al-ḥāra.*[55]

Yet it would be surprising if, while they kept a number of administrative institutions (mostly taxes), the new Ottoman rulers found it expedient to give up the services of the formerly active heads of the quarters. Doubts on this point are strengthened by available information regarding other cities in sixteenth century Syria. As͟htōr[56] mentions that *S͟hayk͟h al-Ḥāras,* according to Ibn

[53] For a different situation in the Hungarian towns where the Turkish element "restait un monde de petites 'colonies' militaires, sans rapports profonds avec les environs" (undoubtedly due to their living in a border province) see Pérenyı, in Todorov, *Studia Balcanica,* p. 29.

[54] Lapidus, *Muslim Cities,* p. 92.

[55] *Sijill* of the religious court (*maḥkama*) of Jerusalem, vol. XLIV, pp. 437–8, dating I Muḥarram 971/21 August 1563.

[56] In As͟htōr, *Rivista degli studi orientalı,* vols. XXXIII–XXXIV (1958–9), pp. 207–9.

Ṭūlūn, were called upon in Damascus to perform certain administrative tasks even after the Ottoman conquest. In Hamat in the same period the *sijill* documents indicate that both the *Shaykh al-Ḥāra* and the *Shaykh zuḳāḳ* were active after the arrival of the Ottomans in the country.[57] While in our defters the *Shaykh al-Ḥāra* is not mentioned, evidence from other sources indicates that, as in other towns in Syria, the *Shaykh al-Ḥāra* was still present, at least in Jerusalem in the first thirty years. The volumes of the Jerusalem *sijill* (the only one left in Palestine for the period under review) which cover the years of the early *taḥrīrs* contain the draft lists of the *taḥrīr* of 945/1538 (copied on 5–6 Rajab 27–8.11.1538). Though the names are copied in an unsystematic, often illegible form, the lists admit a clear-cut conclusion on the foregoing question. Each list of inhabitants, for each of the seven quarters covered, begins: "their *shaykh* is x son of y." In the quarter of Bāb Ḥiṭṭa there were apparently three *shaykhs*.[58] The documents in the *sijill* also tell us something about the appointment and functions of the *shaykh*. He was nominated by the *subaşı* on behalf of the *sanjak bey*. He was vouched for by the inhabitants of the quarter and was regarded as formally responsible for them to the authorities. It seems that this responsibility was not limited to securing the attendance of any one summoned before the authorities (ضمان احضار); it extended to personal liability in any consequences resulting therefrom.[59] The *shaykh* was, formally at least, held responsible for the whole of the quarter, including its non-Muslim elements.[60] There is no indication as to how successful the *shaykhs* were in discharging this responsibility. The fact that they are not referred to in the draft *taḥrīr* twenty-five years later, as well as the total absence of any mention of them in our registers may give some answer to this question. This institution appears to have been kept active by the Ottomans in the cities of Palestine for the

57 ʿAbd al-Wadūd Muḥammad Barghūth, *Liwāʾ Ḥamāt fi al-ḳarn al-sādis ʿashar*, pp. 151–152.

58 The text is grammatically unsatisfactory and reads as follows: محلة باب حطه شيخها عبد الرحيم اليزبكي وعبـــد الرزاق ابن محمود ابن صلاح وحضر[ة] الشيخ باهر و[ا]لكل هو شيخ المحله (*Sijill* of Jerusalem, vol. X, p. 215).

59 وكفل الجماعة المذكورين باطنه شيخ المحلة المذكور باطنه وهو بدر الدين ابن ربيع و [؟] طلب منه احد من المذكورين باطنه وعجز عن احضار كان عليه القيام بما يطلب عليه بالشرع الشريف والقانون المنيف (*ibid.*, pp. 219–20).

60 وكفل المسلم والنصارى شيخهم عبيد المذكور ضمان احضار (*ibid.*, p. 217).

first decades after the conquest. Later on, about the middle of the century, this office probably lost its importance, as the Ottomans became increasingly acquainted with the details of conditions under their rule, and the decreasing population of the cities made it possible to dispense with the services of *Shaykh al-Ḥāra*. This change is probably part of a larger process, in which the officialdom of local origin and authority declined, and was supplanted by the increasingly effective imperial service.

The number of quarters in a town varied between six and eleven[61] (with the notable exception of Safed where twelve additional Jewish quarters are noted). The most outstanding characteristic of the quarters is their flexibility. All of them showed a very substantial capacity to absorb much higher numbers of inhabitants (in many instances fourfold higher) than their initial level, which is an indication of their being rather sparsely populated at the beginning of the sixteenth century. Except for three quarters in Jerusalem, Banī Ḥārith, Banī Zayd, Khawālidī, which were integrated into some of the larger ones during the second half of the century, all the others recur without interruption to the end of the century. In the first half of the century their number did not increase; in the second half there was no change in either their number or their names. Most of the names of quarters remained intact throughout the following four hundred years. It is in this respect that the sense of continuity, which has been described[62] as one of the characteristics of Syrian urbanism in earlier times, seems to have prevailed, at least as far as the quarters are concerned, and the basic structure of the cities remained unchanged. No maps were drawn by the Ottoman authorities, and the only available source (with the exception of the late nineteenth century mapping of Jerusalem and sketching of Nabulus) are town-plans prepared under the British Mandate in the 1920's and 1930's (*Survey of Palestine*, 1925, 1938–9). Ramle is the only town where the nomenclature of the quarters seems to have undergone a very substantial

[61] Trabzon and Mardin had a similar structure of about ten quarters (Gökbılgin, *Belleten*, vol. XXVI (1962), p. 296, Göyünç, *Mardın sancağı*, p. 97). Other references to cities in the sixteenth century illustrate a different composition: Edirne—145 *maḥalle* in 1529 (Gökbilgin, *Edirne ve Paşa Livası*, pp. 37–63); Segedin—20 in 1578 (T. Halası-Kun, *Belleten*, vol. XXVIII (1964), pp. 4–14); Skopje—55 in 1477 (Stoianovich, in Todorov, *Studia Balcanica*, p. 96). The difference may be a result of the cities of Palestine having inherited the classical structure left behind from the early Islamic period, unlike all the above-mentioned examples which had their origin in a different tradition and structure.

[62] Ashtōr, *Rivista degli Studi Orientali*, vol. XXXI (1956), p. 74.

change. All the other plans served as a valuable source for this study.[63]

These quarters were still inhabited and referred to as such even when they underwent, toward the turn of the century, a very profound decline. In the light of all that has been said above, it is almost impossible to reach any firm conclusion as to the average population of so varied a phenomenon as "a quarter." Still, if only the Muslim quarters are taken into account, from among about 180 samples, almost one fourth held less than 300 inhabitants, another fourth ranged between 300 and 600, and the rest had populations above 600. The highest peak reached—and this was by no means unique—was 3,400. In other words, though these were small communities, it would be inaccurate to relate "the order of a thousand people"[64] of Mamluk times to Ottoman Palestine. The *taḥrīr* made after the conquest usually indicates about half the figures cited above; these increase gradually towards the middle of the century, when they reach much higher figures, and then most of them again drop quite sharply.[65]

[63] We would like to offer our thanks to Mr. Candy, Mapping and Charting Establishment, R.E., Map research and library group, for his help and specifically for the reproduction of the town-plan of Safed

[64] Lapidus, in Hourani and Stern, *The Islamic City*, p. 196.

[65] In his article dealing with the premodern Balkan city Tr. Stoianovich (in Todorov, *Studia Balcanica*, p. 96) is of the "impression . . that an average *maḥalla* numbered between 25 and 50 houses in all but the largest and some of the very ancient cities, such as Athens, where it may have been larger." Although on several occasions some corroborating evidence to this effect can be produced from Palestine, one should note that generally speaking this was *not* the case there.

• 3 •

TAXES AND REVENUES

ALL lands and revenues in Palestine fell into one of five classes:

1. *Ḫāṣṣ-i Şāhī* ("Imperial *ḫāṣṣ*," Imperial domain," ID). Whole villages, and the proceeds of many taxes both in towns and villages belonged to the Imperial purse. In some cases, revenues formerly belonging to fiefs or governor's *ḫāṣṣ* or waqf, and then becoming part of the Imperial *ḫāṣṣ*, were known as *ḫāṣṣ-i cedīd*, new *ḫāṣṣ*.

2. *Ḫāṣṣ-i Mīrilivā* (Governor's *ḫāṣṣ*, "Appanage of the Mīr-i Livā," "Appanage of the Governor," AG). The governor of the sanjak received his remuneration in the form of a grant of *ḫāṣṣ*, consisting normally of a number of villages and of the proceeds of certain taxes in the towns in the sanjak.

3. Fiefs. In the Ottoman context, this term is used to designate two main types of grant of the right to collect revenues: the *ziʿāmet* (Z) and the *tīmār* (T).

4. *Mülk*. Freehold real estate, normally of land with buildings or of orchards (*bağçe* or *bustān*), vineyards (*bāğ* or *karm*), and vegetable gardens (*ḥākūra*). This is found almost exclusively in the precincts and immediate surroundings of towns.

5. Waqf (W). Pious or private foundations, for the benefit either of some religious institution or of the founder's family. Waqfs could consist of villages, with their land and revenues, shops and houses in towns, or of certain taxes, the proceeds of which had been consecrated by a ruler to a particular cause. Even in villages wholly assigned to a waqf, certain revenues were reserved as Imperial Domain. An exception to this is villages belonging to waqfs of the two Holy Cities, Mecca and Medina, known as the *Ḥarameyn* which were exempt from taxation.

Taxes were no doubt levied in Palestine from the beginning of Ottoman rule, though our earliest information dates from the *taḥrīr* of 932/1525–6. From the subsequent registers it is clear that in most towns the fiscal machine was only partially active during the first half of the century. This may be a result both of the difficulties in setting up an administration as well as of dislocations in the economy of the country which it took some time to remedy. Whatever the reasons, the relatively low figures of taxes cannot be attributed to a lack of the necessary fiscal regulations. In three towns (Safed, Hebron, Jerusalem) the survey of 1553–4 shows that a very detailed list of taxes was prepared and in fact collected, not only introducing a much greater variety of items, but increasing very substantially the total sum levied. It would seem that around the middle of the century the Ottoman state found it necessary to review its fiscal policy in Palestine, and in many cases make fundamental changes. This might coincide with the first term as grand vezir of Rüstem Pas̱ha (1544–53), who, according to Hammer, "fut le premier grand vizir qui soumit les gouverneurs à des taxes proportionnées aux revenus de leurs provinces."[1] Most probably the reorganization of the fiscal system in Palestine should be viewed as part of an overall development in the Empire. As a result of both more intensive collection and more diversified taxes (and, naturally, also increased economic activity) the rates of increase in the different towns between 1525 and 1555 are 100% (Gaza), 220% (Jerusalem), 300% (Ramle and Safed), 550% (Hebron).

The general and most striking characteristic of the tax picture is a steady, uninterrupted upward curve. This is, perhaps, not altogether surprising in view of the similar demographic developments in the towns during the first decades. Even when the demographic tide began to turn in the second half of the century, to reach quite a low ebb at its end, this is not reflected in the figures for tax revenue. These figures are however given in nominal money of account, in aspers (*aḳçe*).

Almost all figures in the registers are in aspers, the Ottoman silver coin used for all accounting purposes. Though the travellers reveal that a large number of different coins were in circulation in Palestine at the time, the registers only mention two other coins by name. These are: (1) the para—another Ottoman silver coin, of varying value, fixed for this time and place at 2 aspers; and (2) the gold piece—presumably the new Ottoman gold piece, minted in Damascus after the conquest. In the registers of 932/1525–6 the gold piece is deemed to be equivalent to 60 aspers, but by 945/1538–9 it has risen to 80, and in the final *taḥrīr* of our period, that of 1005/1596–7, it has reached 90.

These changes must be seen within the context of economic developments in the Empire as a whole. The depreciation of the silver coinage, the asper, was steadily accelerating during the sixteenth century. Whereas during almost three centuries prior to

[1] Hammer, *Histoire de l'empire ottoman*, vol. VI, p. 260. For some details on taxation in general and in Syria in particular at that time see *ibid.*, pp. 272, 273.

1584 it is said to have lost only 40–50% of its initial value, it was further depreciated by another 50% in the following ten years.[2] The asper underwent both debasement and devaluation, as its silver content was reduced, and the value of silver in relation to gold declined. Unable to curb inflationary pressures caused, *inter alia*, by worldwide developments like the introduction of large quantities of silver from the western to the eastern hemisphere, the Ottoman sultans tried to redress their difficulties by administrative and fiscal measures, which did not stop the general decrease of the public revenue. By the end of the century the asper was little more than a fictitious money of account, and rises in revenue, stated in aspers, may denote not an increase in income but a fall in the value of the money. Unfortunately, the registers say very little about how much was actually collected, and in what coin. With the exception of the *jizya*, the rate of which is fixed by the *Sharīʿa* in gold, the registers give little information about the relation between the asper of account and the various coins actually used (though obviously there must have been a known and accepted procedure), and even less about the gap between the amounts listed and the sums actually received. In spite of this, however, figures are still of some value. The devaluation of the asper, though it may have varied in different parts of the Ottoman Empire, will almost certainly have been much the same in the interlinked cities of a small region like Palestine, and the variations in revenue between the cities are, therefore, of some significance. Devaluation will not, of course, affect the relative importance of individual sources of revenue constituting the global figure for each city at any one date.

The Ottoman administration tried in various ways to meet its urgent need for ready cash. One, widely accepted in the countryside, was to incorporate vacated *tīmārs* in the Imperial domain, and then assign their revenues as tax-farms. Another, less obvious in the registers, was the gradual abandonment of the direct collection of taxes by salaried government commissioners, called *emīn*, and its replacement by a system of tax-farming (*iltizām*), whereby the tax-farmer paid a fixed sum for the right to collect the proceeds of a given tax or area.[3] There is a clear reference to such a transformation

[2] Inalcık, *Belleten*, vol XV (1951), p. 680; Barkan, *Belleten*, vol. XXXIV (1970), pp. 571–3, Cvetkova, in *Etudes historiques*, vol. I (1960), pp. 177–9; Muṣṭafā Nūrī, *Netāʾic ul-vuḳūʿāt*, vol. I, p. 177; Heyd, *Ottoman Documents*, p. 121, n. 3; Barkan, *IJMES*, vol. VI (1975), pp. 11 ff.; Shaw, *Ottoman Egypt*, pp. 167–70.

[3] For a more detailed description of the system see Cohen, *Palestine in the Eighteenth Century*, pp. 179–80; Lewis, "Emīn," *EI*[2].

having occurred in Gaza between 1539–49.[4] One result of the newly established system of *iltizām* was the standardization of figures, though in this respect it appears (in the above-mentioned case, at least) that conditions were not basically different even in earlier years.

As regards the revenue statistics, the towns of Palestine can be divided into two groups, one consisting of Gaza, Safed and Jerusalem, the other of Nabulus, Ramle, and Hebron. The first group, far more populous than the second, provided 70% to 80% of the entire taxes of the six, going up and down between the beginning and the end of the century, respectively. The other group provided the rest. When looked into more closely, the rates of relative increase in each town are very instructive. During the first decade there occurred 20%, 50%, 70%, and 90% increases in Gaza, Jerusalem, Hebron, and Ramle, respectively. During the following decade even higher rates can be noted: 50%, 70%, 120%, 230% in Gaza, Ramle, Hebron, and Jerusalem, respectively. The rate of increase tends to slow down in the 1550's. With the exception of Hebron (25%) it varies from 1% to 10% in all the other towns. In the last thirty years of the century the rate did not exceed 10%. In other words, the sharp rise in these revenues gathered momentum rapidly up to the middle of the century almost identically with the demographic curve. When the latter started dropping it inevitably had a bearing upon the rate of increase, slowing it down very substantially, but until the end of the century it still kept rising, at any rate in aspers of account. Naturally enough, in Hebron, by far the smallest in this respect, the otherwise insignificant changes reach a relatively high percentage, though the actual amounts remain small. On the other hand, even the small relative change in Gaza becomes immensely important in the light of its very high starting point, in fact the highest. Nabulus (for which unfortunately statistics are incomplete) underwent the slowest increase of all: less than 10% during the last sixty years of the century. This may perhaps be coupled with the fact that from the demographic point of view, too, it was an exception in its slow, but steady decrease of recorded population.

The following are the most noteworthy items in the general list.

[4] See below, p. 128.

1. TRADE

A. MARKET TAXES

Iḥtisāb

Of the four main functions of the towns—administrative, religious, industrial, and commercial—the last one was by far the most important as a source of revenue. Although not necessarily always the largest item of income, it can serve as a most valuable indicator to the general developments in the towns. Statements on the yield of market taxes and tolls are unfortunately not presented in a consistent form throughout the *defters*. The yields of several taxes are often given in one lump sum, while the classification differs from one town to another and even in the same town at different dates. Many of the market taxes are included under such general headings as dues payable to the inspector of markets (*iḥtisāb*), weighing and measuring dues (*ḳapan, keyyāliye*), brokerage dues (*simsāriye, dellāliye*), or are simply listed as market taxes without further specification.

Of all the market taxes, the *iḥtisāb* was by far the most important. In the *ḳānūnnāmes* of Nabulus, Gaza and Safed the section dealing with *ʿādet-i iḥtisāb* appears as the opening item, while in Jerusalem it is set forth in great detail in the middle part. The rates vary

TABLE 4

	932/ 1525–6	945/ 1538–9	955/ 1548–9	961–4/ 1553–7	970–5/ 1562–7	1005/ 1596–7
Jerusalem	12,000 ID	12,000 AG		23,000 AG	23,000 ID	
Hebron				3,000 T	7,200[5] ID	9,500[5] ID
Gaza	18,000 ID	27,000 AG	63,000[6] AG	63,000[6] AG		65,000[6] AG
Ramle	1,500[7]	2,000 AG	6,200[8] AG	6,200[8] AG		8,000[8] AG
Nabulus		20,000[9] ID	32,400			33,000
Safed	7,200 AG	15,000 AG		80,000 ID	84,000 ID	

[5] *Iḥtisāb + ḳaṣṣābiye.*

[6] This figure includes the proceeds of the *Ḳapan, Dār al-Wakāla*, the vegetable market and the market for thread and weaving.

[7] *Ihtısāb + ḳaṣṣābiye.*

[8] *Iḥtisāb + Ḳapan + Dār al-wakāla.*

[9] *Iḥtisāb + Ḳapan.*

according to the different items, towns or origins; sometimes (e.g., in Sūḳ al-ᶜAṭṭārīn in Jerusalem or in Sūḳ Shajjāᶜiyya in Gaza) it varies even according to the location of the market where they are sold or the scales on which they are weighed. Although *iḥtisāb* was usually levied on items brought for sale, a fixed sum was collected from various shops or mills independently of the actual volume of their business.

Table 4, above shows the amounts given and the identity of the beneficiary.

Ḳapan[10]

As may be inferred from the table above, the *iḥtisāb* not only covered a very wide range of items, but was often connected and related to some other taxes, notably the *ḳapan*. This term is exten-

TABLE 5

	932/ 1525–6	945/ 1538–9	955/ 1548–9	961–4/ 1553–7	970–5/ 1562–7	1005/ 1596–7
Jerusalem				12,200 W	17,000 ID	
Hebron[11]				2,160	1,800 W	2,000 W
Gaza	300	1,000 AG	63,000 AG	63,000 AG		65,000[12] AG
Ramle	1,200 ID	2,000[13] AG	6,200 AG	6,200 AG		8,000[14] AG
Nabulus		20,000 ID	600 ID			1,000 ID
Safed		1,200 ID		20,000 ID	22,500 ID	

[10] The word already occurs in classical Arabic and Persian, and is probably derived ultimately from the Latin *campana* (scales). The term is applied both to the public scales and to the building where it is housed, hence also to the market place. Most probably this was less important than the main *sūḳs* where in certain cases the rate of taxes levied was much higher (Dozy, *Supplément*, s.v.; Beldiceanu, *Les Actes des premiers Sultans*, p. 178, and n. 1, 2; Cvetkova, *La vie èconomique de villes balkaniques*, p. 21; M. A. Shūshterī, *Farhang-i Fārisi*, p. 517).

[11] In both Jerusalem and Hebron combined with *dār al-khuḍar*.

[12] In the last three entries combined with *iḥtisāb*.

[13] *Ḳaṣṣābiye* + *dār al-wakāla*.

[14] In the last three entries combined with *dār al-wakāla* and *iḥtisāb*. In Istanbul it was called *ḳassāb akçesi* (A. Refik, *Istanbul Hayati*, p. 1). According to one version (ᶜAbd al-Raḥmān Vefīḳ Bey, *Tekālif ḳavāᶜidi*, vol. I, p. 32) it was levied at varying rates of 2–10 pāra on each goat or sheep slaughtered. For rates levied in Jerusalem see Barkan, *Kanunlar*, p. 218; cf. below, p. 102.

sively used in the *ḳānūnnāme* of Jerusalem in the section dealing with *iḥtisāb*. The *ḳapan* served on occasion to determine whether or not a certain commodity was liable to *iḥtisāb*; moreover there were (in Jerusalem, at least) several different *ḳapans*: *muḥtesib ḳapanı* (*ḳapan* of the inspector of markets), *ḳapan-i zeyt* (*ḳapan* of oil), *ḳapan-i ḳuṭn* (*ḳapan* of cotton), etc.[15]

Except for Jerusalem and Safed, the *ḳapan* seems a small source of income, relatively much smaller than the *iḥtisāb*.

Ḳaṣṣābiye

Another tax often combined with *iḥtisāb* was the tax on butchers (*ḳaṣṣābiye*, *ḳaṣṣābān*). The rates were generally half an asper per sheep or goat slaughtered, 2 aspers per ox, 4 per water buffalo.

TABLE 6

	932/ 1525–6	945/ 1538–9	955/ 1548–9	961–4/ 1553–7	970/ 1562–3	1005/ 1596–7
Jerusalem	2,500 ID	3,000 AG		3,000 AG	5,000 ID	
Gaza	6,000 ID	6,000 AG	10,000 ID	10,000 ID		12,000 ID
Ramle	1,500[16]		1,280 ID	1,500		2,000

In Safed a special tax on Jewish slaughtering appears (called *naḥirat al-Yahūd*), which rises from 1,200 aspers in 1525–6 to 6,600 in 1538–9, to 15,500 in 1555–6 and to 17,500 in 1567–8.

Dār al-Wakāla

The fourth element which was, as shown above, closely linked to the *iḥtisāb* was *dār al-wakāla*. This term, the common Egyptian equivalent for the Syrian *k͟hān* was, it seems, used in Southern Palestine intermittently, and is mentioned in another part of Syria, Tripoli. As the *ḳapan* was situated, in some cases at least (Gaza for one) in *dār al-wakāla*, the link is obvious. This tax was apparently levied on behalf of the man in charge of the *k͟hān* (*ṣāḥib*, which could mean owner, lessee, or even just administrator)

[15] In this as in other terms the language of the register uses Turkish, Persian and Arabic words and forms, more or less indiscriminately. *Muḥtesib ḳapanı* means the *ḳapan* of the *muḥtesib* in Turkish; *ḳapan-i zeyt* means the *ḳapan of zeyt* ("olive-oil") with a Persian grammatical form.

[16] *ḳaṣṣābiye* + *iḥtisāb*

as well as the man who actually did the weighing.[17] In addition to the figures mentioned above (Jerusalem, Ramle) it was separately and specifically referred to in Ramle in 1525–6 as 3,200 aspers belonging to the Imperial Domain, while in Gaza the registers mention a *dār al-wakāla* in the Shajjāʾiyya quarter which was given as an appanage to the governor, producing 2,000 aspers in 1525–6 and 3,000 in 1538–9. The same item (referred to as (*dār al-wakāla waʾl ḍamān*)[18] was later integrated into the reassessed *iḥtisāb* as of *ca.* 1548–9 in Gaza and ten years earlier in Ramle.

TABLE 7

	932/ 1525–6	945/ 1538–9	955/ 1548–9	961–4/ 1553–7	970–5/ 1562–7	1005/ 1596–7
Jerusalem	14,500	15,000		38,200	45,000	
Hebron				5,160	9,000	11,500
Gaza	26,300	37,000	73,000	73,000		77,000
Ramle	5,900	4,000	7,480	7,700		10,000
Nabulus		20,000	33,000			34,000
Safed	8,400	22,800		115,500	124,500	
Total	55,100	98,800	113,480	236,560	178,500	132,500

Concluding Remarks on Market Taxes

The above table, combining the different market taxes collected, follows more systematically the general pattern which can be traced in some towns of Palestine. In the course of the century the Ottoman administration seems to have grouped the different taxes related to *iḥtisāb* in one entry. By submerging such details as are available in a single global figure, one may more safely draw some general conclusions.

Although referred to as a town from the very beginning of the century, Hebron was treated by the Ottoman authorities for all practical purposes as a village.[19] Until 1553 taxes were levied there exactly on the same basis as in other villages of Palestine, i.e., in kind, as a percentage of local agricultural produce. Market taxes are not mentioned up to this date, and when they appear they are

[17] "Ve dārülvekâlede ṣatılan . . . iḥtısāb için . . . ve dārülvekâle ṣāḥibı dahi kirāye-i ḫān ve ücret-i ḳapān için ber vech-i iştirāk ḳapāncı ıle bir ʿOsmānī." (Ḳānūn-nāmē-ı livā-i Ghazze)

[18] Lit: "liability", here in the sense of a pledge for items temporarıly deposited in the khān. Cf. s.v. "Ḍamān," *EI*², vol. II, p. 105.

[19] See above, p. 13, and below, p. 112

still in very small figures. During the 1550's commercial activity in Hebron seems to have almost doubled and thereafter continued to grow, though at a slower pace, until the end of the century. Hebron must have developed its economic contacts with its rural and desert hinterland, and also benefited, partially, at least, from the Syrian-Egyptian-Arabian trade. The appearance of a tax on slaughtered animals in the early 1560's indicates a substantial improvement in the standard of living of the local population. Nevertheless, relatively speaking Hebron still showed a rather low volume of commercial activity in its markets. While *iḥtisāb* in Hebron more than doubled in money of account between the middle and the end of the century, the rate of increase in Ramle was about 60% from the beginning of the century to the end. The main increase occurred in 1548–9 (about 25%), to be maintained at a slightly lower rate up to the end of the century, but here, as is Hebron, the total income remained rather low. Much more important in quantitative terms was Nabulus which, here again, made its main leap in 1548–9. In contrast to all the other towns, however, the *iḥtisāb* revenues of Nabulus remained almost unchanged in the subsequent fifty years, thereby suggesting a possible stagnation of commercial activity (or of bureaucratic efficiency or both). Around the middle of the century there is a very substantial increase in *iḥtisāb* revenues in Safed, Gaza and Jerusalem. In the latter two it was in the region of 200%, in Safed 400%. Although some of this is due to the increased consumption of meat in all the three (most conspicuous in Safed), and part of it is to be ascribed to the constant depreciation of the Ottoman currency,[20] the main source of the increase in revenue was a great expansion of the trade on which *iḥtisāb* was levied. One outcome of these developments was that Safed replaced Gaza as the major commercial center by the middle of the century. If we now take the picture as a whole, *iḥtisāb* taxes, which at the beginning of Ottoman rule did not constitute more than 10% of the entire fiscal revenue from the cities, became much more important in the second half of the century, when they rose to about 20% of the total revenue. This is a further indication of the growing importance of the cities as commercial centers, thanks to improved and safer conditions of transport[21] and agriculture, as well as an increasing population consuming the product of the land and engaging in trade.

[20] See above, p. 44.

[21] Cf. the erection of caravansarays by Sinān Pas͟ha in the eighties (M. Bak͟hīt, *Ottoman Province of Damascus*, pp. 258–9; Heyd, *Ottoman Documents*, p. 102.

Grains

Commercial activity was, in fact, far more important than can be deduced from *iḥtisāb* data. Grains were usually brought to a separate market (*bāzār-i ğille*) and were liable to a special tax, referred to as brokerage, measuring or simply grain tax (*keyyāliye, simsāriye-i ğilāl, bāj al-ğilāl, keyyāliye-i muğall*).

TABLE 8

	932/ 1525–6	945/ 1538–9	955/ 1548–9	961–4/ 1553–7	970–5/ 1562–7	1005/ 1596–7
Jerusalem		150 W		720 +8000 W W	360 +8000 W W	
Gaza	6,000 AG	6,000 AG	10,000 AG	10,000 AG		10,000 AG
Ramle	350 ID	720 AG	3,560	3,560		3,560[22]
	1,500[23] ID	1,500 AG	1,500 AG	2,000 AG		2,000 AG
Nabulus		500 ID	1,000 ID			1,500 ID
Safed		1,000[24] ID		5,700 ID		8,300[25] ID

Gaza and Jerusalem seem to have been the most active in this respect, with Nabulus and Ramle lagging far behind. In Jerusalem, at least, this tax was levied at the rate of 1 asper per camel-load and 1/2 asper per mule or ass-load. In the Jewish quarter there was a mill used to grind the incoming grains, its revenues amounting to 480 aspers in 1553–4 and to 1,000 aspers in 1562–3. This indicates an increase in activity, which however does not tally with the general trend shown in the above table. The latter may be better reflected in the revenue from the storehouses of the flour merchants (situated in the Jewish quarter, too) which declined from 600 to 300 aspers over the same period. It is known from Jewish sources that Safed had its own special market for grains,[26] but as this entry includes some further items it is impossible to assess the relative importance

[22] This figure in the last three entries lumps together the taxes levied in the following markets: cotton, vegetables, asses and cattle, "black" tax, grains.

[23] Listed as *Ḥınṭa-i Simsim*, literally "wheat of sesame"—perhaps an error for wheat and sesame.

[24] With brokerage of fruit and of spice merchants.

[25] With "brokerage of spice merchants and of slave market toll," for the last two figures.

[26] Kenaʿanī, *Zion*, vol. VI (1934), p. 185

of grains. Still, these three towns (Gaza, Jerusalem, Safed) had higher yields from *iḥtisāb*. Hebron had a very substantial income from grains, which provided almost the only source of revenue in the first years of Ottoman rule: 4,260 aspers in 1525–6, 6,860 in 1538–9, 6,860 in 1553–4. All of it was waqf (as were the yields of many plots of land near the city).

Dār al-Khuḍar

A special market (*sūḳ al-khuḍar* or *al-khuḍrawāt* or *dār al-khuḍar*) for vegetables was held in Jerusalem, Gaza, Ramle and Hebron. As its revenues are usually combined with the *ḳapan* and *dār al-wakāla* it is impossible to assess the volume of traffic. In Ramle alone this tax was separately recorded, at the rate of 3% of the value of vegetables sold. The records refer only to the years 1525–6 and 1538–9, when the sum of 1,200 aspers was paid annually to the Imperial Domain and to the appanage of the governor, respectively. Later, this entry was combined, as in other towns, with *dār al-wakāla*. This was a natural step, given the difficulties of differentiating between vegetables brought from abroad (onions, garlic, etc.) and sold at the *dār al-wakāla* and those grown locally and sold at the *sūḳ al-khuḍar*.

Fruit

Fruit was liable to a separate brokerage tax (*simsāriyat al-fawākih*), which was collected in the same way as the vegetable tax. The only town in which it received a separate mention was Safed: 830 aspers in 1555–6, 1000 aspers in *ca.* 1567 were collected for the Imperial Domain. Related to this category was the tax on vineyards (*kharāj al-kurūm*) which in 1538–9 was collected in Nabulus at the rate of 5,000 aspers. In Hebron it was levied, probably in kind, at the equivalent rates of 3,000, 3,000, 10,000 aspers in the years 1525–6, 1538–9, 1553–4, respectively. Gaza and Ramle specialized in selling dates, which were grown along the Mediterranean coast between Gaza and al-ᶜArīsh. Most of the produce, naturally, was sold in Gaza, in special baskets (*ḳawṣara*) from which *resm-i ḳawāṣir* accrued to the Imperial Domain as follows:

TABLE 9

	955/1548–9	964/1556–7	1005/1596–7
Gaza	400	400	600
Ramle	100	150	200

Despite the steady increase in the second half of the century, it is obvious that taxes on fruit were only a minor source of revenue. This suggests that the trade in fruit was itself of minor importance in the towns of Palestine.

Animals

Animals were sold in most towns in specially designated markets. Horses, mules, asses, cattle were either grouped in an animal-market (*sūḳ al-dawwāb*) as in Safed, Nabulus, and Gaza, or were brought to separate markets, sometimes bearing a special name: a market of asses or cattle (*sūḳ al-ḥamīr, sūḳ al-baḳar*) in Ramle.

TABLE 10

	932/ 1525–6	945/ 1538–9	955/ 1548–9	961–4/ 1553–7	970–5/ 1562–7	1005/ 1596–7
Jerusalem	800 ID	1,000 AG		2,000 AG	3,000 ID	
Gaza	200[27]	2,150 T	10,000 ID	10,000 ID		
Ramle (asses)		115[28] AG				
(cattle)		25 AG				
Nabulus		400	1,000 ID			1,200 ID
Safed				300 AG	300 AG	

This tax was collected (in Jerusalem, at least) at the following rates: 10 aspers per camel, 4 aspers per horse or mule, 2 aspers per ass or ox, 1/3 asper per sheep or goat. One is surprised by the absence of any animal market in Hebron, especially in view of its agricultural and nomadic hinterland. It may well have been combined with the general entry of *ḳapan*, either for reasons of scribal expediency or because at least part of the animals which brought goods for sale in the market were probably later disposed of at the neighbouring animal market. In other towns, two interesting points emerge. First, there was a steady expansion of trade in animals in four of the towns from the very beginning of the Ottoman rule. The main upsurge in this field also occurred around the middle of the century, when an increase of 100%, 150%, 350% is recorded in

[27] Register 427 gives this figure, whereas register 131 reads (for the same *taḥrīr*) 2,000. Although the possibility of a scribal error cannot be excluded, it may be noted that the latter entry combines *dār al-wakāla* with the animal market, and the two versions may thus still be compatible.

[28] For the following years see above, n. 22.

Jerusalem, Nabulus, and Gaza, respectively. Second, Gaza is a special case not only in relative terms, but also in absolute figures. From the beginning of Ottoman rule, having recovered from the initial shock of the conquest and its aftermath, this trade was resumed on a larger scale, to reach impressive dimensions towards the middle of the century. Like similar trends in the various markets this may be seen as a further indication of the economic revival in Gaza. This unparalleled increase may also reflect the growth of caravan traffic between Palestine and Egypt.

In 1538–9, it will be observed, the revenue from the animal market in Gaza belonged to a *tīmār*. This was very unusual in cities, and disappears in the later *taḥrīrs*, where it is registered as belonging to the Imperial Domain.

Cotton

Separate scales (*ḳapan*) for cotton are mentioned in Jerusalem, Gaza and Ramle. For the one in Jerusalem, which was, naturally, situated in the Sūḳ al-Kaṭṭānīn, information is available for 1553–4 as well as 1562–3. On both occasions 1,500 aspers accrued to the Imperial Domain. For Gaza we have three figures, showing a rise from 400 aspers in 1548–9 to 500 aspers in 1556–7, and to 1,000 aspers in 1596–7. Here, too, the revenue belonged to the Imperial Domain. In Ramle, the register for 1538–9 records a yearly revenue of 1,500 aspers accruing to the governor from both raw and spun cotton. In the three following *taḥrīrs* which cover the second half of the century, the figure for Ramle is combined in one entry with those for grains, vegetable and animal markets, and yielded a total of 3,560 aspers as a *ḫāṣṣ* of the governor. Cotton markets existed only in the southern towns of Palestine. Ramle appears to have been the most important cotton market of the three, although a clear trend of increase can be easily traced in Gaza also. Cotton was brought into these three towns, situated in the midst of the cotton-growing area, on animals (usually camels) to be taxed according to weight, at the rate of 2 aspers per camel-load. In these same three towns no local industry using this raw material is recorded. On the other hand Safed and Nabulus, which both had substantial textile manufactures, had no cotton market. Although most of the textiles manufactured in the last two towns were made of wool rather than cotton, it seems likely that both were used.[29]

[29] In Ḥamāt in the same century there seems to exist ample evidence that the guilds of weavers (*ṭā'ifat al-ghazzālīn, ṭā'ifat al-ḥiyāk*) as well as some others dealt concurrently both in wool and in cotton (ʿAbd al-Wadūd Muhammad Yūsuf, *Majallat al-ḥawliyyāt al-athariyya*, vol. XIX, p. 92).

B. INTERPROVINCIAL TRADE

There was an active export of soap from Jerusalem and Ramle to Egypt through the port of Gaza, as can be deduced both from the registers[30] and the *sijill* of the religious court of Jerusalem. Moreover, a very large percentage of commodities sold in the various markets mentioned above was originally from the Palestinian sanjaks. A distinction, rather difficult to follow in practice, was drawn for taxation purposes between local products and those coming from elsewhere. The *Dār al-Wakāla* seems to have served mainly for the purpose of storing incoming goods.[31] In Ramle these included rice, dates, henna, grape juice, dried onions and garlic. All of these, having arrived there either by sea or by land, were sold at the same place, liable to the payment of a certain proportion (half a *raṭl*) from each load. It is impossible to trace changes in the incidence of this tax, as it is combined with others in the entry for *iḥtisāb*. But one is inclined to relate this tax to the interprovincial and international trade passing through Palestine. Commodities mentioned as reaching Ramle "by sea" presumably came via the port of Jaffa[32] while those coming "by land" were no doubt brought by the caravans from Egypt. These followed an ancient route and an old tradition.[33] We have a complete set of figures for the income accruing to the Imperial Domains from this traffic throughout the century, both in Gaza and in Ramle.

TABLE 11

		932/ 1525–6	945/ 1538–9	955/ 1548–9	964/ 1556–7	1005/ 1596–7
Gaza	Toll on the road to Egypt (*ʿĀdet-i bāc-i*[34] *rāh-i Mıṣr*)	50,000	50,000	80,000	100,000	100,000
	Toll on spices of the Noble Hajj (*Bāc-ı bahār-i ḥācc-i şerif*)	50,000	50,000	50,000	50,000	50,000
Ramle	Road-toll (*bāc-i rāh*)	8,000	30,000	46,740	50,000	55,000

[30] See below, p. 96

[31] Cf. the same institution serving the same purpose in sixteenth-century Ḥamāt in Barghūt, *Liwāʾ Ḥamāt*, p. 53.

[32] See Lewis, "Jaffa in the sixteenth century," *Necati Lugal Armağanı*, pp. 435–46.

[33] Referred to as *bāc-i dirin* ("the old toll") in our registers. For a description of the collection of this tax at Ḳaṭyā in the Mamluk period see Rabie, *Financial system of Egypt*, p. 101.

[34] *Bāc* is an arabicized form of a Persian term *bāẕh*, used in pre-Ottoman times with the meaning of "due," "tax." It was only later that it came to denote an obligatory

The figures for Gaza were probably rounded up for practical considerations or may indicate that these taxes, even when collected by *emīns*[35] were, in fact, farmed out. Although separate entries, the two are intrinsically linked. The second was, as its name clearly indicates, a toll levied on spices arriving from South and South East Asia via Mecca and Cairo. Not only had the spice trade of Egypt not ceased to exist in the sixteenth century,[36] but these very substantial figures on the same item seem to suggest that it was still, in Palestinian terms, impressive.[37] A certain tendency to stagnate, though, can be deduced from a comparison with the first item. During the time of the first *taḥrīr* this tax was collected only at one check-point (*ğafar*),[38] Khān Yūnus, to the south of Gaza. Thereafter and until the turn of the century it was collected at two more points: Gaza and Khān Sdūd. More instructive for our purpose are the figures themselves. They augment at the rate of 60% in 1548–9 and another 40% in the following decade, indicating an important development in this field. What seems to be even more meaningful than the rate of increase is the actual figure. The revenue from these tolls amounted to a fifth of the total tax income from Gaza, about one third if the toll on spices is included. This figure alone exceeded the total revenues from Hebron, from all sources for the same year, and constituted a substantial contribution to the treasury.

In Ramle a toll was levied only on the equivalent of the first entry of Gaza. It was specifically forbidden to levy any tax on spices arriving from Mecca. From the administration's point of view these had already been taxed once in Gaza. This departure from the usual procedure adopted with regard to all other commodities can only be interpreted as an attempt on behalf of the central government to encourage the trade in spices, threatened by the Portuguese incursions, to follow the "classical" route via the Hejaz, Red Sea, and Egypt, leading to Damascus and the north. All other goods were liable in Ramle once again to *bāc-i rāh*[*-i Miṣr*]. Although collected

toll on every commercial transaction involving goods in the cities (also animals) brought from the outside. In the *kānūnnāme* of Süleymān the word was used both as a specific municipal tax and as tax in general. It was usually collected at the gates of towns or in the market itself, as is the case here, and usually paid in coin by the buyer (Köprülü, "Bādj," *EI*², vol. I, pp. 860–2. For many details see Cvetkova, *La vie économique*, pp. 15–25. See also Beldiceanu, *JESHO*, vol. XI (1968), p. 85.

[35] See above, p. 44.

[36] See above, p. 27.

[37] For the increase of spice trade in Mecca and Jedda see Braudel, *La Méditerranée*, vol. I, pp. 498–503; Inalcık, *Belleten*, vol. XV (1951), pp. 663–4, 674

[38] See below, p. 129, n. 38.

at similar rates (the only differences being the absence of any cattle and half the rate paid in Gaza on a donkey-load; from the middle of the century even these were eliminated), the proceeds to the Imperial Domain from Ramle were much lower. Nevertheless, for the early years following the conquest, when relatively low sums accrued from this source as a result of the still unstable state of affairs, the 1530's witnessed a very sharp upsurge (about 300%), and the curve rose steadily to the end of the century.

The rates of this tax did not differ substantially from those fixed for other *ǧafar* posts in Palestine, but the amount collected in Gaza and Ramle was far greater. This means more active traffic between Egypt and Palestine. Although on the face of it there is a striking similarity between the global sum collected in Gaza and the one levied on the sanjak of Safed, one should bear in mind that the latter accrued from six checkpoints, whereas the former was collected only at three. Thus this apparent similarity, which could be a result of parallel *muḳāṭaʿa* (contracts), does not alter our conclusion on the intensity of the trade in the southern part of Palestine.

The figures for Safed are as follows:

TABLE 12

	932/1525–6	945/1538–9	963/1555–6	*ca.* 975/1567–8
Saʿsaʿ	5,700	6,000	21,500	21,500
Jisr Yaʿḳūb	6,000		25,000	25,000
Minya	6,000		23,000	23,000
Jibb Yūsuf	6,000		13,000	13,000
ʿUyūn Tujjār	6,000	7,000	11,500	11,500
Raʾs Ṣūr (Tyre)	1,720	1,400	6,000	6,000
Total	31,420		100,000	100,000

Most of these tolls were collected along the road to Damascus, the highest yield coming from the crossing of the river Jordan at Jisr Yaʿḳūb. Only 6% of the total was collected at what seems to have been a branch route, less frequented, to the Lebanese coast at Tyre (Ṣūr). The total levied here is in fact identical to the sum collected in Gaza in the second half of the century. It indicates the importance of this source of income to the Imperial Domain as compared to other sources or places.

Although incomplete information allows fewer conclusions than in Gaza, some general remarks may, however, be made. Commercial links between Damascus and Palestine were apparently resumed shortly after the Ottoman conquest. Progress was, however, still slow in the first half of the century, and in one case (the road to

Tyre) there was even some decrease during the decade beginning in 1525. However, around the middle of the century a reassessment was apparently made, and new, less stereotyped figures were inserted, indicating an increase of over 200% during thirty years. Here too we find a common phenomenon: a very substantial increase around the middle of the century, indicating improved economic conditions and a higher degree of security.

The rates of *ǧafāre* toll levied at the various checkpoints were:

TABLE 13

	Camel-load	Horse- or mule-load	Donkey-load	White or black male or female slave	Ox or buffalo	Christian traveller	Jewish traveller	Sheep for sale
Gaza	4	2	1	10	3			
Ramle	4	2	1/2	10				
Saʿsaʿ	4	2	1/2	10		10	6	
Jisr Yaʿḳūb	2	1		10		8	6	1 beast per flock
Minya	2	1	1/2			8	6	
Jibb Yūsuf	4	2	1/2	10		8	6	1 beast per flock
ʿUyūn Tujjār	4	2	1/2	10		8	6	1 beast per flock
Raʾs Ṣūr	2	1	1/2	10		8	8	1 beast per flock

Two more conclusions can be drawn from these rates regarding the actual commodities which were transferred, sheep and slaves. Safed was very much dependent for meat upon imports of sheep from Damascus, as stated in a firman dating 990/1582: "as has been customary from olden times to bring sheep from the eastern region to Damascus and Safed and sell them [there]."[39] In contrast to all other commodities, which were not named but were liable to taxation at a certain percentage of their value, sheep "brought to be sold", being a most profitable item to be taxed, were specifically mentioned in the registers and taxed in kind. This trade, apparently very active in the north of Palestine, did not exist in the south, i.e. Gaza and Ramle, where instead oxen and water buffaloes were brought from Egypt for the same purpose.

The second item named in this context was slaves, white and black, male and female. This trade was not apparently directed to Palestine

[39] Heyd, *Ottoman Documents*, p. 134.

as its final destination. The identical rates which are given for the sale of slaves at *ġafar* posts on the ways to both Damascus and Cairo may be a sign of free traffic in this "commodity" in both directions. Palestine served as a halting-place for merchants bringing black slaves from Egypt as well as white slaves from the north to Safed. Official Ottoman documents mention black slaves as being brought from Egypt by slave-merchants travelling with the annual tribute sent to Istanbul; this implies at least a certain continuity.[40] That this phenomenon was more than sporadic is confirmed by the existence in Safed of a special slave-market (*bāzār-i esārā*), the revenue of which was a part of a rapidly rising entry accruing to the Imperial Domain.[41]

Miscellaneous

In Nabulus a tax called *resm-i şeddādiye*, perhaps on loads bound in a special way by the merchants, yielded the Imperial Domain 240 aspers per year in 1538–9, 338 in 1548–9 and 500 in 1596–7.

The extraction of bitumen[42] from the Dead Sea became a regular source of income to the Imperial Domain, yielding 10,000 aspers per year, as is recorded both in 1553–4 and in 1562–3.

2. INDUSTRIES

Trade was by far the most important economic function of the towns of Palestine, and it was usually in commodities brought from outside. In several cases, however, it was linked with local industries. Taxes on industrial production as well as customs and toll duties on industrial products serve as a useful indicator of the development of industry in the period under review.

A. CLOTH AND DYEING

The main center of the textile industry was Safed. In 1525–6 the register shows two dye houses, one contributing 300 aspers

[40] Cf. *ibid.*, pp. 123–4.

[41] Cf. p. 163. For further information on the slave trade, see Shaw, *Ottoman Egypt*, pp. 134–5.

[42] On the extraction of bitumen, also called *al-Ḳafr al-yahūdī*, from the Dead Sea, see Marmardji, *Textes géographiques*, pp 15–18; Fr. Pantaleão de Aveiro, *Itinerario*, pp. 397–8; Luke, *A Franciscan's Narrative*, p. 39; Affagart (*Relation de Terre Sainte*, p. 122) mentions it as a source of "great income" to the governor of Jerusalem.

a year to the Imperial Domain, the other contributing the same amount to the *ziʿāmet* of the Alay Bey. By 1538–9 the revenues of both dye houses belong to the Imperial Domain, and amount to 1,000 aspers a year. The two dye houses are described as being for cloth (*ḳumāş*) and for *çoḳa*[43] (a kind of broadcloth). In 1555–6 there are four dye houses for cloth and *çoḳa*, producing 2,236 aspers, of which 1,000 are for *çoḳa* and 1,236 for cloth. In the late 1560's the same dye houses produced the total sum of 2,250 to the Imperial Domain. In addition there is a stamp duty (*tamǧa-i çoḳa*)[44] on the manufacture of *çoḳa* and of *ḳarziye*,[45] another kind of cloth. The rates were two aspers per *pastav* of *ḳarziye* and four aspers per *pastav* of *çoḳa* giving a total yield of 12,000 aspers (the *pastav* has been estimated at about 37 1/2 yards). The same yield accrued to the Imperial Domain in the late 1560's also.

A third item to be mentioned here is the mill-tax (*resm-i ṭavāḥīn*). This tax was levied on each half-stone[46] at the rate of 30 aspers per year. It was collected from mills initially intended for grains, but actually used primarily, if not exclusively, as a stage in the manufacture of cloth in Safed. Cloth was manufactured in various parts of Palestine, but Safed became the main center. This was helped by a number of factors. One was the proximity of Sidon, the most important functioning port of the southern Levant and used both for the import of raw wool and for the export of finished cloth.[47] Abundant flowing clear water was a necessity in the manufacture and dyeing of cloth at that period, and with the limited exception of Nabulus, only the region of Safed enjoyed this advan-

[43] Čoka vulg čoḫa was "a widely used material in the Turkish Empire. It was in a particularly great demand by the Turkish army since the trousers, overcoats and the raincoats were made from it" (Nagy, *Acta Orientalia*, vol. XVIII (1965), p 301, giving many further details on the term and its use).

[44] Probably identical to *bāc-i bāzār-ı sıyāh* (see p 101, n. 72), which in Jerusalem yielded 2,000 aspers to the appanage of the governor in 1538–9 and 1553–4, while in 1562–3 the same sum went to the Imperial Domain. There is a single entry in Hebron of 250 aspers paid as *siyāh* in 1553–4. Though the "black stamp" was not necessarily applied only on cloth, it seems most likely that this was its main purpose.

[45] A term of early origin, widely used in Middle Eastern and other languages, and of frequent occurrence in Ottoman documents to denote a type of cloth. For different interpretations and the origin of the term see Hamilton and Beldiceanu, *BSOAS*, vol. XXXI (1968), pp. 330–46; Wansbrough, in Dalby, *Language and History in Africa*, p. 95. See below, p. 167.

[46] See below, p. 161, n. 29.

[47] On a substantial trade in cloth in the sixteenth century between the Jews of Safed and Hamat see Barg̱hūt *Liwāʾ Hamāt*, p. 178. On both imports of raw material from and exports of cloth to Europe see Avitzur (citing responsa and other Jewish sources), in Ben-Zvi and Benayahu, *Studies and Texts*, pp. 43–7, 54–6, 67–9.

tage. This town and its vicinity were known for their springs, of which the most plentiful were along Wādī Dilbāy. Not all of the mills listed in our registers can be located precisely, but out of ten mentioned by name, three were specifically situated in Wādī Dilbāy, two of which were the most active and yielded more than a third of the entire proceeds. The water-mills of this Wādī, which later gave it the name "the Wādī of the mills" (*al-ṭawāḥīn*) were perfectly suited for the needs of the weavers. The Jewish immigrants who had brought their skills from Spain to Salonica, thereby turning it into a most prosperous center of textile production, did the same in Safed after the Ottoman conquest. The mechanical fulling mill was the method imported from Spain (known as *batan* in Spanish). Basically, it relied on an abundant flow of water, not only to clean the raw wool, as was usual, but also to drive fulling "hammers" attached to a rotating wheel.[48] The mills of Safed were found to be most suitable for this purpose and were increasingly exploited. Around the middle of the century they paid 9,120 aspers to the Imperial Domain, and almost twice as much about a decade later (16,600 in *ca.* 1567). These are the latest figures at present available.

Second to Safed as a center of weaving and dyeing was Nabulus, where the industry was smaller and differently constituted. The mills in the vicinity of Nabulus (26 in all) were most probably used, as in Safed, for the fulling process, yielding 960 aspers to the Imperial Domain both in 1548–9 and in 1596–7. In contrast, the registers for Nabulus indicate much greater activity among those who practise the *traditional* technique of fulling—the "beaters" (*daḳḳā-ḳīn, daḳḳāḳīn-i ḳumāş*). They paid to the Imperial Domain the sums of 2,400, 2,500 and 3,000 aspers in 1538–9, 1548–9, and 1596–7, respectively. In other words, Nabulus, without the massive influx of Spanish Jews who came to Safed, did not replace old techniques by newly imported ones, and thus, while increasing its production, did so along traditional lines.[49] But there is no doubt about the general trend in this town and in this field. A more advanced stage in the process of cloth-manufacturing and dyeing yielded the Imperial Domain only 200 aspers annually in 1538–9

[48] Avitzūr, in *ibid.*, pp. 46, 56–8, gives a very detailed and instructive description, mainly based on the Responsa literature. He mentions, though (p. 57), "not more than six fulling mills," while in the first half of the sixteenth century there were about ten of them functioning.

[49] والدق هو محاولة لكي الاقمشه بطرقها بمطارق خشبية عريضة مصفحة ورشها بالماء ثم كبسها بمكابس ثقيلة على قطع من الخشب او المعدن
ʿAbd al-Wadūd Muḥammad Yūsuf, in *Majallat al-ḥawliyyāt al-atharıyya*, vol. XIX (1969), p. 93.

and showed an increase of 20% in 1548–9 (240 aspers), reaching the figure of 1,000 aspers in 1596–7.[50]

A further pointer in the same direction was the toll on cloth (*bāc al-ḳumāş*) levied for the Imperial Domain at the rate of 40 aspers per load in Safed—though this may not have been drawn from local industry only. In 1538–9 it yielded 12,000 aspers; a decade later it was one third higher (16,400 in 1548–9), and at the turn of the century (1596–7) it yielded 18,000 aspers.

The third town of Palestine in which a dye-house is mentioned is Gaza. Both in 1538–9 and 1548–9 a revenue of 2,000 aspers is recorded. At the earlier date it belonged to the Imperial Domain, at the later to the waqf of the Bīmāristān of the town. The registers from the second half of the century do not mention the dye-house, though throughout the century there was a special market for spinning and dyeing (*sūḳ al-ghazl waʾl-şibāgha*), suggesting that this trade did not die away.

Jerusalem seems to have had, at least in the second half of the century, some textile and dyeing industry. The register of 1562–3 mentions an income of 240 aspers from a dye-house, which seems to have been similar to the one in Nabulus. On earlier dates 2,000 aspers are recorded as having accrued anually in 1538–9 and 1553–4 to the appanage of the governor, while the same sum in 1562–3 went to the Imperial Domain. This was *bāc-i bāzār-i siyāh*,[51] "black" stamp duty.

B. OLIVE OIL AND SOAP

Olive trees were one of the most ancient and widespread features of Palestine. In spite of the vicissitudes which the economy of the country underwent throughout the ages, they were still regarded in the early Ottoman period as a valuable source of revenue. In two provinces, Safed and Nabulus, the *ḳānūnnāmes* specifically state that "olive [trees] are plentiful in most of the *livā*,"[52] in the others either olive trees or olive oil are explicitly mentioned. Naturally, olives were usually encountered "in the *livā* of . . ." as mentioned above, rather than "in the town of." In many villages (e.g. in the

[50] Al-Nimr, *Taʾrikh Jabal Nābulus*, vol. II, p. 286, mentions twenty dye-houses in Nabulus in an unspecified later date, thus implying a further increase in the years to come.

[51] See above, p. 60, n. 44.

[52] "ammā livā-ı Nābulūsta ekşeriyā zeytūn ziyāde olur." From the *kānunnāme* of Nabulus. For Safed see Barkan, *Kanunlar*, p. 239, translation in Mantran and Sauvaget, *Règlements fiscaux Ottomans*, p. 47.

Sanjak of Jerusalem) olive oil was collected as part of the *ḳism*[53] levy. It was in this form, i.e., olive oil, that this item figure in our registers, notably in Jerusalem and Ramle. In the former a tax on the scales for olive oil (*resm-i ḳapan-i zeyt*) brought in 150 aspers (perhaps an error for 1,500?) in 1538–9, 5,000 in 1553–4, 7,000 in 1562–3. It was collected at the rate of 1 asper per jar, four jars constituting a camel-load. The proceeds of this tax belonged at first to the governor's appanage, but in the register of 1562–3 it appears as "new Imperial Domain." In Ramle the proceeds of the toll on olive oil rose from 1,000 aspers in 1538–9, to 2,070 in 1548–9, to 3,470 in 1556–7. The same figure remained at the end of the century. It was collected at the rate of 1 *mann* per load, and belonged to the governor's appanage. Taxes on olive oil were no doubt levied in other towns also, but are not separately mentioned. They are presumably included under more general headings.

Olive oil was used in Palestine for the manufacture of soap. In the register of Jerusalem 1553–4 (but not earlier) we find a customs duty on loads of soap exported to Egypt. This brought in 11,056 aspers, which at the stated rate of 16 aspers per load means an export in the year of 691 loads. The proceeds of this tax belonged to the waqfs of the Dome of the Rock and Hebron, one third to the former and two thirds to the latter. These figures remained unchanged in 1562–3. Also part of the waqf of Hebron was a soap factory in that town, described as derelict.[54]

C. TANNERIES

The only town with a tannery recorded is Nabulus. It first appears in 1538–9 with a revenue of 960 aspers. By 1548–9 the figure has risen to 1,100, and in 1596–7 it reached 1,500, still paid to the Imperial Domain.

D. MOLASSES AND SWEETS

A special tax on presses (*maʿṣara*), used mainly for making *dibs* (molasses or syrup from fruit) and also for olive oil, was levied in

[53] The main taxes on agriculture in Palestine and Syria were levied by one of two methods, *ḳism* and *dīmūs*. Both methods, inherited from previous times, are probably of very early origin, and are variants of the classical *muḳāsama* and *misāḥa*. In *ḳism* villages the tax was assessed as a share (*ḳism*) of the crop, at a fixed given rate, as distinct from the *dīmūs*, for which the tax was assessed according to the area cultivated. On the latter term see Lewis, *BSOAS*, vol. XVI (1954), p. 484, n. 1.

[54] Interesting details on the processes of manufacture of soap are given in the *ḳānūnnāme* of Tripoli (Barkan, *Kanunlar*, pp. 214–15; Mantran and Sauvaget, *Règlements fiscaux Ottomans*, pp. 69–70).

many villages all over the country. In Jerusalem they were apparently not active in the first half of the century, and are thus regarded as an "additional" (*ḫāric*) Imperial Domain which yielded 930 aspers in 1553–4 and 900 in 1562–3, at the rate of 60 aspers for each of the fifteen functioning presses. In Hebron the rate was slightly higher, 62 per *maʿṣara*. Here too figures are available only for 1553–7, 1562–3, and 1596–7, when the 26 presses were given out as a *tīmār*[55] with an income rising from 1,240 to 1,612 aspers.

In Nabulus the makers of a special sweet paste made of carob fruit (*ḥelva*) paid 1,000 aspers a year to the Imperial Domain in the 1530's and the 1540's; in 1596–7 they had to pay 1,200.

3. AGRICULTURE, STOCK RAISING, FISHERIES

Taxes on these were drawn chiefly from villages, of which they constituted the main revenue. They also appear however in the lists of revenue from the towns, in addition to the usual urban taxes on trade, industry, and services. It has already been mentioned that in at least one town (Hebron), some taxes were collected in kind in the early stages of the Ottoman rule. This suggests a natural market economy with a rudimentary relationship between "town" and "countryside." Between the cities proper and the villages of the countryside there was an intermediate area of vineyards and of fruit and vegetable gardens. These were normally held both as *mülk* or as waqf (made by private individuals from their *mülk*), and fall outside the scope of this work. Extensive stock-raising and fruit growing within the towns seem to be a further sign that at least some traits of village life were still common among parts of the urban population.

A. AGRICULTURE

It is impossible to establish the exact location of the different cultivated lands in the towns: they may have been within the towns and their immediate surroundings, though at least part of them were interspersed among the different quarters. Corroborative evidence to this effect is to be found in many of the *sijills* of Jerusalem; if this was possible in a walled town, it was all the more likely in others which were less precisely delimited. The registers, however, refer these holdings as being either "in the town" (*dāk̲h̲il al-madīna; dāk̲h̲il al-sūr*) or "in the vicinity of the town" (*bi-ẓāhir al-madīna*).

[55] Having an income under 6,000 aspers it was a *tīmār* without *tezkere*, and even among this category is surprisingly low (cf. Lewis, *BSOAS*, vol. XVI [1954], p. 482).

TABLE 14

	932/ 1525–6	945/ 1538–9	955/ 1548–9	961–4/ 1553–7	970–5/ 1562–7	1005/ 1596–7
Jerusalem[56]					570 +440 +450 W W ID	
Hebron[57]	3,000	3,000	3,000 +10,000 W		8,000 W	9,000 W
Gaza[58]	4,455 ID	10,000 ID	12,112 ID	15,500 ID		24,500 ID
Ramle[59]		2,000 AG	2,500			
Nabulus[60]		15,000 ID	18,000 ID			20,000 ID
Safed[61]		2,000 ID	2,500 ID		2,500 ID	

The different entries include orchards, vineyards, vegetable gardens, cultivated plots of land.[62] These smaller items were usually combined under a general heading which had a fiscal common denominator, the payment of the tithe (ʿu̲s̲h̲r), in most cases to the Imperial Domain. Whenever sufficient evidence is available (especially in the case of Gaza, and to a lesser extent in the other towns also), a substantial increase in [output and] revenue is recorded, particularly between the 1530's and the 1550's of the century.

B. STOCK-RAISING

Several towns also paid taxes on livestock. The most commonly encountered taxes are those on sheep, goats, and bees, which are very often inseparable from one another. No reference is made to the exact locality where these animals were kept, but they are specifically referred to as being "of the inhabitants of the town . . ."

[56] Olive trees, vineyards (*karm*), pieces of land (*ḳiṭʿa-ı arż*).
[57] Vegetable-gardens (*ḥākūra*), vineyards and other trees, land.
[58] Vineyards, orchards (*bağçe*).
[59] Land, orchards, vineyards.
[60] Land, vegetable gardens, orchards.
[61] Orchards, vineyards, land.
[62] Various technical terms are used for these, drawn from Arabic, Persian and Turkish: Orchard (*bustān, bağçe*); vegetable-garden (*ḥākūra*); vineyard (*karm, bağ*); plot of land (*ḳiṭʿa-i arż*).

TABLE 15

	932/ 1525–6	945/ 1538–9	955/ 1548–9	961–4/ 1553–7	970–5/ 1562–7	1005/ 1596–7
Jerusalem (sheep and goats)	7,000[63] AG			500 AG	1,000 AG	
Hebron (goats, sheep, and bees)				1,600 ID	1,500 W	1,600 W
Gaza (bees)			3,000 ID	3,000 ID		3,500 ID
(sheep)	6,000 ID		7,000 ID	5,000 ID		5,500 ID
Ramle (sheep, goats, and bees)		1,000[64] AG 500[65] AG	3,087 AG	3,500		3,500 AG
Nabulus (goats and bees)		500[66] ID	1,000 ID			1,500 ID

The rate of taxation was 1/2 asper per goat or sheep,[67] 1 asper per beehive. The towns showing the highest figures are Gaza and Ramle. Safed is the only town in which no stock-raising is recorded. This accords with the references to the importation of sheep to the city from outside,[68] and may be related to the intensive development of the textile industry, which gave Safed a more distinctively urban economy. The people of Safed, like those of the big cities, left cattle-raising to the neighboring nomadic tribes. However, a certain link was still maintained between stock-raising and the town in the form of revenue accruing to the Imperial Domain. This link in Safed was achieved in two different ways: the first was winter-pasturage taxes (*ᶜādet-i ḳis̲h̲lāḳ*) on the bedouin tribes of the immediate vicinity which amounted in 1555–6 as well as ten years later to 4,000 aspers for the Imperial *ḫāṣṣ*, while the same tax levied from the more distant nomads (who roamed in the Biḳāᶜ area, i.e., along the river Jordan) reached the sum of 10,000, belonging to the appanage of the

[63] With the whole district (*nāḥiye*) of Jerusalem.

[64] Bees only.

[65] Sheep and goats only.

[66] Goats only.

[67] Cf. identical rate for Karaman in Beldiceanu, *JESHO*, vol. XI (1968), pp. 50–1.

[68] As far as can be ascertained from the registers used for this work as well as from the *Mühimme* registers studied by Heyd, Safed was the only one of the Palestinian towns which imported sheep in substantial number. See above, p. 58.

governor in the same years. The second category was a special tax levied on water-buffaloes (*resm-i cevāmīs*), raised at the rate of 12 aspers per beast in the whole of the sanjak, which appears only in the early register of 1525–6 as yielding 11,880 to the Imperial Domain.

In Ramle a special tax (*ʿādet-i deştbānī*)[69] was collected for the protection of owners of cultivated lands against incursions by sheep or cattle. The revenue from this item to the appanage of the governor rose from 400 aspers in 1548–9 to 500 aspers in 1596–7.

C. FISHERIES

In the Sanjak of Safed, though not in the town proper, fisheries are known to have existed, the returns of which appear only in the registers of 1555–6 and *ca.* 1567.

TABLE 16

	1555–6	*ca.* 1567
Fisheries at Minya and Tiberias	3,300	3,300
Fisheries in the Baḥr Ḳadas (Ḥūle)	1,700	1,700
Fisheries at Ḳāsimiya	1,000	1,000
Fisheries in the Mediterranean at Tyre	1,000	1,000
Pole-net (*ṭālyān*) fishing at Acre[70]	500	500
Certain fisheries near Tiberias	800	1,200

The same details of most entries were copied in the later register, which implies that when a change is recorded it must have been very conspicuous. Such is the case of the fisheries in the southern part of lake Tiberias, when a rise of 50% in about ten years is noted. It seems to tally in principle (though not in detail) with another indication of a very substantial development of fishing in this lake—the figure of 13,000 aspers mentioned in a firman dated 1560 as the amount actually collected by the *emīn* of Safed "for the fish [caught] in the lake."[71] This provides a measure of the difference

[69] To be found outside Palestine. Cf. J. von Hammer, *Des Osmanischen Reichs Staatsverfassung und Staatsverwaltung*, vol I, p. 254. See below, p. 143, n. 27; see also Beldiceanu, *JESHO*, vol. XI (1968), pp. 37–8.

[70] Probably from the Greek [To] Alianeion, "fishing station." "A kind of fishing station and look-out raised on poles above the water," usually in rather shallow ones—lakes, rivers, bays or straits (H. and R. Kahane, A. Tietze, *The Lingua franca in the Levant*, pp. 477–81). In a special *ḳānūn* in Salonica, the tax on *ṭalyān* was levied according to the quantities sold, and probably upon its erection as well (Cvetkova, *La vie économique de villes balkaniques*, pp. 44–5). The modern Turkish form is *dalyan*.

[71] Heyd, *Ottoman Documents*, p. 141.

between amounts actually collected and the notional figures in the defter. Without the specific reference to a *emīn*, one would have assumed a tax-farm.

4. TAXES ON SHOPS AND OTHER REAL PROPERTY

Trade was usually taxed in accordance with its volume. Its importance in all the towns of Palestine was increasingly reflected in the registers. Shops (*dukkān*) were liable to taxes on a regular basis in Jerusalem, Hebron and Nabulus. In Jerusalem in 1553–4 only 203 out of 350 shops were in use, bringing the waqf 13,637 aspers (with another 100 aspers accruing from a shop which belonged to the K͟hānḳāh Ḥamidiye waqf). Less than ten years later, in 1562–3, the amount collected was 18,000. The increase is due, indubitably, to a general improvement in trade in this town, further corroborated by the reactivation of ten more shops formerly "in ruin." Another indication of this development in Jerusalem is a new entry, a yield of 1,280 aspers from K͟hān al-Faḥm and K͟hān al-S͟hiʿāra in 1562–3. The revenue recorded as accruing to the waqf from 37 shops in Hebron increased from 2,260 in 1553–4, to 2,400 in 1562, to 2,500 in 1596–7, which indicates a rising level of commercial activity. The rate of increase (though lower than in Jerusalem) maintained in the 1550's seems to have slowed down, but the yield was still rising until the end of the century. In Nabulus regular revenue from shops appears only around the middle of the century: three of them yielded 488 aspers in 1548–9 and 500 aspers in 1596–7 to the Imperial Domain. Similarly, the relatively low incomes of K͟hān al-Furn, 60 aspers in 1553–4 falling to 40 aspers in 1562, reached 100 aspers in 1596–7, thus augmenting the income of the waqf.

Usually referred to under the general heading of "shops," was another, special category: wine-shops. Wine-sellers, most probably either Christians or Jews, are separately mentioned in Safed and Nabulus. In Safed the registers of both 1525–6 and 1538–9 record a revenue of 6,000 aspers to the Imperial Domain from wine shops. The disappearance of this item from all the later registers cannot be accidental. The sale of wine has always been regarded as "keeping the Muslim from pious devotion and divine worship."[72] A firman dated 973/1565 states that it was forbidden to bring wine to Jerusalem, and non-Muslims were

[72] *Ibid.*, pp. 160–1 and n. 2.

specifically "warned against advertising and selling" it.[73] Although repeated bans[74] on the sale or importation of wine suggest that this traffic was not discontinued, it is clear that it was not approved, and that revenues from it could not therefore be entered in official records.

Though the night-watches (*ᶜasesān*)[75] were not exclusively at their service, shopkeepers were intended to benefit more than anyone else from their introduction to the towns. Their revenues whenever mentioned (1 asper from any shop locked, 2 *pāras* from a person released from prison) were assigned to the appanage of the governor who, thus, had a personal interest in their successful implementation of their task.

TABLE 17

	932/ 1525–6	945/ 1538–9	955/ 1548–9	961–4/ 1553–7	970–5/ 1562–7	1005/ 1596–7
Jerusalem		2,000		2,000	2,000	
Gaza	8,000	10,000	5,000	5,000		5,000
Nabulus		2,000	2,000			6,000
Safed				7,000	7,000	

Another source of income in the towns was the tax on bathhouses (*ḥammām*).

TABLE 18

		945/ 1538–9	955/ 1548–9	961–4/ 1553–6	970–5/ 1562–7	1005/ 1596–7
Jerusalem	Ḥammām Bāb al-Asbāṭ (W)			14,000	7,600	
	Ḥammām al-Shifāʾ (W)				4,000	
	Ḥammām al-ᶜAyn (W)			16,000	10,000	
	Ḥammām Dāʾūd (W)				735	
	Ḥammām al-ᶜAmūd (W)			347	300	
Hebron	Ḥammām[76] (W)			2,000	6,082	6,500
Nabulus	Ḥammām Rīsh (ID-W)		360			360
Safed	Ḥammām al-Sulṭān (ID)	2,000		1,200	1,200	

A very sharp decline can be noticed in the revenues of all the bathhouses around the middle of the century with the exception of one in Hebron. In Safed it is specifically stated that the bathhouse

[73] *Ibid.*

[74] Heyd, *Ibid.*, n. 2.

[75] See "ᶜAsas," *EI*², Heyd (Ménage, ed.), *Studies*, p. 294. In Konya in the sixteenth century owners of shops used to pay this tax per shop (Beldiceanu, *JESHO*, vol. XI (1968), p. 35).

[76] Another bathhouse is recorded in 1553–4 as derelict.

had been in ruin for some time. One may reasonably assume that there was no change in the sanitary habits of the population, no decrease in the cost of using the baths, and that a decline in the revenue from the bathhouses indicates a decline in population.[77] This can be checked by comparing the figures given for the number of inhabitants, on the one hand, and the revenues from the bathhouses, on the other. The increase, then the stagnation and slight decline of the numbers of the Muslim inhabitants of Safed and Nabulus are reflected in the rise, levelling off and decline of the revenues from the bathhouses. Hebron, for some unknown reason, seems to be an exception to this general rule.

5. TAXES ON *AHL AL-DHIMMA*

The major tax levied on non-Muslims as such was the *jizya*,[78] the poll-tax imposed by Islamic law on Dhimmīs—protected non-Muslims. In the classical Islamic system the *jizya* was due from all male Dhimmīs over the age of puberty, and was assessed at three rates, for the wealthy, those of medium status, and the poor. The rates were four, two and one gold pieces, respectively. Ottoman practice in sixteenth century Palestine, as recorded by the registers, differs from this in two important respects. The *jizya* was levied not from individuals—*ʿalāʾl-ruʾūs* in the official terminology—but from households; and the rate throughout the country is the lowest, of one gold piece. There is no reference at all to the intermediate and higher rates.

The collection of *jizya* by households is attested in other provinces of the Ottoman Empire, in Cyprus, Hungary, and Bulgaria, and is not surprising in view of the fact that the whole Ottoman system of taxation and registration is based on the household as a fiscal unit—the *ʿavārizḫāne*.[79] The single rate of assessment appears to be a survival from Mamluk times. Mamluk rulers not infrequently departed from the classical fiscal system, and the evidence collected by Ashtōr[80] indicates that during the last century of Mamluk rule,

[77] On the correlation between the two elements in 18th Century Acre see Cohen, *Palestine in the Eighteenth Century*, pp. 128–134.

[78] For details on the collection of this tax in different parts of the Ottoman Empire see Neşet Çağatay, *Ankara Üniversıtesı Dıl ve tarih-coğrafya fakültesi dergisi*, vol. V (1947), pp. 493–5. Beldiceanu, *JESHO*, vol. XI (1968), pp. 71–4. For comparative data from Egypt see Shaw, *Financial and Administrative Organization and Development of Ottoman Egypt 1517–1798*, (*Princeton* 1958), pp. 151–67.

[79] Cf. "Awārid," *EI*².

[80] Strauss (Ashtōr), *Tōledōth ha-Yehūdim*, vol. II, pp. 266 ff.

the three rates of assessment virtually disappeared, and were replaced by a single *jizya* of one gold piece plus a fraction to cover collection costs.

TABLE 19

	932/ 1525–6	945/ 1538–9	955/ 1548–9	961–4/ 1553–7	970–5/ 1562–7	1005/ 1596–7
Jerusalem	19,080	32,560		51,920 (ID) 11,360 (W)	53,920	
Hebron (W)		2,160		640	880	880
Gaza	21,180	31,040	38,000	35,440		34,380
Ramle (ID)	1,560	2,640	7,280	6,000		6,560
Nabulus						
Safed (ID)	31,310[81]			94,000	160,600	

According to the register of 1525–6 the *jizya* was levied at a rate of sixty aspers per household, but as from the next register (1538–9), it became eighty aspers, at which rate it was maintained up to the end of the century. In practice it seems that even this rate was not heeded very scrupulously. A comparison between the *ḳānūn nāme* of Gaza in the register dating 965/1558 and the one appended to the register of 1005/1596–7 reveals that no substantial modifications were introduced except from one item; the latter notes that an extra 5 and 10 aspers for Christians and Jews, respectively, should be added to the *jizya* paid by them.[82] The register for Nabulus 1596–7 has a similar paragraph in its *ḳānūnnāme,* without any reference to Jews, which may be regarded as a scribal error. In both cases it is specifically stated that the new additional tax was decreed after the accession of the new Sultan, who can not have been Süleymān the Magnificent (as these changes were not mentioned in the registers of his time). The reference is probably to Selīm II (1566–74). The two increases in the rate of the *jizya* as stated in aspers in the course of the century do not imply extortionate taxation of the *Dhimmīs*. The increases should rather be seen within the context of the continuing depreciation of the Ottoman silver currency in relation to gold. According to the *Sharīʿa* the rate of the *jizya* is fixed in gold, and there is some evidence that it was at some times and places at least collected in gold (*sikke-i ḥasane*). Like all other sources of income, however, it is stated for accountancy purposes in silver aspers, and the increases in the rate are more apparent than real. The two increases in the

[81] "*Jizya* of the Christians of the *liwāʾ*".

[82] See above, p. 11, n. 40.

rates of *jizya* during the century do not imply any maltreatment of the *D̲himmis* but should be seen in the context of the continuous depreciation of the Ottoman currency,[83] as an attempt to maintain the legal gold rate of taxation, stated in aspers.

The *jizya* belonged to the *Bayt al-māl*, and, unlike some other revenues, was never granted to fief-holders or holders of *ḫāṣṣ*. Occasionally, however, a part of the *jizya* revenues of a city is included in an imperial waqf. Thus in Jerusalem, a proportion of the *jizya* is assigned to the waqf of the Dome of the Rock; in Hebron the *jizya* belongs entirely to the waqf of Hebron.

Another tax levied specifically on Christians and Jews is the toll or "protection" (*ğafāre*) duty collected at various check-posts (usually either a bridge or a caravanserai) on the high roads. This was usually at the rate of eight aspers per Christian and six per Jew (but also ten and six, eight and eight, respectively).[84] Although the *ḳānūn* of Jerusalem separately stipulated "merchants" and "pilgrims," the rate was identical for both categories and it seems that this was done in order to prevent any evasion of payment. The original aim seems to have been the collection of a poll-tax from all pilgrims to Jerusalem. Those who came via Nabulus had to pay to the Imperial Domain, in addition to all *ğafāres* listed above, a special "toll on Christians, Jews and other unbelievers" at the rate of 16 aspers upon their arrival and departure. The proceeds as recorded were 20,000 aspers in 1538–9, 22,000 in 1548–9, 23,000 in 1596–7. A toll collected at varying rates[85] from Christian pilgrims visiting the Church of the Holy Sepulchre in Jerusalem brought in the following yearly amounts to the waqf of the Dome of the Rock: 40,000 aspers in 1525–6, 80,000 aspers in 1538–9, 120,000 in 1553–4 and in 1562–3.[86] An additional tax on the Frankish pilgrims who came to the Holy Sepulchre, known as "the tax of the citadel" (*resm-i ḳalᶜe*), was levied at the rate of 50 aspers per person. Both in 1553–4 and in 1562–3 it yielded 3,000 aspers annually to the waqf of the Dome of the Rock.

6. REVENUES OF A RELIGIOUS CHARACTER

Hebron and Jerusalem, the two most venerated towns of Palestine in the eyes of Islam, had, as a result, some additional taxes and

[83] See above, pp. 43–4.

[84] Cf. above, p. 58.

[85] The rates are given in the *ḳānūnnāme* of Jerusalem (Barkan, *Kanunlar*, p. 219; Mantran and Sauvaget, *Règlements fiscaux Ottomans*, pp. 40–2).

[86] For further details see p 95.

collections of a specific public religious character. First and foremost was the *simāṭ* of Hebron, the soup-kitchen, in which free meals were distributed to the poor three times a day. This custom, which predated the Ottoman conquest,[87] was adopted by the new rulers. The only statistics available for the *simāṭ* are for 1553–4, when it received 10,000 aspers from the *ḫizāne* of Egypt as well as 2000 *mudd* of wheat for the preparation of bread. There is no satisfactory answer as to the reason for the disappearance of these items. One is, however, inclined to suppose that the custom was maintained, though it underwent a certain metamorphosis: Instead of payments in kind it followed the general pattern of economic development and was levied in coin during the second half of the century.[88] This was apparently the meaning and purpose of the entry "offertory" (*ṣundūḳ al-nudhūr*) which first appears in the Cave of Machpela in 1562 at the rate of 7,783, later to be repeated in 1596–7 at the rate of 8,000 aspers per year. A similar offertory was established in the same time at the Mosque of the Rock in Jerusalem, and its yield in 1562–3 was 1,200 aspers to the waqf. A less substantial, though by no means insignificant source of income to the waqf were belongings left behind by deceased persons who had come as pilgrims to the Holy Places of Jerusalem and Hebron or stayed there permanently, either as "sojourners" (*mujāwir*) or as "recipients of stipends" (*erbāb-i veẓāʾif*).[89] These yielded the waqf of Hebron 200 aspers in 1553–4, 500 in 1562–3, and 1,000 aspers in 1596–7. As for Jerusalem, the same category brought in 500 aspers in 1553–4 and 4,000 in 1562–3.

7. *BAYT AL-MĀL* AND *BĀD-I HAVĀ*

Of a more general character, common to all the towns of Palestine, were revenues accruing to *Bayt al-māl* from the properties of missing people, slaves, or stray animals. Those consisted of heirless and unclaimed property and dues for recovering stray cattle, runaway

[87] See below, p. 113, n. 25.

[88] This inference is reinforced by substantial evidence which however comes from a later period. See Cohen, *Palestine in the Eighteenth Century*, pp. 266–9.

[89] Both terms are to be read in the religious context: the first refers to Muslims living in or at the expense of a religious place (usually a *zāwiya* or a *madrasa*) for pious reasons. The second does not, as became the case for later and post-Ottoman usage, mean those who hold formal official positions; it refers, like the former term, to people who lived in or around holy or religious places and received from the state a permanent stipend (*vaẓife*) calculated on a daily basis, usually formally but also involving some service in a religious capacity. Such arrangements are commonly encountered in the Holy Shrines in the Hejaz and in Palestine.

slaves, etc. They belonged to the state treasury (*Bayt al-māl*). If their value was 10,000 aspers or less, they were assigned to the appanage of the governor of the sanjak; if more than 10,000, or if they came from persons in the Sultan's service, they were claimed by the Imperial Domain. The latter category included the feudal cavalry (*sipāhī*), the garrison troops (*mustāḥfiẓ*) and the "Slaves of the Porte." Two categories were exempt from this rule; *sipāhis* holding privileged grants of the kind known as free (*serbest*) timars, and certain waqfs, namely those in favour of the *ḥarameyn* (the holy places in Mecca and Medina), the Dome of the Rock, and Hebron. On such timars and waqfs this income did not go to the treasury but was retained by the beneficiaries.[90]

Usually linked with this entry were the revenues known collectively as *bād-i havā,* literally "wind of the air,"[91] a general term for irregular and occasional revenues from fines, fees, registration charges, and other casual sources of income. Whereas in free tīmārs it belonged to the tīmār holder, in other tīmārs it was either shared by him with the *ḫāṣṣ,* or more frequently reserved entirely to the *ḫāṣṣ* in which case it might be either retained as Imperial *ḫāṣṣ* or granted as *ḫāṣṣ* to the governor.

TABLE 20: Bayt al-Māl

		932/ 1525–6	945/ 1538–9	955/ 1548–9	961–4/ 1553–7	970–5/ 1562–7	1005/ 1596–7
Jerusalem	up to 10,000 (AG)		9,000		12,000	12,000	
	over 10,000 (ID)	13,000			15,000	15,000	
Hebron		combined with Jerusalem					
Gaza	up to 10,000 (AG)		7,000				
	over 10,000 (ID)	10,000	20,000	47,487	47,487		55,000[9]
Ramle			4,000 (AG)	10,000	10,000		12,000
Nabulus (ID)				6,000			6,500
Safed (ID)					10,000	10,000	

[90] See Lewis, "Bād-ı Hawā," *EI*², vol. I, p. 850, "Bayt al-Māl," vol. I, pp. 1147–8, "Ḥaramayn," vol. III, pp. 175–6; Inalcık, "Ḍarība (3)", *EI*², vol. II, pp. 146–8. Contrary to the statement in *EI*² s.v. Ḥaramayn, in sixteenth century Palestine this term was used only of Mecca and Medina and not applied to Jerusalem and Hebron. This is clear from a number of passages in the registers and *Sijills* for example in a firman of Shaʿbān 998/July–August 1590, cited in the *sijill* register of Jerusalem, vol. 71, p. 113: "Safed ve Küds-i Şerīf ve Nābulūs ve Gazze ve Ramlede vākıʿ olan Ḥaramayn-i Şerīfayn evkāfına ve ḥażret-i Ḫalīl ür-Raḥmān ve Ṣaḫra-i Mübāreke ve tevābiʿı evḳāfına muḥarrer taʿyīn edıp."

[91] The name is probably related to the classical Islamic *ṭayyārāt* and to the Byzantine *aerikon,* and expresses the same idea as the English word windfall. Lewis, "Bād-i Hawā" in *EI*², vol I, p. 850. Inalcık, "Osmanlılarda Raiyyet rüsumu,"

TABLE 21: Bād-i Havā

	932/ 1525–6	945/ 1538–9	955/ 1548–9	961–4/ 1553–7	970–5/ 1562–7	1005/ 1596–7
Jerusalem (AG)	20,000	27,000		33,000	33,000	
Hebron		combined with Jerusalem				
Gaza	50,000[93]	10,000	24,128	24,134		28,134
Ramle		8,800	57,724	57,724		59,724[94]
Nabulus (AG)		5,000[95]	26,500			40,000
Safed (AG)	30,000[96]	10,000		16,500	20,000	

Belleten, vol. XXIII (1959), pp. 594–5) regards it as one out of the three categories into which all taxes to which the reʿāyā are liable, are divided: *çift resmi veleváḥiḳi; aʿşar; bâdihavâ*. See also Inalcık, *Suret-i Defter-i Arvanid*, pp. xxvii–xxviii; Kaldy-Nagy, *Acta Orientalia*, vol. XIII (1961), p. 34; Beldiceanu, *JESHO*, vol. XI (1968), p. 85.

92 The three last entries: "Town and district (*nāḥiye*) of Gaza."

93 "Of the whole *liwāʾ* of Gaza."

94 "The town of Ramle and the district of Gaza and Ramle" for the last four entries.

95 + *Bād-i Havā* of two districts, which amounts to another 30,000 aspers.

96 Pertaining to the whole *liwāʾ* of Safed.

PART II

THE TOWNS

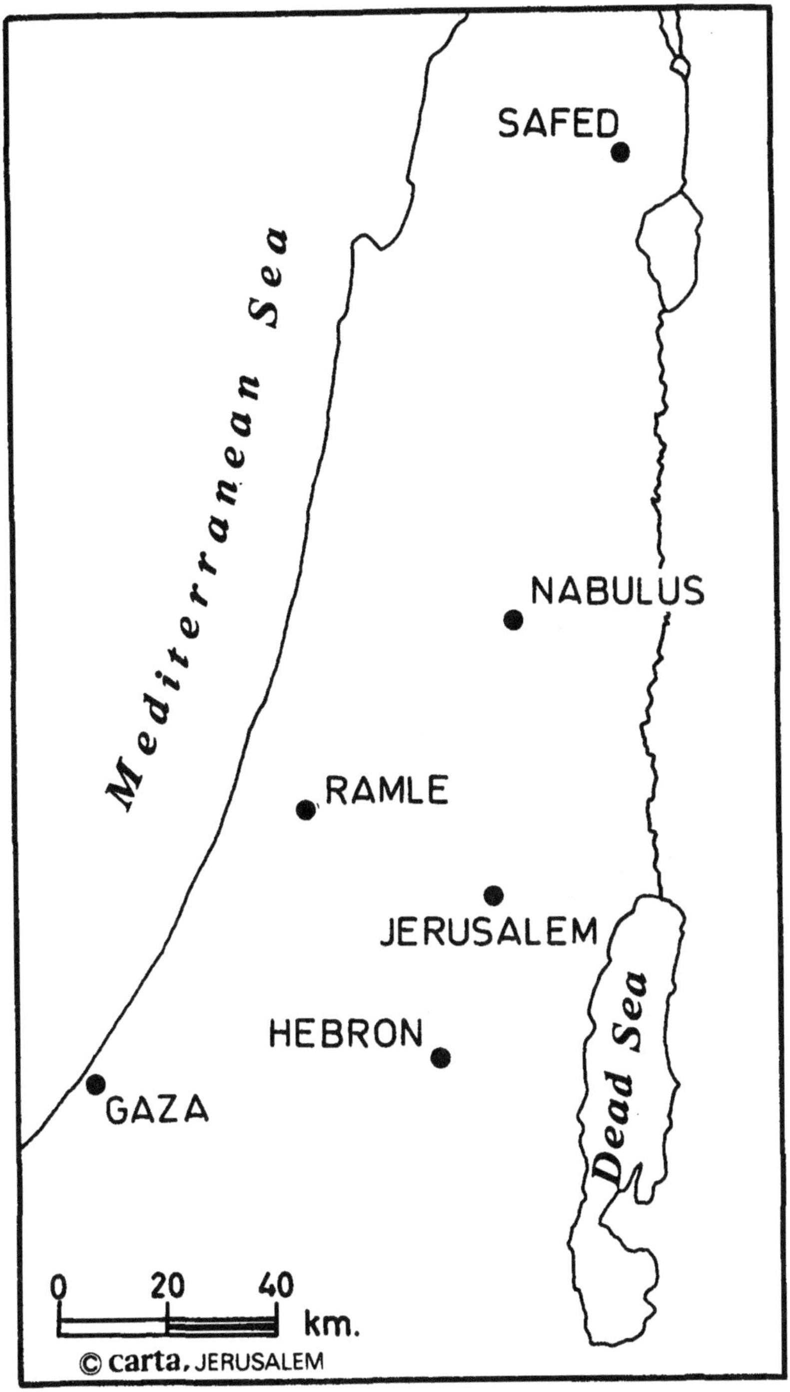
SAFED
Mediterranean Sea
NABULUS
RAMLE
JERUSALEM
HEBRON
GAZA
Dead Sea
0 20 40
km.
© carta, JERUSALEM

1. Palestine

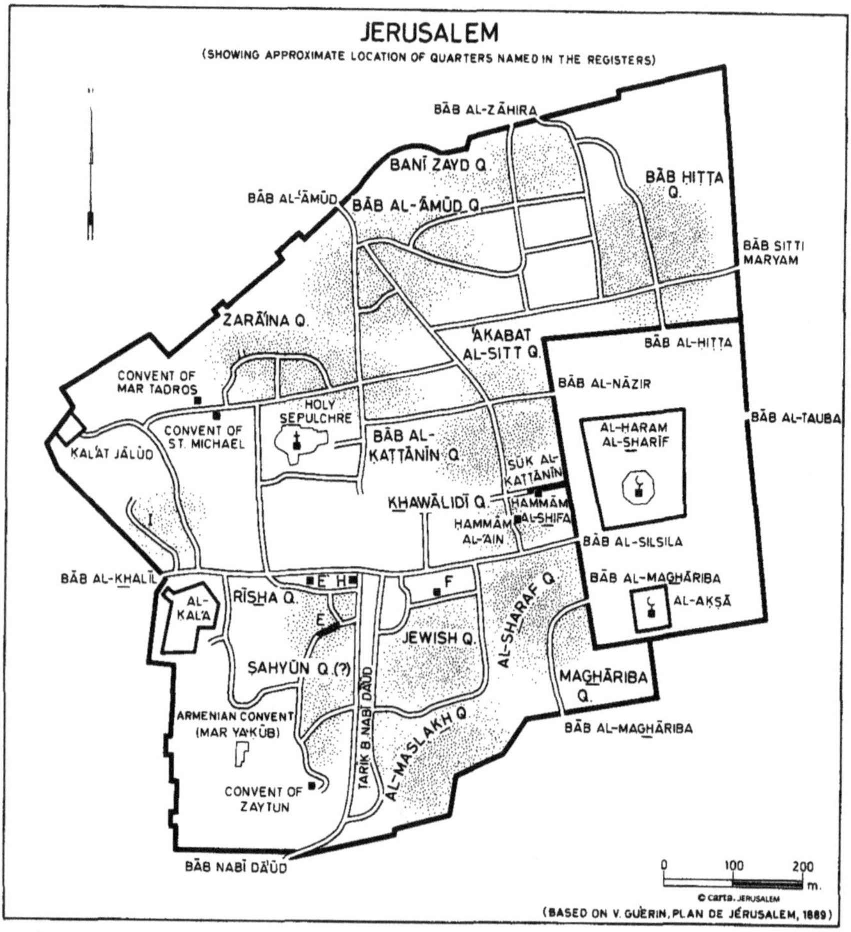
JERUSALEM
(SHOWING APPROXIMATE LOCATION OF QUARTERS NAMED IN THE REGISTERS)
BĀB AL-ZĀHIRA
BANĪ ZAYD Q.
BĀB ḤIṬṬA Q.
BĀB AL-ʿĀMŪD
BĀB AL-ʿĀMŪD Q.
BĀB SITTI MARYAM
ZARĀʾINA Q.
ʿAKABAT AL-SITT Q.
BĀB AL-ḤIṬṬA
CONVENT OF MAR TADROS
BĀB AL-NĀZIR
HOLY SEPULCHRE
BĀB AL-ṬAUBA
CONVENT OF ST. MICHAEL
BĀB AL-ḲAṬṬĀNĪN Q.
AL-ḤARAM AL-SHARĪF
ḲALʿAT JĀLŪD
SŪK AL-ḲAṬṬĀNĪN
KHAWĀLIDĪ Q.
ḤAMMĀM AL-SHIFĀ
ḤAMMĀM AL-ʿAIN
BĀB AL-SILSILA
BĀB AL-KHALĪL
E H
F
BĀB AL-MAGHĀRIBA
AL-ḲALʿA
RĪSHA Q.
AL-AḲṢĀ
E
JEWISH Q.
AL-SHARAF Q.
ṢAHYŪN Q.(?)
MAGHĀRIBA Q.
ARMENIAN CONVENT (MAR YAʿKŪB)
ṬARĪK B. NABĪ DĀʾŪD
AL-MASLAKH Q.
BĀB AL-MAGHĀRIBA
CONVENT OF ZAYTUN
BĀB NABĪ DĀʾŪD
0 100 200 m.
© carta. JERUSALEM
(BASED ON V. GUÉRIN, PLAN DE JÉRUSALEM, 1889)

2. Jerusalem

• 4 •

JERUSALEM قدس شريف

1. QUARTERS AND INHABITANTS

REGISTER 427 OF 932/1525–6

Quarter of:

Bāb al-Ḥiṭṭa[1] باب الحطه 1 Imam, 110 households

Bāb al-Ḳaṭṭānīn باب المطانين 102 households,[2] 1 bachelor

Zarāʿina[3] رراعنه 110 households

Rīsha[4] in the city of Jerusalem ريشه 15 households

Banī Ḥārith[5] بنى حارث 7 households

ʿAḳabat al-Sitt[6] عقبه ست 24 households

[1] Lies north of the Temple Mount (cf. Map 2). One of the largest quarters in Mamluk times. For several versions as to the possible meaning of the name see Mujīr al-Dīn, *Al-Uns al-jalīl*, vol. II, pp. 381–2, 405; French translation by Sauvaire, pp. 130–2.

[2] Three of whom are referred to as shaykh, another as kadi.

[3] Thus in Mujīr al-Dīn, *Al-Uns al-Jalīl*, vol. II, p. 404 and all the defters. H. Sauvaire, in his translation *Histoire de Jérusalem*, p. 180, probably using another manuscript, reads *Darâʾéneh*. The only location mentioned by Mujīr is that it lies west of the Christian quarter (*Ḥārat al-naṣārā*), "outside the town" (*bi-ẓāhir al-balad*). If it was indeed outside the walled city the name is probably that of a bedouin tribe. On the other hand the quarter of Bāb al-ʿAmūd comes, according to the same source, next to it. This quarter was also called "the quarter of Banī Saʿd," and derived its name from a nomadic tribe also designated Banī Zarāʿina. Cf. *sijill* of Jerusalem, vol. XVII, p. 196 (952/1545–6): Maḥallat Banī Zarāʿina al-maʿrūfa bi-Maḥallat Banī Saʿd.

[4] "The Feather." Toward the end of the fifteenth century it was a part of the Jewish quarter (Mujīr al-Dīn, *Al-Uns al-jalīl*, vol. II, p. 403). In 1865 Wilson identified it in the northern part of the Armenian quarter, which at his time was called "ḥāret Deir as Surîan" (Wilson, *Survey of Jerusalem*, 1 day, 18.4.1865. Cf. Map 2, E). However, two days later he came across the same name ("as an old Moslem told us") somewhat to the north of it (Cf. Map 2, E_1).

[5] According to Mujīr al-Dīn, (*Al-Uns al-jalīl*, vol. II, p. 403), this quarter was outside the town near the *ḳalʿa*.

[6] Formerly "*ʿAḳabat al-Sūḳ*" which lay west of Bāb al-Nāẓir (Cf. Map 2). Toward the end of the eighth century A.H./fourteenth century A.D., Al-Sitt Tanshaq bint ʿAbd Allāh al-Muẓaffariyya built a large building, *dār al-sitt*, which in its turn lent its name to the whole quarter (Mujīr al-Dīn, *Al-Uns al-jalīl*, vol. II, pp. 404, 409).

Khawālidī[7] حوالدى 11 households

Sharaf,[8] also called ʿAlam سرف نام ديكر علم 89[9] households

Bāb al-ʿĀmūd[10] باب العامود 78 households, 1 bachelor

Banī Zayd[11] بنى زيد 46 households

The community of Maghribīs[12] in Jerusalem مغاربه 31[13] households
The Maghribī community in Jerusalem, Maghribīs who are sojourners (*mujāwir*). Saladin constituted the quarter they inhabit with all its limits, as a *waqf*, and gave the said community a decree

[7] Wilson, *Survey of Jerusalem* (Vth day, 27.4) identified "the street nearest to . . . Jaffa Gate and leading in a North-West direction . . . called ṭarîk hârat al-Waʿriyé, or al-Jawâlidé or al-Jawâlidiye . . . which names are family names" (Cf. Map 2, I). One could easily read ج for ح, as such errors occur in our registers However, in view of the fact that such a Muslim quarter is unlikely in the Christian part of the city (even though leading to Ḳalʿat al-Jalūd), the Khawālidī quarter should probably be located as it appears in the register—i.e., between ʿAkabat al-Sitt and Ḥārat Sharaf. It is there, in the street leading from Bāb al-Silsila, that the Khālidi family either owned or was responsible for various properties and waqfs,

[8] At the turn of the fifteenth century these two names seem to have designated two separate quarters: al-ʿAlam, after ʿAlam al-Dīn Sulaymān, also called ibn al-Muhadhdhab (d. 770 A.H.); and al-Sharaf (also called Ḥārat al-Akrād), after Sharaf al-Dīn Mūsā (Mujīr al-Dīn, *Al-Uns al-jalil*, vol. II, p. 402). We learn from this register that the two quarters became one early in the sixteenth century, either before or just after the Ottoman occupation. "A tomb of a Waly with an inscription" (Cf. Map 2, F) which explicitly identifies the two as one and the same person, indicating that Sharaf al-Dīn was a descendant of (that?) ʿAlam, whereas the actual name of the quarter was due to the fact that he was regarded as a descendant of the prophet (*sharif*).

هذه الحاره حازت شرفا وابتهاجا بجوار الصالحين
((لا)) سيما هذا الولي الشرفي علمي الاصل عين العارفين
رحمه الله عليه دايما وعلى اسلافه في كل حين

(Wilson, *Survey of Jerusalem*, II day, 20.4).

[9] One *nāʾib ḳalʿa*, one son of the *nāʾib ḳalʿa* are listed. See above, p. 38.

[10] See Map 2.

[11] In the northern part of the city, south of Bāb al-Zāhira (cf. Map 2). A street by the name of "al-Saʿdiyyin", which according to Mujīr al-Dīn, (*Al-Uns al-jalil*, vol. II, p. 405) was within this quarter, is the Saʿadiye quarter, which Wilson located just south of Bāb al-Zāhira. The component "Banī Zayd" appears in several villages in the Sanjak of Jerusalem: Ḳarāwā Banī Zayd, ʿAṭṭāra Banī Zayd, Mazāriʿ Banī Zayd. All of these are, as it seems, references to a bedouin tribe which as late as 1480 could still break into the city and release some of their relatives which had been kept prisoner there (Schefer, *Le Voyage*, pp. xviii–xix). Schefer tells us that the governor engaged them in battle in the northern part of the city, near Bāb al-Asbāṭ where, as the name of the quarter indicates, some of them were already settled.

[12] Living in a separate quarter, Ḥārat al-Maghāriba, as is indicated in later registers. This quarter lay west of Bāb al-Maghāriba (cf. Map 2).

[13] Most of whom are designated either *shaykh* or *sayyid*.

(*marsūm*) saying that the property left by anyone who died without heir should be inventoried and handed over to the *zāwiya.* The Sultans who came since that time accepted this, gave decrees, and thus confirmed its validity. It has now been confirmed as valid as above stated.[14]

Communities of Christians and Jews[15]

Melkite quarter ملكيه 96 households

Christian Jacobite quarter يعاقبه النصارى 15 households

Community of Syrians (*Suryān*) سريان 8 households

Community of Jews يهودان [199 households]

REGISTER 1015 OF *ca* 945/1538–9

Quarter of:

S͟haraf شرف 266[16] households, 27 bachelors, 5 imams

Bāb al-Ḳaṭṭānīn باب القطانين 128 households, 7 bachelors, 3 imams

Bāb al-ʿĀmūd باب العمود 101 households, 14 bachelors, 2 imams

Community of Döger,[17] dependent on the said quarter, 15 households, 1 imam

Zarāʿina زراعنه 159[18] households, 4 bachelors, 3 imams

In the convent (*dayr*) of the Franks in this quarter, 19 monks

Banī Ḥārit͟h بنى حارث 9 households

In Dayr Zaytūn, 3[19] households

[14] Heirless estates normally escheated to the treasury (see above, pp. 73–4). Privileges of this kind, amounting to recognition as a corporate entity, are very rare in Islamic history. For a similar arrangement in Egypt see A. S. Tritton, *Materials on Muslim Education*, pp. 123–124.

[15] For further details see Pantaleão de Aveiro, *Itinerario*, pp. 105, 200–8, 255–61; C. F. Beckingham, in *Journal of Semitic Studies*, vol. VII (1962), pp. 325–38; M. Is͟h-S͟halōm, *Christian Travels*, pp. 280–1. Many descriptions of Jewish life were written by Jewish residents and visitors throughout the century, cf. Yaʿari, *Letters*, pp. 162–6 (1521); 167–78 (1517–23); 180–1 (mid-century); 188–9 (1584). See above, p. 29, n. 38.

[16] 10 holders of the title *s͟hayk͟h*, *muʿallim* or *sīdī* (Coll. for *sayyid*); 8 holders of the title *ḥajjī*. Also listed are a son of *nāʾib al-kalʿa* and a son of *k͟hādim al-Ṣak͟hra*. Lit.: "the servant of [the mosque of the] Rock." This was a religious attendant in charge of the maintenance of the mosque. On the term see Dozy, s.v. (p. 355). There were several attendants at the Dome of the Rock, cf. n. 29. See also "*aḥad al-sāda al-k͟huddām bi'l-Masjid al-Aḳṣā*" in the *Sijill*, vol. LXXVII, p. 61, dated 1003/1594–5. See p. 15.

[17] Turcoman tribe, see above, p. 18.

[18] Fifteen of them are listed under the designation *al-mujāwir*.

[19] Only one of them is referred to specifically as a monk (*rāhib*).

In Dayr Andreas, 3 monks

In Dayr Mār Yaʿḳūb,[20] 15 monks

Banī Zayd بنى زيد 117 households, 1 bachelor, 3 imams

Community of Döger, in the said quarter, 7 households, 1 imam

Community [sic] of ʿAḳabat al-Sitta عقبه الستة 34 households, 1 bachelor, 1 imam

Bāb al-Ḥiṭṭa باب الحطه 166 households, 19 bachelors, 3 imams, 8[21] sharifs

Community of Maghribīs مغاربه 69 households,[22] 1 bachelor, 1 imam

Community of Syrians سريانى 13 persons

Khawālidī جوالدى 16 households, 1 imam

Rīsha and Ṣahyūn ريشه وصهيون 81 households, 1 bachelor, 2 imams [85 names listed]

Community of Christians in the said quarter, 12 persons

Community of Melkite Christians ملكيه 107 persons—85 households, 20 bachelors, 2 blind

Community of Coptic Christians قبطيان 32 persons—26 households, 6 bachelors

Community of Jews in the city of Jerusalem يهودان

In the Sharaf quarter شرف 94 persons—85 households, 9 bachelors

Mashlakh[23] quarter مسلخ 47 persons—43 households, 4 bachelors

[20] Reads: Yākūb. For an earlier reference see Marmardji, *Textes géographiques*, p. 188. Although not stated specifically, this was an Armenian church (explicitly referred to as such in the next *taḥrir*, p. 83). On the history of this church, more commonly referred to in western languages as St. James, see Sanjian, *Armenian Communities in Syria*, pp. 12–13. Sanjian mentions "small enclaves" of Armenians in Mamluk Palestine, *inter alia* in Ramle and Gaza (p. 20) He suggests that "this state of affairs continued until the Ottoman conquest"; after the conquest, as is shown by the *taḥrirs*, Armenians were left only in Jerusalem. For further details on St. James Cathedral cf. A. Antreassian, *Jerusalem and the Armenians*

[21] Ten *sharifs*, 6 *shaykhs*, 9 *ḥajjis* are listed.

[22] Ten *hajjis* and *sidis*, 1 son of *nāʾib kalʿa* are listed.

[23] "Quarter of the slaughter house", the south-western corner of the Jewish quarter (cf. Map 2,B), was bordered by ṭarīḳ bāb nabī Daʾud from the west in Wilson's

Rīsha quarter الريشه 102 persons—96 households, 6 bachelors

REGISTER 289 OF 961/1553-4

Quarter of:

Sharaf شرف 340 households, 25 bachelors, 3 imams, 1 blind man

Bāb al-Ḳaṭṭānīn باب القطانين 215 households, 16 bachelors, 1 imam, 2 *muezzins,* 2 jundīs

Bāb al-ʿĀmūd باب العمود 429[24] households, 32 bachelors, 1 imam

Döger community in Bāb al-ʿĀmūd quarter, 18 households, 4 bachelors

Bāb al-Ḥiṭṭa باب الحطه 362 households, 22 bachelors, 1 imam[25]

Community of Ayyūbiyya in the said quarter, from among the *Jundiyān-i Ḥalḳa,*[26] 26 households [25 names listed]

Zarāʿina زراعنه 280 households, 28 bachelors

Rīsha and Ṣahyūn ريشه وصهيون 168 households, 3 bachelors

Maghāriba مغاربه 84 households, 11 bachelors

Community of Shaykh Aḥmad Maghribī in the said quarter, 32 households

ʿAḳabat al-Sitta عقبة الستة 39 households, 4 imams,[27] 2 attendants (or eunuchs?)[28] (*khādim*), 1 doorkeeper (*bawwāb*)[29]

Communities of Christians in Jerusalem

Syrian quarter سرياني 22 households, 4 bachelors

time. "There had been in former years (some ten years ago) the place where beasts were butchered for the market" (Wilson, IInd day, 20.4.1865). From register 516 it can be concluded that this quarter, which lay between Sharaf and Rīsha, was also known as Wusṭā ("the middle [quarter]").

24 Nine *ḥādim-ı ḥażret-ı Mūsā* listed. Lit.: "servants of [the mosque of] Moses", situated half-way between Jerusalem and Jericho.

25 Imām of al-Aḳṣā mosque. Among the names listed are also a *khaṭib*, a *khādım* and a *bawwāb* of al-Aḳṣa, as well as a *shaykh al-ḥaram*.

26 I.e., members of the *Jund al-Halḳa,* the Mamluk army in Syria and Palestine. When compared to the other two main towns, Gaza and Safed, the number of *Jundīs* in Jerusalem is strikingly low. This may be an indication of the relative administrative unimportance of Jerusalem in Mamluk time.

27 Three in al-Aḳṣā mosque, 1 in Ṣakhrat Allāh.

28 See above, p. 15.

29 Both this *bawwāb* and one of the two *khādims* serve in al-Ṣakhra.

In Dayr Mār Yaᶜḳūb, of the Armenian community, 54 households

Dayr Zaytūn, 1 monk

Dayr Andreas, 1 monk

Community of Coptic[30] Christians قبطيان 43 households, 4 bachelors

Community of Melkite Christians ملكية 135 households, 14 bachelors, 3 madmen

Community of Christians from the village of Bethlehem, who live in Jerusalem—Their *kharāj* [is for] 30 households, 3 bachelors

Community of Christians from the village of Bayt Jālā, who live in Jerusalem—Their *kharāj* is assigned to [the waqf of] Hebron 19 households

In Dayr Minda,[31] where the Ethiopian community live, 30 persons

[30] Several names are designated *al-Miṣri* (the Egyptian).

[31] Toward the end of the Mamluk period the Ethiopian community in Jerusalem attained its greatest prosperity. Almost immediately after the Ottoman conquest they started to emigrate to Europe in separate groups throughout the first five years, and when Bartolomeo de Salignac visited Jerusalem in 1522 there were no Ethiopians left (C. F. Beckingham, *Journal of Semitic Studies*, vol. VII (1962), p. 332; E. Cerulli, *Etiopi in Palestina*, vol. II, pp. 395–8). It is not surprising, therefore, that no Ethiopians were recorded in the first *taḥrir*, carried out three years later. But they came back. Various accounts from the 1530's indicate their reappearance in Jerusalem (Cerulli, *Etiopi in Palestina*, vol. II, pp. 410–12). In the 1560's, i.e., a short time preceding this register, the Ethiopian community of Jerusalem possessed two chapels (The Chapel of the Mocking and a chapel in the rotunda of the Holy Sepulchre). The recurring references to this, though conclusive, do not furnish any hint as to the exact name of this dayr. Two vague and ambiguous references to two more churches (The Chapel of Abraham's sacrifice and a chapel called St. Mary of Golgotha) do not seem to be conducive to a satisfactory solution (Beckingham, in *Journal of Semitic Studies*, vol. VII (1962), p. 332; Cerulli, *Etiopi in Palestina*, vol. II, pp. 19–20). There may, still, be a possibility of reading منده as (sayyida), which may tally with St. Mary's chapel. An Arabic manuscript in the library of the Vatican refers to the Chapel of السيدة (al-Sayyida) which is located near the Chapel of St. Constantin (al-Ḳiddīs Ḳusṭanṭīn), also called the Chapel of the Patriarch (Kanīsat al-Baṭriyark) near the Holy Sepulchre, next to *Ḥammām al-sayyida*, to the east of the House of Pilate (Vat. Arabo, 286, pp. 80a–82b). The main difficulty is that the manuscript speaks of it as a Greek Orthodox church without any reference to Ethiopians.

In Dayr Sīḳ,[32] of the community of Greeks (*Rūmīyān*), near the the Dead Sea (*Baḥr-i Lūṭ*), 20 persons

In Dayr Ḳumāma,[33] community of Greek Christians, 9 persons

In Dayr of the Serbs[34], Community of Greek Christians, 15 persons

In Dayr Mār[35] ?. . . ās, 1 monk

In Dayr Ḥiżr, 1 monk

In Dayr Ṣahyūn,[36] community of Frankish Christians, 14 persons

[32] Later known as Mār Sāba. Cf. Mujīr, vol. II, p. 433; Marmardji, *Textes géographiques*, p. 74, quoting Ibn Baṭūṭa to that effect. An Orthodox monk, Sophronius, who visited it in 1547, speaks of fifty monks in the monastery of Mar Saba (Khitrowo, *Itinéraires russes*, p. 273). The decline in their number in less than a decade may well be a result of their hardships, and many if not all of the "missing" monks may have moved to Dayr Sirb (see note 34). Another monk, Clément, who also toured the vicinity of Jerusalem, mentions the fact that in 1547 all the other important Greek Orthodox monasteries, except for Mār Sāba, were deserted. In point of fact, the information of our register tallies to a very large extent with the foregoing (Khitrowo, *Itinéraires russes*, pp. 267–8).

[33] Literally garbage, midden. This is probably a derisive pun on *al-Ḳiyāma*, the Resurrection—the Arabic name of the Church of the Holy Sepulchre. Some Muslim authors claim that *Ḳumāma* was the true name, and that the place was originally a garbage heap (see Canard, *Byzantion*, vol. XXXV [1965], pp. 20–21). On the earlier use of the term Ḳumāma, see Gaudefroy-Demombynes, *La Syrie*, p. 11, and Marmardji, *Textes géographiques*, pp. 31, 179–88.

[34] Mujīr al-Dīn (*Al-Uns al-jalīl*, vol. II, p. 40) mentions *Bāb Dayr al-Sirb* as one of the northern gates of Jerusalem. See also Ashtōr, *Yerushalayim*, vol. II (1955), p. 75, n. 33; Miquel, *Bulletin d'études orientales*, tom. XVI (1961), pp. 7–13, map, D; Marmardji, *Textes géographiques*, p. 184. A Russian merchant, Posniakov, who travelled in Jerusalem in the late 1550's of the sixteenth century, offers a reasonable explanation of the presence of Greek Orthodox monks (Serbs are Orthodox, after all) there: "The monks of St. Saba lived then in the Serbian Convent of St. Michael where they had taken refuge when their hospice in Jerusalem had been ruined twice by the Turks, and confiscated" (Moore, *Ancient Churches of Old Jerusalem*, pp. 79–80). If it is St. Michael, the Orthodox Convent of Guérin, *Jérusalem* (Paris, 1889) (no. 21 in his map, U in our map), then the road which leads from it to the northern wall may have once led to a gate. On the Serb monastery, see further Archimandrite Kallistos Miliara, *Hoi Hagioi Topoi en Palaistinê. . .*, vol. I (Jerusalem, 1928), p. 467 ff, vol. II (1933), p. 46 ff.

[35] ىا ىاس misread by the scribe for مار الياس (Mār Eliās)

[36] It seems odd, though, that this register, dated 1553–4, fails to mention the fact that at this stage there were no more Frankish Christians in Dayr Ṣahyūn. Many Christian accounts (C. L. Harry [H. C. Luke]), *A Franciscan's narrative*, pp. V, 21; Moore, *Ancient Churches of Old Jerusalem*, p. 77, citing the monk Boniface; Peradze, *Georgica*, nos. 4–5 (1937), p. 222; Ms. Vat. Arabo, p. 81) refer very clearly

In Dayr Laḥm,[37] of the Frankish community, 3 persons

In Dayr Muṣallaba,[38] community of Georgian Christians,[39] 15 persons

Community of Jews in Jerusalem, 107[40] households, 3 bachelors

In Maslakh quarter مسلخ 79[41] households, 3 bachelors

Community of Jews in Rīsha quarter ريشه 138[42] households, 7 bachelors, 1 madman

to the expulsion of all these from their monastery on Mount Zion in the years 1551–2. However, the very same number of monks can be traced in the following *tahrir* (p. 90) when they hold possession of Dayr al-ᶜAmūd monastery by an explicit Ottoman authorization (for further details see Moore, *Ancient Churches of Old Jerusalem*, pp. 77, 80; Peradze, *Georgica*, nos. 4–5 (1937), pp. 222–3).

[37] Most probably the Church of Nativity, situated in Bethlehem (Bayt Laḥm). The small number of priests is striking in view of its importance to Christianity, and is due to the lamentable conditions into which this church declined. As a Franciscan monk who visited the place in 1553–4 puts it: "Everything is now in ruins except those holy places which are underground" (H. C. Luke, *A Franciscan's narrative*, p. 34 and note).

[38] For earlier references in Arabic sources see: Marmardji, pp 78–79; Ashtōr, in *Yerushalayim*, vol. II (1955), pp. 71–2. Mujīr al-Dīn (*Al-Uns al-jalīl*, vol. II, p. 402) spells it *al-muṣallabiyya*. This is the Monastery of the Cross, which lies in a shallow valley one and a half miles west of the city walls. It was founded about the year 1038 by the Georgian monk Prochorus. From accounts of sixteenth-century pilgrims, we learn that at this time the monastery was "beautiful and large possessing many cells" (according to one version, as many as 365), and that it was the seat of a Georgian bishop. In the course of the nineteenth century it passed into the hands of the Greeks, and was later a theological college of the Orthodox Patriarchate of Jerusalem (See G. Peradze, *Georgica*, nos 4–5 (1937), pp. 181–246; Luke, *Anatolica*, p. 161; D. A. Qip'shidze, *Izvestiya Kavkazskogo Istoriko-Arkheologicheskogo Instituta*, vol. II (1927), pp. 31–68).

[39] The Georgians who enjoyed a privileged status under the Mamluks underwent (probably because of this as well as other reasons) a decline in Jerusalem. As a result of their misfortunes they had to sell their monasteries to the Franciscans. The most conspicuous, though by no means single, example was their removal, upon a French initiative, sanctioned by an Ottoman firman, from their monastery (St. John), to be sold to the Franciscans. Devoid of any reinforcements or assistance from Georgia, they were forced to evacuate all their convents, with this one left as their only refuge by the end of the century (Peradze, *Georgica*, nos. 4–5 (1937), pp. 181, 216, 222–3; Moore, *Ancient Churches of Old Jerusalem*, pp. 77–80).

[40] Three listed as blind men.

[41] Five listed as *askināzī*.

[42] One of whom is listed as *Ketḫüdā-i Yahūdiyān*. *Ketḫüda* is the Turkish form of the Persian *Kat-khudā*, "lord of the house," often used in Ottoman administration to designate high officials, representatives of these or of different common groups (i.e. *Kapıcılar Ketḫüdāsı*, *Ketḫüda-ı Bevvābin*, etc.). Here it is used to designate the "intendant of the Jews," more often referred to as *Shaykh al-Yahūd*, (the elder of the Jews), who was recognized by the local governor and population as the representative of the local Jewish community.

REGISTER 516 OF 970/1562–3

Quarter of:

Sharaf شرف 375 households, 19 bachelors, 21 *muʿīdīn, müderrisīn,*[43] *khaṭībs,* imams and muezzins, 1 blind [415 names listed]

Bāb Ḳaṭṭānīn باب قطانين 166 households, 13 bachelors, 19 *khaṭībs,* imams, muezzins, etc., 1 cripple [198 names listed]

Rīsha ريشه 189 households, 1 cripple [188 names listed]

Maghāriba مغاربه 130 households,[44] 2 bachelors

Bāb al-ʿĀmūd باب العمود 386 households, 2 bachelors, 1 sharīf, 1 blind man [390 names listed]

ʿAḳabat al-Sitt عقبة الست 50 households [49 names listed][45]

Bāb al-Ḥiṭṭa باب الحطه 308 households, 52 bachelors, 20 sharīfs, 48[46] *müderrisīn, khaṭībs,* imams, *khādims,* muezzins, etc. [421 names listed]

Community of *Ayyūbiye* in the said quarter of Bāb al-Ḥiṭṭa, from among the *Ajnād-i Ḥalḳa,* 19 households, 3 bachelors

Zarāʿina زراعنه 306 households, 4 bachelors [321 names listed]

Community of Melkite Christians ملكيه 99 households [98[47] names listed, 6 of which are termed as bachelors]

Community of Melkite Christians from among the community of Bayt Rīmā (*Rīmāwiyyīn*), 15 households, 5 bachelors[48]

Community of Melkite Christians (*Melkiyye-i naṣārā-i Rūm*) from the countryside (*baladiyyīn*), 13 households, 8 bachelors

[43] Lit: "One who teaches" seems to have had a specific meaning in the sixteenth century. The usual term for "teacher" was *muʿallim* or *muḥaṣṣil,* while *mudarris* was probably used specifically for teaching in a *madrasa* (cf. *waẓifat tadrīs al-Madrasa al-ʿUthmāniyya* in the *sijill* of Jerusalem, vol. LXXVII, p. 64, for the year 1003/1593–4).

[44] Seventeen of whom are designated al-Maghribī, one as *shaykh al-Maghāriba,* one as *gharbī.*

[45] Including one *shaykh ʿimāret,* one *naḳīb ʿimāret,* one *bawwāb ʿimāret,* one *kātib ʿimāret.*

[46] About thirty are either *shaykh* or *mevlānā;* some, as specifically noted, serve either in al-Aḳṣā or al-Ṣakhra mosques.

[47] Two specifically designated Maronites (*Mārūni*).

[48] From here onward the register lists only the names, omitting the totals.

Community of Melkite Christians from Hebron (*Khalīliyyūn*) who live in the city of Jerusalem, 4 households, 3 bachelors

Community of Melkite Christians from the village of Bayt Jālā who live in the city of Jerusalem, 21 households, 1 bachelor

Community of Christians from the village of Bayt Laḥm who live in Jerusalem, 26 households, 1 bachelor, 1 blind

Community of Jews in the city of Jerusalem in the quarter of Rīsha, 51 households, 5 bachelors

In the quarter of Wusṭā[49] ("the middle quarter"), 40 households, 6 bachelors

In the quarter of Sharaf, 146 households, 1 bachelor

Community of Christians in Jerusalem[50]

Syrian community, 19 households, 5 bachelors

In Dayr Mār Yaʿḳūb from the Armenian community, 31 households, 3 bachelors

Dayr Zaytūn, 7 monks

Dayr Andreas, 7 monks

Community of Copts, 53 households, 8 bachelors

Dayr Sīḳ, the community of Greeks (*Rūmīyān*), near the Dead Sea, 31 monks

In Dayr Muṣallaba, community of Georgian Christians, 15 persons

In Dayr ʿĀmūd in the hands of Frankish monks who live there in accordance with a Noble order and a legal document (*ḥüccet-i şerʿiye*), 14 monks.

In Dayr Bayt Laḥm, community of Franks, 4 monks

In Dayr Ḳumāma, community of Greeks (*Rūmīyān*), 7 monks

[49] See above, note 23. This may also be a misreading of *al-maslakh*.

[50] Since the Christian and Jewish communities of Jerusalem have already been listed in this register, it would seem that this section, although simply headed "Christians", refers to the foreign residents. It will be noted that it consists largely of monasteries and their occupants.

In Dayr Mār Eliās, 3 monks

Dayr Mayda(?),[51] where the Ethiopian community live, 20 monks

REGISTER 515 OF 1005/1596–7[52]

Quarter of:

Sharaf شرق 150 households, 9 bachelors

Bāb Ḳaṭṭānīn باب قطانين 150 households, 12 bachelors

Rīsha ريشه 163 households, 11 bachelors

Maghāriba مغاربه 126 households, 7 bachelors

Bāb al-ᶜĀmūd باب العمود 188 households, 19 bachelors [274 households, 19 bachelors listed]

ᶜAḳabat al-Sitt عقبة الست 24 households

Bāb al-Ḥiṭṭa باب الحطه 226 households [316 names listed]

Community of Ayyubiyye from among the *Ejnād-i Ḥalḳa* in the said quarter of Bāb al-Ḥiṭṭa, 18 households, 3 bachelors

Zarāᶜina زراعنه 223 households, 15 bachelors [234 names listed]

Community of Melkite Christians, 42 households

[51] See above, note 31.

[52] For an unknown reason no more details are recorded in this register. Whereas the Muslim population at this date is most probably given *in toto*, the scribe omitted the Jewish and most of the Christian inhabitants of this city. Even the last item recorded here seems to be incomplete.

TABLE 1
Quarters and Population of Jerusalem
(h = households, b = bachelors, r = religious, d = disabled)

	932/1525–6				*ca.* 945/1538–9				961/1553–4				970/1562–3				1005/1596–7			
	h.	b.	r.	d.	h.	b.	r	d.	h.	b.	r.	d.	h.	b.	r.	d.	h.	b.	r	d.
									Muslims											
Bāb al-Ḥiṭṭa	110	—	1	—	166	19	11	—	362	22	1	—	308	52	68	—	316	—	—	—
Jundīs	—	—	—	—	—	—	—	—	26	—	—	—	19	3	—	—	18	3	—	—
Bāb al-ᶜAmūd	71	1	—	—	101	14	2	—	429	32	1	—	386	2	1	1	274	19	—	—
Döger group	—	—	—	—	15	—	1	—	18	4	—	—	—	—	—	—	—	—	—	—
Bāb al-Ḳaṭṭānīn	102	1	—	—	128	7	3	—	215	16	3	—	166	13	19	1	150	12	—	—
Jundīs	—	—	—	—	—	—	—	—	2	—	—	—	—	—	—	—	—	—	—	—
Banī Ḥārith	7	—	—	—	9	—	—	—	—	—	—	—	—	—	—	—	—	—	—	—
Banī Zayd	46	—	—	—	117	1	3	—	—	—	—	—	—	—	—	—	—	—	—	—
Döger	—	—	—	—	7	—	1	—	—	—	—	—	—	—	—	—	—	—	—	—
Khawālidī	11	—	—	—	16	—	1	—	—	—	—	—	—	—	—	—	—	—	—	—
Rīsha	15	—	—	—	81	1	2	—	160	3	—	—	189	—	—	1	163	11	—	—
Zarāᶜina	110	—	—	—	159	4	3	—	280	28	—	—	306	4	—	—	223	15	—	—
Sharaf or ᶜAlam	89	—	—	—	266	27	5	—	340	25	3	1	379	19	21	1	150	9	—	—
ᶜAḳabat al-Sitt	24	—	—	—	34	1	1	—	39	—	7	—	50	—	—	—	24	—	—	—
Maghāriba	31	—	—	—	69	1	1	—	84	11	—	—	130	2	—	—	126	7	—	—
community of Sh Aḥmad	—	—	—	—	—	—	—	—	32	—	—	—	—	—	—	—	—	—	—	—
Total	616	2	1	—	1,168	75	34	—	1,987	141	15	1	1,933	95	109	4	1,444	76	—	—

	932/1525–6				*ca.* 945/1538–9				961/1553–4				970/1562–3				1005/1596–7			
	h.	b.	r.	d.	h.	b	r.	d.	h.	b.	r.	d.	h.	b.	r.	d	h.	b	r.	d.
									Christians											
Melkites	96	—	—	—	85	20	—	2	135	14	—	3	99	—	—	—	42	—	—	—
Melkites from the countryside	—	—	—	—	—	—	—	—	—	—	—	—	13	8	—	—	—	—	—	—
Syrians	8	—	—	—	13	(in Bāb al Ḥiṭṭa)		—	22	4	—	—	19	5	—	—	—	—	—	—
Jacobites	15	—	—	—	12	(in Risha-Ṣahyūn			—	—	—	—	—	—	—	—	—	—	—	—
Copts	—	—	—	—	26	6	—	—	43	4	—	—	53	8	—		—	—	—	—
Christians of Bayt Rīmā (Melkites)	—	—	—	—	—	—	—	—	—	—	—	—	15	5	—	—	—	—	—	—
Armenians	—	—	—	—	—	—	—	—	54	—	—	—	31	3	—	—	—	—	—	—
Christians of Hebron (Melkites)	—	—	—	—	—	—	—	—	—	—	—	—	4	3	—	—	—	—	—	—
Christians of Bethlehem	—	—	—	—	—	—	—	—	30	3	—	—	26	1	—	2	—	—	—	—
Christians of Bayt Jālā	—	—	—	—	—	—	—	—	19	—	—	—	21	1	—	—	—	—	—	—
Monks	—	—	—	—	—	40	—	—	—	110	—	—	—	108	—	—	—	—	—	—
Total	119	—	—	—	136	66	—	2	303	135	—	3	281	142	—	2	42	—	—	—

TABLE 1 (contd.)

	932/1525–6				*ca.* 945/1538–9				961/1553–4				970/1562–3				1005/1596–7			
	h.	b.	r.	d.	h.	b.	r.	d.	h.	b.	r.	d.	h.	b.	r.	d.	h	b.	r.	d.
										Jews										
S͟haraf	199 (Sharaf, Maslakh, Risha together)	—	—	—	85	9	—	—	107	3	—	—	146	1	—	—	—	—	—	—
Maslak͟h					43	4			79	3	—	—	40	6	—	—	—	—	—	—
Ris͟ha		—	—	—	96	6	—	—	138	7	—	1	51	5	—	—	—	—	—	—
Total	199	—	—	—	224	19	—	—	324	13	—	1	237	12	—	—	—	—	—	—
Muslims	616	2	1	—	1,168	75	34	—	1,987	141	15	1	1,933	95	109	4	1,444	76	—	—
Christians	119	—	—	—	136	66	—	2	303	135	—	3	281	142	—	2	42	—	—	—
Jews	199	—	—	—	224	19	—	—	324	13	—	1	237	12	—	—	—	—	—	—
[Jundīs]	—	—	—	—	—	—	—	—	28]	—	—	—	[19	3]	—	—	[18	3]	—	—
Total	934	2	1	—	1,528	160	34	2	2,614	289	15	5	2,451	249	109	6	—	—	—	—

2. TAXES AND REVENUES[53]

	932/1525–6	*ca.* 945/1538–9	961/1553–4	970/1562–3
Revenue of tax on the Church of the Sepulchre (*resm-i Dār al-Ḳumāma*) in the city of Jerusalem.[54] Waqf of the Sultan Suleyman for the reading of sections [of the ḳurʾān] in the [Mosque of] the Noble Rock, entirely.				
per year	40,000	80,000	120,000	120,000
Revenue of tax on measuring corn (*resm-i key vāliyet al-muğall,* or *ğilāl*). From each camel-load one ʿosmānī [asper], from each mule- or donkey-load 1/2 ʿosmānī is taken. Measuring tax (*resm-i keyl*). Waqf of the Rock of God, in accordance with the Noble Order (*ḥükm-i şerif*), entirely.				
per year		150[sic][55]	8,000	8,000
Revenue of tax on the scales (*resm-i ḳapan*)[56] in k͟hān al-wikāla and the vegetable building (*dār al-k͟huḍar*), in the city of Jerusalem. Waqf of the Rock, entirely.				
per year			12,000	17,000

[53] After the lists of quarters and inhabitants, the registers give lists of taxes and revenues. In dealing with the latter we follow basically the same order of *defters* as considered in the former. The fullest and most detailed list is that contained Register 289. We have therefore taken this register as basis, and given the text and translation of the headings as shown there, adding the amounts recorded in the earlier and later lists. Information for the year 970/1562–3 is to be found in registers 342 and 346 also, but except for one entry (the bathhouse of Bāb al-Asbāṭ, recorded only in register 342) it is combined and best presented in Register 516. Register 515, as mentioned already in note 52, is defective: the last part of the *taḥrir* is missing, thus statistics regarding taxes and revenues levied at the end of the century are unfortunately unavailable. The translation is slightly abridged by the omission of titles and honorifics. Except where otherwise stated, all amounts are given in aspers (*akçe-i ʿos̱mānī*). One para at this date equals two aspers.

[54] A tax paid by Christians visiting the Church. The tariff is given in the *ḳānūnnāme* of Jerusalem (Turkish text in Barkan, *Kanunlar*, p. 217; French translation in Mantran and Sauvaget, *Règlements fiscaux ottomans*, pp. 35–42 (the translation and annotation pre-date recent research). For references to the actual sums paid on different dates in the sixteenth century see Dudon, *St. Ignatius of Loyola*, p. 84 (in 1523); Luke, *A Franciscan's Narrative*, p. 27 for the early 1550's; Ray, *A Collection of Travels*, vol. I, p. 316 (in 1575); Zuallart, *Le voyage de Jérusalem*, vol. I, p. 82 (in 1586); de Hault, *Le voyage de Hierusalem*, p. 48 (in 1593).

[55] The earlier figure is probably an error, of a kind that is not uncommon in the registers. The second figure indicates 8,000 camel-loads or 16,000 donkey-loads in Jerusalem.

[56] On the *ḳapan* see B. Lewis, *Notes and Documents*, pp. 20 and 41. See above pp. 47–8.

Taxes and Revenues (contd.)

	932/1525–6	*ca.* 945/1538–9	961/1553–4		970/1562–3	
Revenue of [dues from] shops (*dakākin*) in the city of Jerusalem. Waqf of the Rock.						
			In Use 203 doors	Ruined 147 doors	In Use 213 doors	Ruined 137 doors
per year			13,637		18,000	
Revenue of storehouses for flour-merchants (*maḫāzin-i dakkākịn*) in the city of Jerusalem. Waqf of the Rock in the Jews' quarter, entirely.						
per year			600		300	
Revenue of corn (*muğall*) in the neighborhood of the Ḥaram al-S̲harīf. Waqf of the Rock, entirely.						
per year			700		360	
Revenue [of dues] from the Frankish pilgrims who come to the Church of the Sepluchre (Dār al-Ḳumāma), in accordance with ancient custom. Waqf of the Rock.						
per person			50		50	
per year			3,000		3,000	
Revenue of dues on consignments of soap (*resm-ı aḥmāl-i ṣābūn*),[57] going from the city of Jerusalem to Egypt. Waqf of the Rock and of Hebron, entirely.						
Each consignment 16 ᶜosmānīs						
per year			11,056[sic]		11,055	
of which						
			Portion of the waqf of the Rock	Portion of the waqf of Hebron	waqf of the Rock	waqf of Hebron
			3,685	7,370	3,685	7,370
Revenue of bathhouse (*ḥammām*) of Jerusalem, in the city, known as Hammām al-ᶜAmūd.[58] Waqf of the Rock, entirely.						
per year			347		300	
Revenue of a mill in the city of Jerusalem, in the Jews' Quarter. Waqf of the Rock, entirely.						
per year			480		1,000	

	932/1525–6	*ca.* 945/1538–9	961/1553–4	970/1562–3
Revenue of property left behind (*mukhallafāt*) by *Mujāwirs* of the Haram-i Sherīf.[59] Waqf of the Rock, in accordance with the Noble Order (*ḥükm-i şerīf*), entirely.				
per year			500	4,000 including recipients of stipends (*erbāb-i vaẓāʾif*)[60] in Jerusalem
Revenue of leases (*aḥkār*)[61] in the city of Jerusalem, waqf of the Rock, entirely.				
per year			11 doors 400	11 doors 212
Revenue of bathhouse of al-ʿAyn[62] in the city of Jerusalem, in Bāb al-Ḳaṭṭānīn. Waqf of the Rock.				
			16,000	10,000
			Portion of the waqf of the Rock: 12 *ḳirāṭ* per year 8000; Portion of the waqf of Deñiz: 12 *ḳirāṭ* per year 8000	Portion of the waqf of the Rock: 12 *ḳirāṭ* 5000; Portion of the waqf of the amir Deñiz for his madrasa in Bāb al-Silsila: 12 *ḳirāṭ* 5000

57 See above, p. 55.

58 Probably that known as "the bathhouse of the Patriarch" (*Batrık ḥammāmı*), which, as Evliya Çelebi, (*Seyāḥatnāme* (Istanbul, 1314), vol. IX, p 488) says, was frequented mostly by Christians because of its proximity to their quarters.

59 On the privilege of the Maghribī *mujāwirs*, see above, n. 14.

60 "Religious judges who were granted a daily stipend by the stste-treasury" *hükkām-i şerʿiyye ḫazīne-i devletten vaẓife-i yevmıye ile muvaẓẓaf* (Muṣṭafā Nūrī, *Netāʾic ul-vuḳūʿāt*, vol. I, p. 23).

61 The *ḥikr* is a form of lease, sometimes a kind of waqf See Dozy, *Supplément*, s.v.; Maḳrīzī, Khiṭaṭ, vol. II, p. 114; *EI*[1] s.v. "Waqf" (by E. Heffening) vol. IV, pp. 1096–1103.

62 There were two *ḥammāms* near *Bāb al-kaṭṭānīn: Hammām al-ʿayn* and *Hammām al-shıfāʾ*. The former was built by Amīr Tankız al-Nāṣirı, who is referred to here as amīr Deniz (Golvin, in *Institut Français de Damas, Bulletın d'études orientales*, vol. XX (1967), pp. 101–117. See also "The *Ḥammām al-ʿayn*" which is known as "the ḥammām of Tankız" (*Sijill* of Jerusalem, vol. VIII, p. 203 for the year 945/1538–9). As the name of this bathhouse appeared without any diacritical signs it was mistaken by the scribe of the register for *al-sitt* (this time, also, without any diacritical points). Although there later appears to have been a bathhouse (mentioned both by Evliya Çelebi and Wilson) by the name of "Ḥammam Sitti Maryam", it was near St. Stephan's gate, and should therefore not be confused with that mentioned above.

Taxes and Revenues (contd.)

932/1525–6	*ca.* 945/1538–9	961/1553–4	970/1562–3
Revenue of poll-tax (*jizya*) of Christians, Syrians, Copts and Jews in the city of Jerusalem, apart from Christians of Bethlehem and Bayt Jālā residing in the city.			
19.080	32,560	791 persons from each 80[63] Total 63,280 of which Portion of the Rock, as fixed (*ber-vech-i makṭuʿ*)[65] 142 persons Remainder of the waqf of the Rock From the community of Jews in the city of Jerusalem. *Makṭuʿ* 85 persons 80 from each Total 6,800 From the community of Armenians in the city of Jerusalem. *Makṭuʿ* 15 persons 80 from each Total 1,200 From the community of Melkite Greeks in the city of Jerusalem. *Makṭuʿ* 15 persons 80 from each Total 1,200 From the community of Copts in the city of Jerusalem. *Makṭuʿ* 10 persons Total 800 From the community of Christians from Bayt Rīmā (*Rīmāwwiyyin*) in the said city 13 persons Total 1,040	53,920[64]

	932/1525–6	*ca.* 945/1538–9	961/1553–4	970/1562–3
			From the community of Hebron Christians in the said city. 4 persons 80 from each Total 320	
			Remainder Apart from the portion of the Waqf of the Noble Rock, Imperial Domain (*Ḫāṣṣ-i Şāhī*). 649 persons 80 from each Total 51,920	

Treasury revenues (*Bayt al-māl*)[66] and property of absent and missing persons (*māl-ı ğā'ib* and *māl-i mefḳud*)[67] above ten thousand, with *Bayı al-māl* of *Sipāhīs, Mustaḥfiẓ* and *Ghūlāms*[68] of the Sultan, with their male and female slaves, apart from the portion of runaway slaves from free tīmārs, and waqfs of the Ḥarameyn, the Rock and Hebron.[69]

	932/1525–6	*ca.* 945/1538–9	961/1553–4	970/1562–3
Imperial Domain per year	13,000		15,000	15,000

[63] The *jizya* (in Ottoman usage usually called *kharāj*) was fixed in this period at one gold piece. On the rate of the asper to the gold piece see above, p. 71.

[64] Calculated on the same basis of 80 aspers for the total of 674 tax-payers.

[65] An arrangement whereby a tax was paid as an agreed global sum.

[66] In the Ottoman state the distinction was carefully maintained between the private treasury of the Sultan and the public treasury. The term most commonly applied to the state treasury was *mīrī*. The term *bayt al-māl* was normally restricted in common Ottoman usage to a certain group of revenues belonging by law to the public treasury. These consisted of various categories of forfeited, escheated and unclaimed property. The most important were properties belonging to missing and absent people. See above, p. 74.

[67] "If his heir is outside the country and his place [of abode] is unknown, that man is called *mefkūd*" (*Ḳānūnnāme-i Āl-i ʿOsmān, Tarih-ı Osmanı Encümenı mecmuası ilavesi* (Supplement) (Istanbul, 1329), p. 21). "His belongings (*metrūkāt*) will be left in possession of a custodian (*başi elinde*) for one year, to be handed over thereafter to the *Bayt al-Mālci* (*ibid.*).

[68] H. Inalcık, "Ghulām," EI^2, vol. III, pp. 1085–91.

Taxes and Revenues (contd.)

	932/1525–6	*ca.* 945/1538–9	961/1553–4	970/1562–3
Revenue of scales for cotton (*Ḳapan al-ḳuṭn*), in the cotton market. From each camel-load one para scales tax (*resm-i ḳapan*) is taken. From horse, mule and donkey loads the tax is collected at the rate of one para per camel-load.				
Imperial Domain per year			1,500	1,500
Revenue of bitumen (*ḥummar*)[70] which comes out of the Dead Sea once a year and is poured on to the shore. Hitherto collected as external.				
Imperial Domain, outside the Defter[71] per year			10,000	10,000
Revenue of presses (*maᶜṣara*) in the city of Jerusalem.	15 doors			
Imperial Domain outside [? the Defter] per year			930	900 (60 per each)
Revenue of black market toll (*bāc-i bāzār-i siyāh*)[72] the details of which are written in the *ḳānūnnāme*.				
Appanage of the governor of the sanjak (*Ḫāṣṣ-i Mīr-i Liwā*) per year		2,000	2,000	2,000 (ID)
Revenue of tax (*bāc*) on the market for horses (*bāzār-i esb*) camels, mules, donkeys and cattle. From the sale of a camel 10 aspers, of a horse or mule 4, of a donkey or an ox 2, of sheep and goats 1 asper for every three.				
Appanage of the governor. per year	800	1,000	2,000	3,000 (ID)

	932/1525–6	*ca.* 945/1538–9	961/1553–4	970/1562–3

Revenue of tax on the scales for olive oil (*resm-i ḳapan-i zeyt*). One asper duty is collected for each jar, when the jars are big, so that four jars make a camel-load. When the jars are small the duty should be calculated and collected at the rate of 4 aspers per camel-load.

Appanage of the governor per year		150[sic]	5,000	7,000 (ID)

Treasury revenues and property of absent and missing persons and stray cattle and runaway male and female slaves and riding animals in the cities of Jerusalem and Hebron, up to 10,000; apart from the portion of the runaways of the free tīmārs, the waqfs of the Harameyn, the Rock and Hebron, and the sojourners (*mujāwir*) of Ḥaram al-Sharīf.[73]

[70] See above, p. 59, n. 42.

[71] *Ḫāric ez defter*. Inalcık (*Defter-i sancak-ı Arvanid*, pp. xxv–xxvi) mentions two categories of items which, according to a collection of *ḳānūns* from the seventeenth century, can be thus termed: Villages and *mezraʿas* which were not included in the original *icmāl* and *mufṣṣal* during the *taḥrīr* of the *defter-i ʿatiḳ*, as well as newly established or newly settled places. To these two categories of lands and persons one should add products (sources of income) which were nonexistant during the initial *taḥrīr*.

[72] This item, which appears in various forms in a number of *ḳānūns* and registers, has given rise to some confusion. It has been taken as a tax on black slaves, as an illicit levy or a levy on illicit transactions, and, by amending *siyāh* to *sıpāh*, as a tax levied on military purchases or assigned to military beneficiaries. None of these explanations is convincing. Fekete, who, too, first read it *sipāh* (*Siyāqat-Schrift*, vol. I, p. 89) was unsure of his reading and therefore added a footnote, (p. 90, n. 34) suggesting the possibility of *siyāh*. However, in his later work he reads it only *siyāh* without any doubt throughout the scores of references (Fekete and Kaldy-Nagy, *Rechnungsbücher*, pp. 17–382 *passim*). That the adjective *sıyāh* applies to *bāc* and not to *bāzār* is clearly shown by the innumerable texts, including Jerusalem register 346 of 970/1562–3, in which it is listed simply as *bāc-i siyāh* (Cf. Halası-Kun, *Belleten*, vol. XXVIII [1964], p. 16). The *bāc-i siyāh* (in some parts of the Empire called *tamğa-i siyāh*) was a tax levied in markets on goods brought into the city for sale. The name probably refers to a black stamp given as receipt presumably by the *muḥtesib* (Beldiceanu, in *JESHO*, vol. XI, (1968), p. 95). In the nineteenth century it probably changed its name to *resm-i tamğā ve-iḥtısāb* (Osman Nuri, *Mecelle-ı umūr-i belediye*, pp. 356–357). See *EI*^{2}, s.v. Bādj (by M. F. Köprülü); Barkan, *Kanunlar*, index, s.vv. *bac-i bazar, bac-ı siyah, kara bazar bac-i, tamga-i siyah*; S. Jikyā, *Defter-i Kurjistan*, p. 3. For details on the actual collection of this tax in other cities see F. Dalsar, *Bursada ıpekçilik*, p. 242; Goyünç, *Mardin Sancağı*, pp. 129, 142. In the register of 970/1562–3 this and the two following items, as well as the butchers' tax and the *ıḥtisāb* have been transferred from the governor's appanage to the Imperial Domain and were consequently termed *ḫāṣṣ-i cedīd*.

[73] See above, p. 74.

Taxes and Revenues (contd.)

	932/1525–6	*ca.* 945/1538–9	961/1553–4	970/1562–3
Appanage of the governor				
per year		9,000	12,000	12,000
Revenue of inspection of the markets (*Iḥtisāb*) of the city of Jerusalem, details of which are recorded in the *ḳānūnnāme*.[74] Subject entirely to the weights [or measures] of the *iḥtisāb*.				
Appanage of the governor.				
per year	12,000	12,000	23,000	23,000 (ID)
Revenue of tax for the night-watch (*resm-i ʿasesān*)[75] and the watch-prison (*maḥbes-i ʿasesiye*). One asper is collected from every shop that is locked. Two paras are collected from any arrested person who is released.				
Appanage of the governor				
per year		2,000	2,000	2,000
Revenue from butchers (*Ḳaṣṣābān*) of the city of Jerusalem. For two sheep or two goats one asper is collected; for a water-buffalo 2 paras; for an ox 1 para, when they are slaughtered.				
Appanage of the governor				
per year	2,500 (*maḳṭūʿ*)	3,000	3,000	5,000 (ID)
Occasional revenues (*bād-i havā*)[76] and bride-tax (*resm-i ʿarūsāne*)[77] of the cities of Jerusalem and Hebron, with half of the fines (*niyābet*)[78] and bride-tax of the districts (*nāḥiye*) of Jerusalem and Hebron, apart from the free tīmārs.				
Appanage of the governor				
per year	20,000	7,000 (city of Jerusalem only) 20,000 (districts of Jerusalem and Hebron and the city of Hebron with fines and penalties and bride-tax)	33,000	33,000

	932/1525–6	*ca.* 945/1538–9	961/1553–4	970/1562–3
Revenue of sheep tax (*resm-i ağnām, ᶜādet-i ağnām wa'l-miᶜze*) of the city of Jerusalem. From 2 sheep one asper is collected; from a flock one para. One asper from every two lambs is collected.				
Appanage of the governor per year	7,000 (with the whole district)		500 (city only)	1,000 (city only)
Revenue of bathhouse in Bāb al-Asbāṭ in Jerusalem. Waqf of Salāḥ al-Dīn Yūsuf b. Ayyūb for his madrasa in Jerusalem. Entirely.				
per year			14,000	7,600
Eastern and Western Markets. Waqf of the K͟hānḳāh Hamdiye. Shops. 6 (1 in use, 5 ruined)				
per year			100	
Revenue of K͟hān al-Faḥm, K͟hān S͟hiᶜāra and a dye-house (*maṣbag͟ha*).[79] Waqf of the Holy Rock.				
per year				1,520 (K͟hān al-Faḥm 1120; K͟hān S͟hiᶜāra 160; Dye-house 240)

[74] See *EI*² s.v. "Ḥisba II" (by R. Mantran) vol. III, pp. 489–90.; Heyd, *Studies*, pp. 229–34.

[75] See above, p. 69.

[76] See above, p. 74, n. 91.

[77] Also called *ᶜArūs resmi, resm-i ᶜarūs, ᶜādet-i ᶜarūsi*, etc. The standard rates were sixty aspers on girls and forty or thirty on widows and divorcees (Lewis, "ᶜArūs Resmi," *EI*², vol. I, p. 679). See also Kaldy-Nagy, *Acta Orientalia*, vol. XIII (1961), p. 34. Cf. *Ḫidmat al-ᶜUrs* in the Mamluk time, Sauvaget, *Bulletin d'etudes orientales*, t. XII (1948), p. 52.

[78] The term *niyābet-i cürüm ve cināyet* is used for fines and similar penalties, imposed with the authorization of a deputy (*nā'ib*) appointed by the kady of the area. Also called *cerā'im ve cināyet, cerā'im, niyābet-i cürum ve cināyet*, and prevalent in many parts of the Ottoman Empire in the sixteenth century (for a very detailed list of crimes and misdemeanors which this term comprises see Beldiceanu, *JESHO*, vol. XI (1968), pp. 54, 87. See also Inalcık, *Belgeler*, vol. II (1967), p. 79; Gökbilgin, *Edirne ve Paşa livası*, p. 19; Barkan, *Kanunlar*, p. 286; Inalcık, "Ḍarība," *EI*², vol. II, p. 147; Heyd, "D͟jurm," p. 604). Inalcık, *Defter-i Sancak-i Arvanid*, pp. xxvii–xxviii; Fekete, *Siyaqāt-Schrift*, vol. I, p. 81, n. 19. For several suggestions as to the possible interpretation of the term see Heyd, *Studies*, p. 276.

[79] Wilson's Dyers' market; see Map 2, H.

Taxes and Revenues (contd.)

	932/1525–6	*va.* 945/1538–9	961/1553–4	970/1562–3
Revenue of rent (*Kirāye*) of olive-trees in the city of Jerusalem. Waqf of the Noble Rock				
per year				570
Revenue of 6 vineyards in the vicinity of Jerusalem. Waqf of the Noble Rock.				
per year				440
Revenue of the bathhouse of al-Shifā[80] in the city of Jerusalem. Waqf of the Noble Rock.				
per year				4,000
Revenue of the bathhouse of Dāʾūd[81] in the city of Jerusalem, in the Jews' Quarter. Waqf of the Noble Rock.				
per year				735
Revenue of the offertory (*ṣundūk al-nudhūr*) in the Mosque of the Rock. Waqf of the Noble Rock.				
per year				1,200
Revenue of leases (*aḥkār*) of 12 pieces of land within the walls (*ḫandaḳ-i sūr*) of Jerusalem, which were not [written down] in the "old register" and were introduced into the "new register."				
Imperial Domain				
per year				450

[80] "The bath of the healing." Evilya Çelebı, (*Seyaḥātnāme*, vol. IX, p. 488) mentions the names of six bathhouses, but gives some details only about this one (*Şifa ḥammāmi*) of which he says "because of its being old [the oldest?], each and every sick man who enters it is cured in accordance with God's order (*biemrillâh*)." For a very detailed descriptıon of this *ḥammām* wıth many pıctures see Golvın, *Bulletin d'etudes orıentales*, tom. XX (1967).

[81] Possibly Map 2-G, which at Wilson's time was known and used as a *masbana*, soap-manufactory, but as he notes "was formerly known under the name of al-Ḥammâm al-Jamal." It was located rather close to the street of Nabi Daʾud.

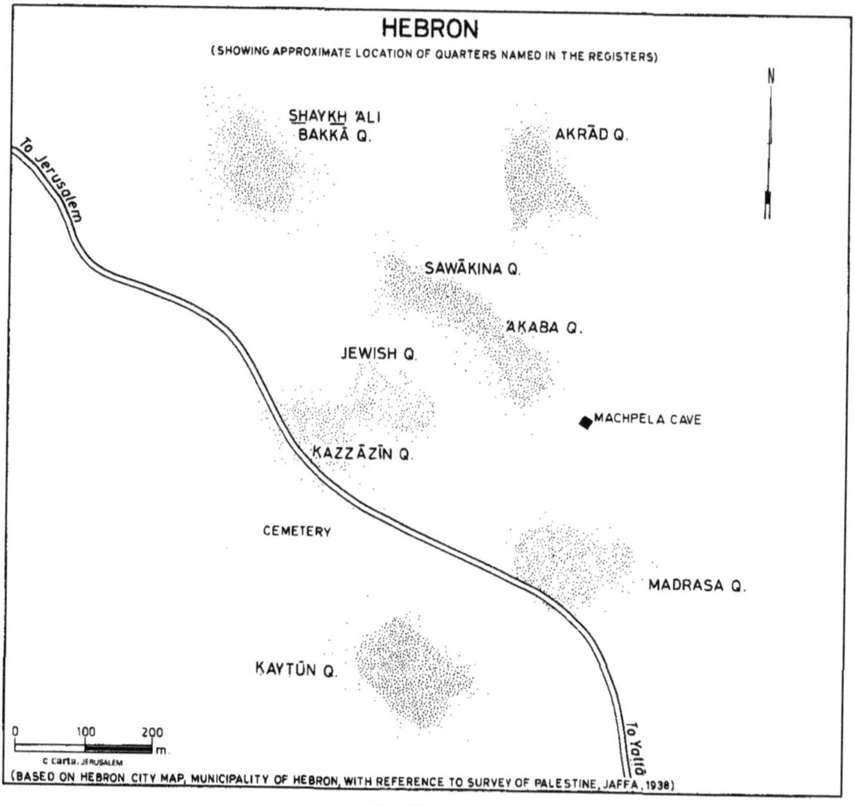
HEBRON
(SHOWING APPROXIMATE LOCATION OF QUARTERS NAMED IN THE REGISTERS)
N
SHAYKH 'ALI BAKKĀ Q.
AKRĀD Q.
To Jerusalem
SAWĀKINA Q.
'AKABA Q.
JEWISH Q.
MACHPELA CAVE
KAZZĀZĪN Q.
CEMETERY
MADRASA Q.
KAYTŪN Q.
To Yaffā
0 100 200 m.
c carta, JERUSALEM
(BASED ON HEBRON CITY MAP, MUNICIPALITY OF HEBRON, WITH REFERENCE TO SURVEY OF PALESTINE, JAFFA, 1938)

3. Hebron

·5·

HEBRON خليل الرحمان

1. QUARTERS AND INHABITANTS[1]

REGISTER 427 OF 932/1525–6

Quarter of:

Shaykh ʿAlī Bakkā[2] Yamānī[3] سبع على بكا يمانى 17 households

Ḳayṭūn[4] سطون 17 households[5].

Ḥabābina[6] حبابنه 22 households

[1] Described by a traveller who visited it in 1533–4 as follows: "Ebron est ung petit bourg où y a environ 100 maisons" (Affagart, *Relation de Terre Sainte*, p. 140). For earlier years see also Gaudefroy-Demombynes, *La Syrie*, p. 62, n. 2; Ḳalḳashandī, *Ṣubḥ al-Aʿsha*, vol. IV, pp. 102–3. Marmardjı, *Textes géographiques*, pp. 59–70; Le Strange, *Palestine under the Moslems*, pp. 309–27. For a description of the city in the seventeenth century cf. Evliya Çelebi, *Seyāḥatnāme*, vol. IX, pp. 504–13.

[2] The northeastern part of the city (cf. Map 3). There is an interesting similarity between this and the case of Jāmiʿ al-Abyaḍ quarter in Ramle: here, too, it is a quarter detached from the rest of the city (cf. Mujīr al-Dīn, *Al-Uns al-jalil*, vol. II, p. 425) and by far the smallest throughout the century. The quarter takes its name from Shaykh ʿAlī al-Bakkāʾ, d. 670/1271–2 (see his biography as well as the reason for this peculiar title in Mujīr al-Dīn, *Al-Uns al-jalil*, vol. II, pp. 492–3). Evliya Çelebi (or perhaps his editors) erroneously refers to the same person as Şeyh Aliyyüd Dekâvî (*Seyaḥātnāme*, vol. IX, p. 513). In the second half of the nineteenth century the quarter was called "Haret ech-Cheikh," and was still separated from the rest of the city by several orchards (V. Guérin, *La Terre S^te^*, vol. II, p. 274).

[3] The population of Palestine in the sixteenth century "from Jerusalem to Tripoli" was divided between Ḳaysīs and Yamanīs (cf. firman dated 979/1571 in Heyd, *Ottoman Documents*, p. 86, n. 1. See also above, p. 17, n. 57). This division was not only a matter of real or imagined descent, but rested on substantial differences which led at times to violent clashes. For obvious reasons, the tensions were deeper in the countryside than in the towns, and greater among nomads than among peasants. Hebron was in an area which was still, to a large extent, semi-nomadic. It served the tribes as a market centre, and attracted a tribal population. Unlike all the other cities of Palestine, Hebron still kept the differentiation Ḳaysī/Yamanī in some of its quarters, although in later registers these terms do not recur.

[4] The southwestern part of the city (cf. Map 3), also called "Raʾs Ḳayṭūn," i.e. "The hill (head) of Kayṭūn." Mujīr al-Dīn, (*Al-Uns al-jalil*, vol. II, p. 425) mentions that it was "detached from the city on its west."

[5] Three of whom are designated Ḳaysī or ibn Ḳays.

[6] Misread by the scribe; should read: Jabārina ("Those who come from Bayt Jibrīn"). Although Mujīr al-Dīn (*Al-Uns al-jalil*, vol. II, p. 425) writes "al-Jabbāriya

Ḥāfiẓ al-Dīn حافظ الدين 14 households

Ḳazzāzīn[7] قزازى 15 households

Akrād[8] Ḳaysī[9] اكراد قيسي 48 households

REGISTER 1015 OF *ca* 945/1538–9

Quarter of:

Ḳazzāzīn قزازين 170 households, 76 bachelors, 2 *sharīfs*, 4 imams [255 names listed]

Shaykh ʿAlī Bakkā شيخ على بكا 46 households, 20 bachelors, 2 imams

Al-Wuṣṭā and al-Ḳayṭūn الوسطا و القيطون 229 households, 52 bachelors, 4 *sharīfs*, 5 imams

Al-Madrasa and al-ʿAḳaba and al-Shaʿābina[10] المدرسة والعقبه والشعابنه 155 households, 50 bachelors, 1 *sharīf*, 5 imams

Al-Akrād الاكراد 135 households,[11] 29 bachelors, 2 *sharīfs*, 4 imams

[181 names listed]

Al-Yahūdā[12] (Jews) اليهودا 20 persons: 20 households, 1 blind man [20 names listed]

which was known in the past as Ḥārat al-Fustuka," both the French translation by Sauvaire and Muṣṭafā al-Dabbāgh, *Bilādunā Filasṭīn* (vol. V, part 2, pp. 108–9) call it al-Jabārina. Local tradition locates it where the present al-ʿAkāba quarter lies (cf. Map 3).

[7] "The glassmakers," the southern part of the city (cf. Map 3), called by Mujīr al-Dīn (*Al-Uns al-jalīl*, vol. II, p. 425) al-Zajjājīn. Hebron has always been famous for its glass industry. It is for this reason that we find it difficult to agree with Heyd, in *Yerushalyim*, vol. IV (1952), p. 179 and n. 39, who prefers to read *ghazzāz* ("silk-seller" or "spinner") rather than *ḳazzāz* in Jerusalem because, as he rightly mentions, glass was not used for windows. It was, however, used for utensils and other purposes.

[8] "The Kurds," overlooking the north and northeast of the Cave of Machpela (Mujīr al-Dīn, *Al-Uns al-jalīl*, vol. II, p. 425; cf Map 3). See above, pp 36–7.

[9] See above, note 3. Although the Kays-Yaman rivalry was, by definition, a feud among Arab tribes, even this aspect of it was not fully preserved in Ottoman Palestine. It was related to non-Arab tribes, too, as is shown by this and other examples (cf. Baer and Hoexter, "Ḳays ʿAylān", *EI*², vol. IV, pp. 833–5), which is a further indication of this division being political and social rather than genealogical.

[10] All three quarters lay to the south and west of the Cave of Machpela (cf. Map). Local tradition locates al-Shaʿābina in the al-Sawākina quarter. No local explanation of the name was available.

[11] Seven are designated as *al-Miṣri*, three as *al-Jaʿbar*, one as *al-khaṭib*.

[12] North of the Ḳazzāzīn quarter (cf. Map 3). It seems that no substantial change occurred with regard to this community as an immediate result of the Ottoman

HEBRON

Community of Christians, 7 persons[13]

REGISTER 289 OF 961/1553-4

Quarter of:

Wusṭā وسطى 154 households, 1 imam

Shafāyina and al-Madrasa شفاينه والمدرسه 79 households

ᶜAḳaba عقبه 90 households

Ḳazzāzīn قزازى 143 households

Ra'ˀs Ḳayṭūn راس قيطون 88 households

Fustuḳa فستقه 99 households

Akrād اكراد 247 households [only 207 names listed]

Shaykh ᶜAlī Bakkā شيخ على بكا 69 households

Community of Jews in Hebron belonging to the said [quarter] 8 households.[14] *Jizya* [at the rate] of 80 [aspers] each—total 640. Waqf of Hebron

occupation. At the turn of the fifteenth century a Jewish traveller found about twenty Jewish families and in 1522 another Jewish traveller mentions about ten (Bassola, [1522] in Yaᶜari, *Massaᶜōt*, p. 147 and Obadiah de Bertinoro (1487–90) cited in Ben Zvi, *Eretz Israel*, p. 150). It is most likely, therefore, that the first *taḥrīr* carried-out in 1525–6, which lists no Jews or Christians, was incomplete.

[13] Mujīr al-Dīn (*Al-Uns al-jalīl*, vol. II, p. 425) mentions a small Christian quarter in the city (Ḥārat al-Naṣārā). It seems that the negligible Christian community which had dwindled away just prior to the Ottoman occupation or at about that time no longer justified the further use of the term in the eyes of the local inhabitants. However a community of Christians "from Hebron," twenty-three families, appears in Gaza in the 932/1525–6 *taḥrīr*. Even the last remnants did not stay for very long in Hebron and they do not figure in the next *taḥrīr*, dated 1553–4. It is interesting to find a similar number of Christian families (five) though under different names, reappearing in Ramle between the *taḥrīrs* of 955/1548–9 and 964/1556–7, while two more new Christian families "from Hebron" reappear in Gaza in 955/1548–9 (the other twenty-three families having left the city, as is shown by the census of 945/1538–9). Unless one takes these seven families as identical with those which left Hebron after 945/1538–9 (which in view of the different names seems very doubtful) these must be regarded as yet another group which had left Hebron prior to this date.

[14] A substantial part of the Jewish community had left the city since the last recorded *taḥrīr* (1538–9). Two Jewish families "from Hebron" appear in Gaza in 1548–9, to be joined later by a third one, and throughout the second half of the century, they are referred to as "[originally] from Hebron". (Their names, however, do not tally with those first listed. This may be due either to some inaccuracy in the original list of Jews of Hebron or to the defective way in which they were copied in the register, no. 1015. This makes it very hard to draw any meaningful conclusion from this discrepancy.)

REGISTER 516 OF 970/1562

Quarter of:

Fustuḳa فستقه 98 households, 23 bachelors [99 households, 29 bachelors listed]

Ḳayṭūn قيطون 77 households, 31 bachelors

Sha'ābina شعابنه 141 households, 33 bachelors, 1 blind man [142 households,[15] 32 bachelors, 1 blind man listed]

Shaykh 'Alī Bakkā شيخ على بكا 46 households, 18 bachelors, 1 cripple

Ḳazzāzīn قزازين 155 households, 7 bachelors, 3 blind men, 2 cripples, 1 madman [173 names listed]

Akrād اكراد 304 households, 12 bachelors, 1 blind man [302 households,[16] 12 bachelors, 2 *sharīfs* listed]

Wusṭā وسطى 155 households, 3 *sharīfs* [153 households, 1 *khaṭīb*, 3 *sharīfs* listed]

Yahūdiyyān يهوديان 11 households at the rate of 80—total 880. Waqf of Hebron

REGISTER 515 OF 1005/1596–7

Quarter of:

Fustuḳa فستقه 78 households, 22 bachelors

Ḳayṭūn مطمون 102 households [112 names listed]

Sha'ābina شعابنه 42 households [one of which is listed as *sharīf*]

Shaykh 'Alī Bakkā شيخ على بكا 65 households

Ḳazzāzīn قزازين 123 households [2 listed as blind men]

Akrād اكراد 180 households

Wusṭā وسطى 90 households [one listed as imam, *khaṭīb* and a Hanefite *müderris*][17]

Yahūdiyyān يهوديان 11 households. Waqf of Hebron

[15] Two of which are designated Ṭurahbāy. See p. 17 above.

[16] One of which is designated Ṭurahbāy.

[17] See above, p. 89, n. 43.

TABLE 2
Quarters and Population of Hebron

	932/1525–6				*ca.* 945/1538–9				961/1553–4				970/1562				1005/1596–7			
	h.	b.	r.	d.	h.	b.	r.	d.	h.	b.	r.	d.	h.	b.	r.	d.	h.	b.	r.	d.
									Muslims											
Shaykh ᶜAlī Bakkā	17	—	—	—	46	20	2	—	69	—	—	—	46	18	—	1	65	—	—	—
Al-Kayṭūn	17	—	—	—	229	52	9}	—	88	—	—	—	77	31	—	—	112	—	—	—
Al Wusṭā	—	—	—	—			}	—	154	—	1	—	155	—	3	—	90	—	—	—
Ḳazzāzīn	15	—	—	—	173	76	6	—	143	—	—	—	160	7	—	6	121	—	—	2
Al-Akrād	48	—	—	—	146	29	6	—	247	—	—	—	304	12	—	1	180	—	—	—
Ḥafiẓ al-Dīn	14	—	—	—	—	—	—	—	—	—	—	—	—	—	—	—	—	—	—	—
Shaᶜābina	22	—	—	—	155	50	6}	—	79}	—	—	—	142	32	—	1	41	—	1	—
Al-Madrasa	—	—	—	—			}	—	}	—	—	—	—	—	—	—	—	—	—	—
Al-ᶜAḳaba	—	—	—	—			}	—	90	—	—	—	—	—	—	—	—	—	—	—
Fustuka	—	—	—	—	—	—	—	—	99	—	—	—	99	29	—	—	78	22	—	—
Total	133	—	—	—	749	227	29	—	969	—	1	—	983	129	3	9	687	22	1	2
									Jews											
Al-Yahūd	—	—	—	—	20	—	—	1	8	—	—	—	11	—	—	—	11	—	—	—
									Christians											
Community of Christians	—	—	—	—	7	—	—	—	—	—	—	—	—	—	—	—	—	—	—	—
Total	133	—	—	—	776	227	29	1	977	—	1	—	994	129	3	9	698	22	1	2

2. TAXES AND REVENUES[18]

	932/1525–6	*ca.* 945/1538–9	961/1553–4	970/1562	1005/1596–7
1. Revenue of the town[19] of Hebron, waqf of Hebron.[20] Entirely.					
(a) Wheat					
per year	3,000 (10 *ghirāra*)[21]	4,800 (10 *ghirāra*)	4,800 (10 *ghirāra*)		
(b) Barley					
per year	1,260 (6 *ghirāra*)	2,060 (6 *ghirāra*)	2,060 (6 *ghirāra*)		
(c) Tax on vineyards and other trees (*kharāj al-kurūm ve ashjār-i sā'ire*)					
per year	3,000	3,000	10,000		
2. Tax on [sheep and] goats and bees (*resm-i maᶜz ve naḥl* or *resm-i aghnām ve miᶜza ve naḥl*					
per year			1,600 (ID)	1,500 waqf of Hebron	1,600 waqf of Hebron
3. [Dues from] shops (*dakkākin*), 37 doors					
per year			2,260	2,400 waqf of Hebron	2,500 waqf of Hebron
4. Revenue of tax on the scales (*ḳapan*) and the vegetable building (*dār al-khudar*) in the cit of Hebron					
per year			2,160	1,800 waqf of Hebron	2,000 waqf of Hebron
5. Revenue of Khān al-Furn[22] in the city of Hebron			60	40 waqf of Hebron	100 waqf of Hebron

[18] Compiled from the following registers: 427, 1015, 289, 516, 515. The order followed, basically was that of registers 289 and 516.

[19] In the earliest register (no. 427 of 932/1525–6) Hebron is listed as a town, and designated *şehir* the normal Ottoman administrative term. In later registers this is replaced by *madina*, an Arabic wor which is not part of the standard Ottoman technical vocabulary. This change seems contrary to th general trend, which was to replace Arabic by Turkish terms. The fiscal pattern of Hebron is rural, no urban, in that the last includes taxes on agricultural products stated in kind, with notional monetar equivalents. This is standard practice in the villages, but does not normally occur in towns. From all thi it may be inferred that as regards its effective fiscal and perhaps also administrative status Hebron was a village, and that the use of the Arabic term *madina*, in place of the customary Ottoman administrativ terms *şehir* or *ḳaṣaba* indicates that its urban status was purely honorific, in recognition of its religiou importance.

[20] Lit.: "Of Abraham" (*sayyidunā Khalil*).

[21] The *ghirāra Ḳudsi* was three times the *ghirāra* of Damascus, the capacity of which was a little mor than 250 litres. Cf. Lewis, *Notes and Studies*, p. 17.

[22] "Khān of the oven (*furn*)" most probably, even though register 342 reads: *al-ᶜarab*. Register 28 reads: "half of Khān al-farrān".

Taxes and Revenues (contd.)

	932/1525–6	*ca.* 945/1538–9	961/1553–4	970/1562	1005/1596–7
6. Part of the revenue of Furn (?) al-Sūḳ ("the bakery in the market") in the city of Hebron per year			600		
7. Revenue of K͟hān al-Amīr in the city of Hebron			derelict		
8. Revenue of "black" (*siyāh*)[23] in the city of Hebron			250		
9. Revenue of soap-factory in the city of Hebron			derelict		
10. Lease (*ḥikr, aḥkār*) of houses in the city of Hebron per year			338 (7 doors)	472 (13 doors) waqf of Hebron	472 (13 doors) waqf of Hebron
11. Revenue of bathhouse (*ḥammām*) in the city of Hebron per year			2,000	6,082 waqf of Hebron Entirely	6,500 waqf of Hebron Entirely
12. Revenue of another bathhouse			ruined		
13. Revenue of property left behind (*muk͟hallafāt*)[24] by sojourners (*mujāwirīn*), recipients of stipends (*erbāb-i vaẓā'if*) and pilgrims (*wāridīn*) coming to visit the waqf of Hebron, in accordance with the Noble Order (*ḥükm-i şerīf*) per year			200	500 waqf of Hebron	1,000 waqf of Hebron

14. Part of the Imperial Domains of Jerusalem, waqf of Hebron, established as waqf for the *simāṭ*[25] of Hebron in accordance with the exalted Order of the Sultan.

[23] See Jerusalem, p. 101, n. 71.

[24] This entry is slightly modified in the two later registers, where it is termed as "Treasury revenues (*bayt al-māl*) . . . of pilgrims to the cave of Machpela."

[25] A free soup-kitchen which is probably related to the tradition of Abraham's hospitality. Mujīr describes it as follows: "*al-simāṭ al-karīm* . . . one of the wonders of this world: the people of the town (*balad*) and those who come from outside eat from it. It is bread which is prepared daily and is distributed in three [fixed] times [every day]" (Mujīr al-Dīn, *Al-Uns al-jalīl*, vol. I, p. 59, where further details are given). For other dishes handed out (lentils, for instance) in the *simāṭ*, vol. II, pp. 606, 443. For further details vol. II, pp. 440, 667, 672, 677, 679, 683. See also the French translation by Sauvaire, p. 257, n. 1. In the tenth century the *simāṭ* was called *ḍiyāfa* (Gaudefroy-Demombynes, *La Syrie*, pp. 62–3, n. 2). See also Bassola in A. Ya'ari, *Massa'ōt*, p. 147.

Taxes and Revenues (contd.)

	932/1525–6	*ca.* 945/1538–9	961/1553–4	970/1562	1005/1596–7
Wheat *mudd*[26] (Jerusalemite *mudd*)			2,000		
15. Revenues of some vegetable-gardens (*ḥākūra*) and other waqfs in the city of Cairo in accordance with the register of the waqf of Hebron per year			3,000		
16. Poll-tax (*jizya*) of the Jews and Christians in the city of Hebron, waqf of Hebron 80 from each person		2,160 27 persons	640	880	880[27]
17. Part of the revenues of the treasury (*ḫizāne*) of Egypt. Waqf of the Sultan for the *simāṭ* of Hebron per year			10,000 in coin		
18. Revenue of tax on presses (*maᶜṣara*) of molasses (*dibs*) in the city of Hebron. 20 rising to 26 doors, 62 aspers on each per year			1,240 (Tīmār of . . . and Ilyās	1,612 (Tīmār of Yūnis)	1,612 (Tīmār of Ḥiżr and Muḥammad ᶜAbd Allāh)
19. Revenue of inspection of the markets (*iḥtisāb*), tax on butchers (*ᶜādet-i ḳaṣṣābān*) and market-toll (*bāc-i bāzār*) in the city of Hebron. Tīmār, later New Imperial Domain (*Ḫāṣṣ-i cedīd*) per year			3,000 (Tīmār of Yūsuf)	7,200	9,500
20. Revenue of the offertory (*ṣundūḳ al-nudhūr*) in the cave of Machpela and the districts (*nāḥiye*)of Hebron. Waqf of Hebron per year				7,783	8,000

26 One *müdd* = 20 *kile* of Istanbul; 1 *kile* = 25.5 kg of wheat (Heyd, *Ottoman Documents*, p. 125, n. 3; p. 131, n. 2). It is, however, very doubtful whether this could serve as anything more than an indication, as the *müdd* tends to vary quite substantially from one place to another and from one commodity to another (cf. Beldiceanu, *JESHO*, vol. XI [1968], p. 90; Kaldy-Nagy, *Acta Orientalia*, vol. XXI [1968], pp. 197–8). Nowhere have we come across the specific measurement or weight of the *müdd* of Jerusalem. If, as suggested by Hinz, the *müdd* is calculated at the rate of 77 kg = 100 litres, then the *müdd* of Jerusalem could be estimated at the former figure (W. Hınz, *Islamic Masse und Gewichte*, pp. 45–6).

27 Calculated at the same rate of 80 aspers.

Taxes and Revenues (contd.)

	932/1525–6	*ca.* 945/1538–9	961/1553–4	970/1562	1005/1596–7
21. Land of the city of Hebron known as Ḥabrūn, Ḥibrā or the house of Abraham (Bayt Ibrāhīm),[28] waqf of ᶜAlam al-Dārī al-Anṣārī. Entirely.				Revenue: *Ḳism* of 1/4 and tax [on trees] (al-kharāj) 8,000	Revenue: *Ḳism* of 1/4 and tax [on trees] (al-kharāj) 9,000
22. *Mezraᶜa* of Dhū al-Rām (al-Rūm?) near the city of Hebron				Revenue: *Ḳism*[29] of 1/4 and tax on trees 12,000	Revenue: *Ḳism* of 1/4 and tax on trees 12,000
				Share of waqf of Hebron: 18 *ḳirāṭ* 9,000 Share of tīmār of Yūnis: 6 *ḳirāṭ* 3,000	Share of waqf of Hebron: 18 *ḳirāṭ* 9,000 Share of tīmār of Hiżr and Muḥammad ibn ᶜAbd Allāh: 6 *ḳirāṭ* 3,000
23. *Mezraᶜa* of Ḳilkis[30] near the city of Hebron				Revenue: *Kism* of 1/4 648 (Tīmār of Yūnis. Entirely)	Revenue: *Ḳism* of 1/4 650 (Tīmār of Ḥiżr and Muḥammad ibn ᶜAbd Allāh)

[28] For earlier references in Arabic sources to these names of the city see: Marmardji, *Textes géographiques*, pp. 48–50, 64–6; Ḳalḳashandī, *Ṣubḥ al-aᶜshā*, vol. IV, p. 102.

[29] Lit. "share" or "sharing," the most prevalent system used in assessing the tax levied as a share of the crop at the rate of 1/3, 1/4, 1/5 and 1/6, according to the fertility and situation of the land. This word may be read either as a noun (*ḳism*—"share") or as a verbal noun (*ḳasm*—"sharing"). Gramatically, the former seems more likely, in view of the contexts in which the term occurs (*ḳism min al-rubᶜ*, etc.). Ottoman officials do not, however, seem to have been concerned about Arabic grammar, and the form *ḳasm* seems to be preferred by modern Turkish historians.

[30] About 2 1/2 miles south of Hebron.

Taxes and Revenues (contd.)

	932/1525–6	*ca.* 945/1538–9	961/1553	970/1562	1005/1596–7
24. Treasury revenues (*bayt al-māl*) and property of absent and missing persons (*māl-j ğā* and *māl-i mefḳūd*) and stray cattle and runaway male and female slaves in the city Hebron, up to 10,000; apart from the portion of the runaways of the free tīmārs, the waq of the two Noble Cities (*Ḥarameyn*) and the Rock, and apart from sojourners of the Ḥara al-Khalīl				AG of Jerusalem, together wi the treasury revenues of Jerusale	
25. Occasional revenues (*bād-i havā*) and bride-tax (*resm-i ᶜarūsāne*) of the city of Hebr together with occasional revenues of the district (*nāḥiye*) of Hebron, apart from free tīmā				Constitute one category with tl Occasional revenues of Jerusalei AG of Jerusalem	

• 6 •

GAZA غزة

1. QUARTERS AND INHABITANTS[1]

REGISTER 427 OF 932/1525–6

Quarter of:

Fikr Tuffāḥ[2] فكر تفاح 6 imams, *khaṭībs* and *faḳīhs*, 74 households

Dār al-Khuḍar[3] دار الخضر 4 imams, *khaṭībs* and *faḳīh*, 43 households, 3 bachelors

Ṣabbāgha[4] صباغه 3 imams, *khaṭībs* and *faḳīhs*, 57 households, 6 bachelors

Zaytūn[5] زيتون 5 imams, *khṭībs* and muezzins, 54 households, 30 bachelors

Burjuliyya[6] برجليه 11 imams, *khaṭībs* and *faḳīhs*, 141 households, 2 bachelors

[1] For different versions as to the origin of the word, as well as the history of the town in earlier years cf. Gaudefroy-Demombynes, *La Syrie*, pp. 50–2. Marmardji, *Textes géographiques*, pp. 154–7; Le Strange, *Palestine under the Moslems*, pp. 441–3. Affagart, (*Relation de Terre Sainte*, p. 61), describes it as larger than Jerusalem, though its population was then (1553–4) by far scantier. Mujīr al-Dīn (*Al-Uns al-jalīl*, vol. II, p. 422) describes it as "one of the best towns of Palestine." For further details on Gaza as seen in 1561 by German travellers see Ish-Shalōm, *Christian travels*, pp. 288–9.

[2] The scribe erroneously took the ḥ to be f; this name is *Ḥikr tuffāḥ* or *Ḥikr al-tuffāḥ*, as a reference to apple (*tuffāḥ*) orchards, for which, according to local tradition (cf. ʿĀrif al-ʿĀrif, *Taʾrikh Ghazza*, p. 255) the place was famous. This quarter constitutes the northeastern part of the city (cf. Map 4).

[3] "The vegetable house", the north-western part of the Zaytūn quarter. Within this quarter are the Greek-Orthodox church and the Mosque of Kātib al-Wilāya, on the gate of which ʿĀrif, (*Taʾrikh Ghazza*, p. 339) read an inscription relating its construction to Aḥmad ibn Kātib al-Wilāya, dated the first ten days Dhū al-Ḳaʿda 995 (5–14.10.1587). Local tradition tells of an old well which used to supply both the mosque and the inhabitants of the quarter with water.

[4] Probably not *Ṣabbāgha*, dyers, but a distorted form of *Dabbāgha*, tanners. A part of the Tuffāḥ quarter, probably its southern (cf. slaughter house in our map) which was famous for its tanneries (ʿĀrif, *Taʾrikh Ghazza*, p. 255).

[5] "The Olives quarter." The southeastern part of the present Zaytūn quarter (cf. Map 4), which has always been famous for its olive trees.

[6] The southeastern part of the present Daraj quarter (cf. Map 4) in which are the Great ʿUmari Mosque (*al-Jāmiʿ al-ʿUmarī al-Kabīr*), al-Sayyid Hāshim Mosque and

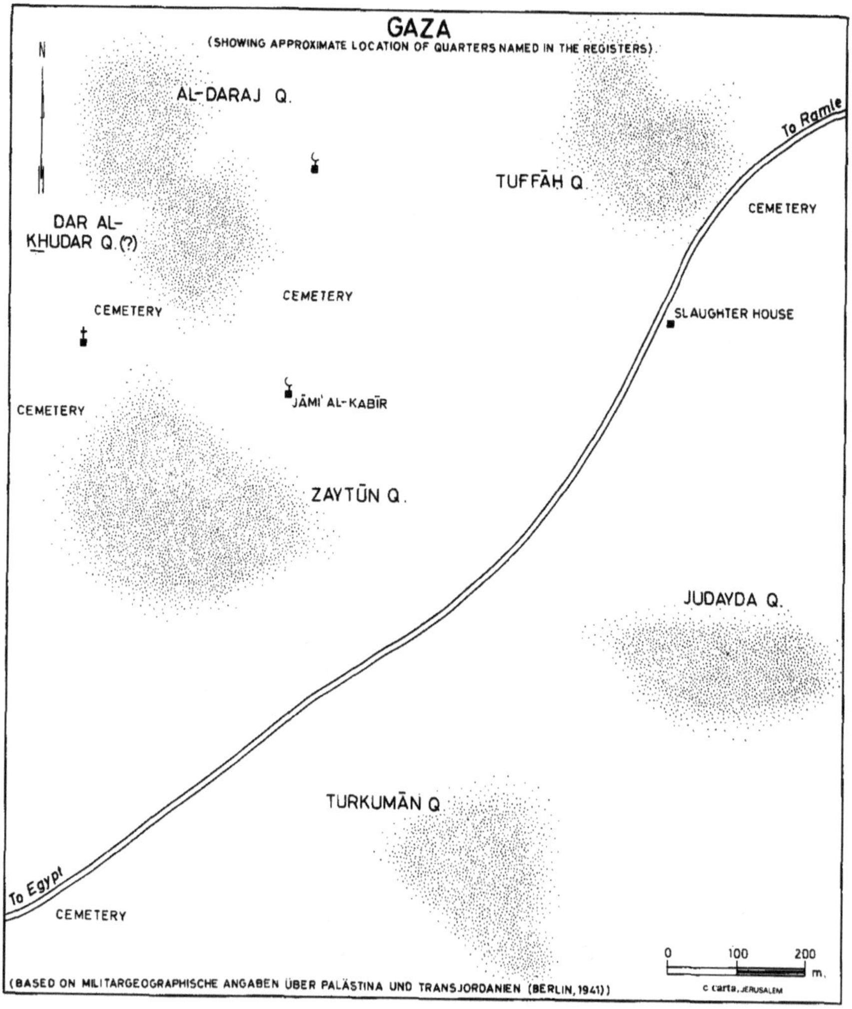
GAZA
(SHOWING APPROXIMATE LOCATION OF QUARTERS NAMED IN THE REGISTERS)
N
AL-DARAJ Q.
TUFFĀḤ Q.
To Ramle
CEMETERY
DAR AL-
KHUDAR Q.(?)
CEMETERY
CEMETERY
SLAUGHTER HOUSE
CEMETERY
JĀMI' AL-KABĪR
ZAYTŪN Q.
JUDAYDA Q.
TURKUMĀN Q.
To Egypt
CEMETERY
0
100
200
m.
(BASED ON MILITARGEOGRAPHISCHE ANGABEN ÜBER PALÄSTINA UND TRANSJORDANIEN (BERLIN, 1941))
c carta, JERUSALEM

4. Gaza

Turkumān[7] تركمان 89 households
Akrād[8] اكراد 90 households
Naṣārā[9] نصارى 82 households
Community of Shawābika,[10] 28 households
Community of Rizḳ-Allah,[11] 35 households
Community of Wādah (Wādī?)[12] 16 households
Community of al-Jabbāra,[13] 25 households

al-Zahra school, formerly the residence of the governor. Local tradition relates the name of the quarter to a part of the old walls of Gaza, studded with towers (*burj*). It is just possible that the name may derive from Birzāl, a Berber tribe of the Zenāta group. The Fatimids brought many Berbers including Zenāta to Syria and Palestine. The etymology of the name remains, however, uncertain. In the second half of the nineteenth century, it was already called "*Haret ed-Deredj* . . . la ville haute ou . . . la ville proprement dite; son nom lui vient des escaliers par lesquels on y monte" (Guérin, *La Terre Sainte*, 2e partie, p. 251).

[7] The southeastern part of the city (cf. Map 4), in which the old Ibn ʿUthmān mosque and the famous Munṭār hill are located. Most probably it took its name from the descendants of the Turcoman garrison which was stationed in the city during Mamluk times (Gaudefroy-Demombynes, *La Syrie*, p. 52, citing al-ʿUmarī's *Masālik al-Abṣār*). ʿĀrif, *Taʾrīkh Ghazza*, p. 256) relates the name to the Turcoman tribes which settled there in the thirteenth century.

[8] The southeastern and lower part of the city, which is known as *al-Sajjāʿiyya*, *al-Shajjāʿiyya*, or *Shajjāʿiyyat al-Akrād* (cf. Judeida in Map 4). This was said to take its name from Shujāʿ al-Dīn ʿUthmān ibn ʿAlakān al-Kurdī, who was killed in 637 A.H. in the vicinity of Gaza during a battle against the Crusaders (Maḳrīzī, *Khiṭaṭ*, vol. III, p. 82, cited in Dabbāgh, *Bilādunā Filasṭīn*, vol. I, part I, p. 53). Another version (*ibid.*, n. 2) gives al-Sajjāʿiyya, a village in al-Maḥalla al-Kubra in Egypt as the place of origin of the inhabitants. Despite its inherent improbability, Dabbāgh adopts the latter version on grounds of the way the inhabitants pronounce the word (s rather than sh). Our registers, which refer to it as *Akrād* ("Kurds") or sajjāʿiyyat al-Akrād, confirm the first interpretation. A fragment of an inscription below the lintel of the entrance door of the Shaykh ʿAlī al-Maghribī mosque, founded in 786/1384–5, *al-maʿrūfa bi'l-sajjāʿiyya* ("known as al-Sajjāʿiyya"). This, according to Mayer, had been "the commercial, and to a certain extent, residential quarter as opposed to the northwestern and higher quarter, where the residence of the Governor was located, the Main Mosque, the biggest caravanserai and other buildings of a more or less official character" (Mayer, *Journal of the Palestine Oriental Society*, vol. XI [1931], p. 150).

[9] A part of the present Zaytūn quarter (cf. Map 4) in which the Greek Orthodox Christians erected their church in 425 A.D.

[10] Originally from Shawbak, on the Ḥajj route, east of the river Jordan.

[11] Named after the head of the family, Rizḳ-Allah Mājid, who is listed first.

[12] Probably named after an ancestor, Wādī Faḍl, whose son ʿĪsā is listed first. Another possibility is that this is a shortened form for Wādī Mūsā, their place of origin (near Petra). This latter interpretation is corroborated by register 546, which specifically states Wādī Mūsā (see below, p. 125).

[13] Reading *Jabbāriyya*, as is clearly written in the later registers, i.e., originally from Bayt Jibrīn.

Community of peasants (*fellāḥīn*) of the Noble Rock (*Ṣaḫrā-i Şerīfe*),[14] 19 households

Community of Hebron[ites], 23 households

Community of Copts, 5 households

Community of Samaritans, 25 households

Community of Jews,[15] 95 households

REGISTER 1015 OF *ca.* 945/1538–9

Quarter of:

Burjuliyya برجلية 415 households, 80 bachelors, 8 *sharīfs*, 7 imams [511 names listed]

Dar al-Khuḍar with the quarter of Ṭabbāʿīyya (Ṭabbāgha?) دار الخضر مع طباعيه 138 households,[16] 23 bachelors, 3 imams, 1 blind man

Ḥikr Tuffāḥ حكر تفاح 211 households, 38 bachelors, 5 *sharīfs*, 5 imams

Shajjāʿat al-Akrād شجاعه الاكراد 278 households, 25 bachelors, 4 imams [291 names listed]

Turkumān تركمان 181 households, 19 bachelors, 3 imams [204 names listed]

Zaytūn زيتون 108 households, 17 bachelors, 2 imams [128 names listed]

[14] There were, of course, no peasants living on the Temple Mount in Jerusalem. The register refers here to peasants from lands the income of which belonged to the Waqf of the Noble Rock, probably in Bayt Rīma (cf. p. 137).

[15] Among whom 31 Maghribīs, 7 Frankish, 2 Shāmīs are listed. According to an account of a Jewish traveller who visited Gaza in the early 1520's there was a Jewish silversmith and another who was a spice dealer (David Reubeni's diary (1522–1525), a Bodleian MS. published in Eisenstein, pp. 143–5). Some Jews, to judge by the responsa of the first half of the century, were land owners who lived by agriculture (Braslavski, *Studies*, p. 162). But most of the Jewish community of Gaza, which had increased as a result of the Sephardic immigration, was engaged mainly in the flourishing commerce to and from Egypt (Ben Zvi, *Eretz Israel*, p. 167, quoting several *responsa* to this effect).

[16] Two of them are listed as "... son of *Shaykh al-Balad*." See p. 38.

Naṣārā نصارا 115 households (*jizya* at the rate of 80 per person)

Community of Copts among the Christians, 5 households, 2 bachelors (*jizya* at the rate of 80)

Community of Rizḳ Allah, 30 households, 5 bachelors (*jizya* at the rate of 80)[17]

Community of Wādah among the Christians, 19 households (*jizya* at the rate of 80)

Community of Shawbak among the Christians, 19 households, 7 bachelors (*jizya* at the rate of 80)

Community of Jabbārina among the Christians, 20 households, 7 bachelors (*jizya* at the rate of 80)

Community of Taḳāʿina[18] from the mountains of Jerusalem, 6 persons (*jizya* at the rate of 80)

Community of the Noble Rock among the Christians, 20 households, 7 bachelors [18 households, 8 bachelors listed] (*jizya* at the rate of 80 per person, total 2,080)

Community of the Noble Rock, inhabitants of Cairo,[19] 10 persons (at the rate of 80 each, total 800)

Community of Samaritans, 15 persons (*jizya* at the rate of 80)

Community of Jews,[20] 98 persons

[17] The first on the list is Rizḳ-Allah veled-i Tūmā. At least ten households and two bachelors listed are doubtless either sons or grandsons of Tūmā.

[18] Formerly inhabitants of the village of Taḳūʿ near Bethlehem, where there were still 4 Christian families left at this stage. During the previous *taḥrīr*, held about thirteen years earlier, there were still 55 Christian families in that village.

[19] The appearances, disappearances, and reappearances of this group in the registers, taken with this allusion to Cairo, may indicate that they were part of the Bayt Rīmā community who migrated to Egypt and then returned to Gaza sometimes between 1525 and 1538.

[20] No longer distinguished according to their place of origin, as in the previous *taḥrīr*, 13 years earlier.

REGISTER 265 YEAR 955/1548-9

Quarter of:

Zaytūn زيتون 1 imam, 162 households, 20 bachelors [2 imams, 1 *muḥaṣṣil*,[21] and 2 muezzins[22] are listed, among others]

Community of *jundiyān-i ḥalḳa* who were *jundīs* in the time of the Mamluks (*Çerākise*) and who now live in the above-mentioned quarter, 18 households, 4 bachelors

Burjuliyya برجله 2 imams, 527 households, 5 *sharīfs*, 41 bachelors [the names listed include, among others, 1 blind man, 1 *jundī ḥalḳa*, 12 *ʿālim muḥaṣṣil*]

Community of *jundiyān-i ḥalḳa* who were a part of the *jundī* corps (*jundī ṭāʾifesi*)[23] in the time of the Mamluks and who now live in the quarter of Burjulīyya, 20 households, 9 bachelors

Sajjāʿiyyat al-Khrād[24] سجاعيه الاكراد 1 imam, 406 households, 7 bachelors [10 names listed as *sharīfs*, 2 as imams, 1 *farrāsh -i masjid*,[25] 5 *muḥaṣṣils*]

Community of Jews, 116 households, 5 bachelors [2 designated as "from Hebron", 2 "in Jerusalem," 1 blind man]

Community of *jundiyān-i ḥalḳa* who were a part of the *jundī* corps in the time of the Mamluks and who now live in the quarter of Sajjāʿiyya, 17 households, 22 bachelors [one of the *muḥaṣṣils* listed above is termed *jundī ḥalḳa*, as well]

Community of Samaritans, 18 households, 2 bachelors

Dar al-Khuḍar دار الخضر 1 imam, 161 households, 3 bachelors [among others there are 2 *muḥaṣṣils*, 2 sons of *shaykh al-balad*, 2 muezzins, 1 *mutawallī* listed]

---

[21] Not used here in the ordinary fiscal sense of the term (cf. Gibb and Bowen, *Islamic Society*, vol. I, part I, p. 201, n. 1; Pakalın, *Osmanlı tarih deyimleri ve terimleri sözlüğü*, s.v.). It seems to denote a student or apprentice-scholar,—*muḥaṣṣil*—"étudiant, disciple, l'opposé de *muʿallim*, professeur", as in the Western Arabic texts cited by Dozy, *Supplément*, vol. I, p. 295). Cf. the modern use of *taḥṣil* in the sense of education.

[22] One of them in Jāmiʿ Kabīr mosque.

[23] See above p. 18. Both the Perso-Turkısh (*jundiyān*) and the Arabic (*ajnād*) forms are used here alternately to designate members of the *jund al-ḥalḳa*.

[24] About 10 persons are still designated *al-Kurdī*, 8 *al-Miṣrī*.

[25] "One who lays mats ... a sweeper or servant of a mosque (Redhouse, *Turkish and English Lexıcon*, p. 1371). Here, from the context presumably an attendant in a religious building (as for ınstance, is the case in Mecca).

Community of *jundiyān-i ḥalḳa* who were a part of the *jundī corps* in the time of the Mamluks and who are now retired (*ber vech-i taḳāʿud*) in the quarter of Dār al-Khuḍar, 8 households

Ḥikr Tuffāḥ حكر تفاح 1 imam, 2 muezzins, 247 households, 21 bachelors, 3 blind men [274 names listed, among whom there are 1 *muḥaṣṣil* and 1 *kadi* serving as a *nāʾib*][26]

Community of *jundiyān-i ḥalḳa* who were a part of the *jundī* corps in the time of the Mamluks and who now live in the quarter of Tuffāḥ, 12 households, 10 bachelors

Turkumān تركمان 5 imams, 5 bachelors, 1 muezzin, 195 households [among them: 2 muezzins, 3 imams, 3 *muḥaṣṣils* listed]

Community of *ejnād-i ḥalḳa* in the above-mentioned quarter of Turkuman who were a part of the *Jundī* corps in the time of the Mamluks and who now live in the above-mentioned quarter, 27 households, 38 bachelors

Naṣārā نصارا 116 households, 3 bachelors (*jizya* at the rate of 80)

Community of Coptic Christians, 5 households (*jizya* at the rate of 80)

Community of Rizḳ Allah, 34 households (*jizya* at the rate of 80)

Community of Wādah among the Christians, 24 households [1 listed as a blind man] (*jizya* at the rate of 80)

Community of [people from] Shawbak, 46 households, 1 bachelor [1 listed as a blind man] (*jizya* at the rate of 80)

Community of Jabbārina, 40 households, 1 bachelor [1 listed as a blind man] (*jizya* at the rate of 80)

Community of Taḳāʿina from Jerusalem Mountain, 8 households [2 listed as "from Hebron"] (*jizya* at the rate of 80)

Community of the Noble Rock among the Christians in Gaza, 42 households, 4 bachelors [41 households, 4 bachelors listed] (*jizya* at the rate of 80)

Community of the Noble Rock living in Cairo (*mütemekkin*), 10 households (*jizya* at the rate of 80)

[26] The usual procedure was usually the very opposite. *Nāʾib*, lit.: "deputy," was usually supposed either to help or replace the kadi when he did not or could not attend a case.

REGISTER 304 OF 964/1556–7

Quarter of:

Zaytūn زيتون 160 households, 10 muezzins, imams and *khaṭībs*, 1 *sharīf*, 5 invalids and blind men

Community of *jundiyān-i ḥalḳa* who were a part of the *jundīs* in the time of the Mamluks and who now live in the above-mentioned quarter, 15 households

Burjuliyya برجليه 453 households, 58 bachelors, 9 *sharīfs*, 9 invalids, blind men, and madmen, 9 imams, muezzins, and *khaṭībs*

Community of *jundiyān-i ḥalḳa* who were a part of the *jundī* corps in the time of the Mamluks and who now live in the above-mentioned quarter 35 households

Shajjāʿiyya شجاعيه 380 households, 15 *sharīfs*, 15 imams, *khaṭībs*, muezzins, and *muḥaṣṣils*, 5 invalids and blind men [412 names listed]

Community of *ajnād-i ḥalḳa* who were *jundīs* in the time of the Mamluks and who now live in the above-mentioned quarter, 34 households

Dār al-Khuḍar دار الخضر 128 households, 2 *sharīfs*, 15 bachelors, 19 *khaṭībs*, muezzins, imams, and *muḥaṣṣils*, 8 blind men and madmen [170 names listed]

Community of *jundiyān-i ḥalḳa* who were a part of the *jundī* corps in the past and who now live in the above-mentioned quarter, 10 households

Ḥikr Tuffāḥ حكر تفاح 254 households, 4 *sharīfs*, 3 imams, *khaṭībs*, and muezzins, 5 bachelors

Community of *jundiyān-i ḥalḳa* who were a part of the *jundī* corps in the time of the Mamluks and who now live in the above-mentioned quarter, 9 households

Turkumans تركمانان 207 households, 1 *sharīf*, 3 *khaṭībs*, imams, and muezzins [220 names listed]

Community of *ajnād-i ḥalḳa* who were a part of the *jundī* corps in the time of the Mamluks and who now live in the above-mentioned quarter, 70 households [69 names listed]

Naṣārā نصارا 96 households, 2 blind men [99 names listed] (at 80)

Community of Rizḳ Allah, 38 households (*jizya* at 80)

Community of the Christians of Wādī Mūsā, 26 households

Community of the Christians of Shawbak, 43 households, 2 blind men (*jizya* at 80 ᶜ*osmānī*)[27]

Community of Jabbārina, 51 households [1 monk listed] (*jizya* at 80)

Community of Taḳāᶜina who came [from] Jerusalem, 9 households (*jizya* at 80), 2 households "from the *reᶜāya*[28] of Hebron"

Community of Christians of the Noble Rock, 75 households [1 blind man listed] (*jizya* at 80)

Community of Jews, 78 households; 3 households, all three of them pertaining to the waqfs of Hebron

Community of Samaritans, 18 households

REGISTER 546 OF 1005/1596–7

Quarter of:

Zaytūn زيتون 9 *khaṭībs*, imams, and muezzins, 53 households, 12 bachelors, 5 blind men and invalids [only 77 names listed]

Community of *jundiyān-i ḥalḳa* who were a part of the *jundī* corps in the time of the Mamluks and who now live in the above-mentioned quarter, 17 persons

Burjuliyya برجليه 156 households, 35 bachelors, 13 *khaṭībs*, imams, and muezzins, 9 *sharīfs*,[29] 14 blind men, madmen, and invalids

Community of *jundiyān-i ḥalḳa* who were a part of the *jundī* corps during the time of the Mamluks and who now live in the above-mentioned quarter, 31 persons

Shajjāᶜiyya شجاعيه 7 *sharīfs*, 11 imams, *khaṭībs*, and muezzins, 125 households, 10 bachelors [10 *sharīfs* listed, one of which holds the title of *naḳīb al-ashrāf*]

[27] Akçe-i ᶜOsmānī = Ottoman asper.

[28] Contrary to the common belief *reᶜāyā* does not mean non-Muslims. In classical usage this word, with the connotation of flocks, was used of the generality of the ruler's subjects. In Ottoman usage it was specialized to mean those who were not members of the ruling establishment. It thus included urban civilians as well as peasants, though in practice the latter is the most common meaning. (cf. Heyd, *Ottoman Documents*, p. 49, n. 4: "In many of our texts, however, *reᶜāyā* may mean not only peasants but tax-paying subjects in general.")

[29] Referred to as *sayyid*, see p. 15.

Community of *ajnād-i ḥalḳa* who were *jundīs* in the time of the Mamluks and who now live in the above-mentioned quarter, 24 persons

Dār al-Khuḍar دار الخضر 69 households, 23 bachelors

Community of *jundiyān-i ḥalḳa* who were in the past a part of the *jundī* corps and who now live in the above-mentioned quarter, 9 persons[30]

Ḥikr Tuffāḥ حكر تفاح 5 *khaṭibs* and muezzins, 86 households, 15 bachelors

Community of *jundiyān-i ḥalḳa* who were a part of the *jundī* corps in the time of the Mamluks and who now live in the above-mentioned quarter, 10 persons

Community of Turkumans تركمانان 5 *khaṭībs*, imams, and muezzins, 67 households, 18 bachelors

Community of *jundiyān-i ḥalḳa* who were part of the *jundī* corps in the time of the Mamluks and who now live in the above-mentioned quarter, 50 persons

Community of Christians (*Naṣārā*) نصارا 1 blind man, 94 households (*jizya* at 90)

Community of Rizḳ Allah, 35 households [36 names listed] (*jizya* at 90)

Community of Christians of Wādī Mūsā, 15 households

Community of Christians of Shawbak, 31 households (*jizya* at 90)

Community of Jabbāriyya, 6 blind, invalid, and lame, 38 households

Community of Taḳāʿina who came from Jerusalem, 9 persons, 2 persons of the *reʿāyā* of Hebron

Community of Christians of the Noble Rock, 70 households (*jizya* at 90)

Community of Jews, 70 persons, 3 households, all three of them pertaining to the waqfs of Hebron

Community of Samaritans, 8 households

[30] Two of whom are referred to as "*shaykh* of the family of al-Anṣārī."

TABLE 3
Quarters and Population of Gaza

	932/1525–6				*ca.* 945/1538–9				955/1548–9				964/1556–7				1005/1596–7			
	h.	b.	r.	d.	h.	b.	r.	d.	h.	b.	r.	d.	h.	b.	r.	d.	h.	b.	r.	d.
									Muslims											
Hikr Tuffāḥ	74	—	6	—	211	38	10	—	247	21	3	3	254	5	7	—	86	15	5	—
Jundīs	—	—	—	—	—	—	—	—	12	10	—	—	9	—	—	—	10	—	—	—
Dār al-Khuḍar	43	3	4	—	{138	23	3	1	157	3	5	—	128	15	21	8	69	23	—	—
Jundīs	—	—	—	—					8	—	—	—	10	—	—	—	9	—	—	—
Dabbāgha (Ṣabbāgha?)	57	6	3	—					—	—	—	—	—	—	—	—	—	—	—	—
Zaytūn	54	30	5	—	108	17	2	—	158	20	5	—	160	—	11	5	53	12	9	5
Jundīs	—	—	—	—	—	—	—	—	18	4	—	—	15	—	—	—	17	—	—	—
Burjuliyya	141	2	11	—	415	80	15	—	522	32	19	1	453	58	18	9	156	35	22	14
Jundīs	—	—	—	—	—	—	—	—	21	9	—	—	35	—	—	—	31	—	—	—
Turkumān	89	—	—	—	181	19	3	—	193	5	8	—	216	—	4	—	67	18	5	—
Jundīs	—	—	—	—	—	—	—	—	27	38	—	—	70	—	—	—	50	—	—	—
Shajjāʿiyyat al-Akrād	90	—	—	—	278	25	4	—	389	7	18	—	380	—	30	5	125	10	18	—
Jundīs	—	—	—	—	—	—	—	—	17	22	—	—	34	—	—	—	24	—	—	—
Total	548	41	29	—	1,331	202	37	1	1,769	171	58	4	1,764	78	91	27	697	113	59	19

TABLE 3 (Contd.)

	932/1525–6				ca. 945/1538–9				955/1548–9				964/1556–7				1005/1596–7			
	h.	b.	r.	d.	h.	b.	r.	d.	h.	b.	r.	d.	h.	b.	r.	d.	h.	b.	r.	d.
									Christians											
Naṣārā	82	—	—	—	115	—	—	—	116	3	—	—	97	—	—	2	94	—	—	1
Community of Rizk Allah	35	—	—	—	30	5	—	—	34	—	—	—	38	—	—	—	36	—	—	—
Community of Shawbak	28	—	—	—	19	7	—	—	45	1	—	1	43	—	—	2	31	—	—	—
Community of Wādī Mūsā	16	—	—	—	19	—	—	—	23	—	—	1	26	—	—	—	15	—	—	—
Community of Jabbārina	25	—	—	—	20	7	—	—	39	1	—	1	51	—	—	—	38	—	—	6
Peasants of the Noble Rock	19	—	—	—	18	8	—	—	42	4	—	—	74	—	—	1	70	—	—	—
Peasants of the Noble Rock in Cairo	—	—	—	—	10	—	—	—	10	—	—	—	—	—	—	—	—	—	—	—
Community of Hebron	23	—	—	—	—	—	—	—	2	—	—	—	2	—	—	—	2	—	—	—
Community of Copts	5	—	—	—	5	2	—	—	5	—	—	—	—	—	—	—	—	—	—	—
Community of Takā^cina	—	—	—	—	6	—	—	—	6	—	—	—	9	—	—	—	9	—	—	—
Total	233	—	—	—	242	29	—	—	322	9	—	3	340	—	—	5	295	—	—	7
									Jews											
	95	—	—	—	98	—	—	—	115	5	—	1	81	—	—	—	73	—	—	—
									Samaritans											
	25	—	—	—	15	—	—	—	18	2	—	—	18	—	—	—	8	—	—	—
Total	901	41	29		1,686	231	37	1	2,224	187	58	8	2,203	78	91	32	1,073	113	59	26

2. TAXES AND REVENUES[31]

	932/1525–6	*ca.* 945/1538–9	955/1548–9	964/1556–7	1005/1596–7
1. Toll on the road to Cairo (*ʿādet-i bāc-i rāh-i Mişr*) [collected] in the city of Gaza, K͟hān Yūnus[32] and K͟hān Sdūd apart from the old toll (*bāc-i dirīn*).[33] Hitherto in charge of commissioners (*emin*),[34] now removed by Imperial Order. According to the "old register" [the following] is to be collected at each check-post (*ğafar*): 4 Ottoman aspers from each camel-load for the *Mīrī*;[35] 2 Ottoman aspers from each mule-load; 1 Ottoman asper from each donkey-load; 10 Ottoman aspers from each black slave, male or female, who are brought[36] for sale; 3 Ottoman aspers from each ox or water-buffalo.[37] ID.					
per year	50,000[38]	50,000	80,000[39]	100,000	100,000
2. Toll on spices accompanying the Noble Ḥajj (*bāc-i bahār-i ḥacc-i şerif*) in the event of its going via Gaza. ID.					
per year	50,000[40]	50,000	50,000	50,000	50,000[41]
3. Treasury revenues (*Bayt al-Māl*) and property of absent and missing persons (*māl-i ğāʾib* and *māl-i mefḳūd*) with runaway slaves and stray cattle in the city of Gaza. Entirely. ID.					
per year	10,000	20,000[42]	47,487 (both in the city and in the district (*nāḥiye*) of Gaza)	47,487	55,000
4. Treasury revenues and property of absent and missing persons up to 10,000. AG.					
per year		7,000			
5. Revenue of butchers (*ḳaşşāb*)[43] in the city of Gaza					
per year	6,000	6,000 AG	10,000 ID	10,000 ID	12,000 ID
6. Revenue of the market for horses, donkeys, camels, cattle, goats, sheep and other beasts					
per year	200	2,150 (Timār of Ibrāhim Jenki)	10,000 ID	10,000 ID	12,000 ID
7. Sheep-tax (*resm-i ğanam, ʿādet-i ağnām*) of the inhabitants of the city of Gaza. ID.					
per year	6,000[44]		7,000	5,000	5,500

Taxes and Revenues (contd.)

	932/1525–6	*ca.* 945/1538–9	955/1548–9	964/1556–7	1005/1596–7
8. Bee-tax (*resm-i naḥl*) of the inhabitants of the city of Gaza					
per year			3,000	3,000	3,500
9. Brokerage-due (*dellāliye*)[45] on the market of criers and sellers of cast-off clothes (*Sūḳ al-Khallāʿiyya*[46] *wa dellāliya*). ID.					
per year			4,000	10,000	12,000

[31] The following text is based on Register 546, with additional items inserted from other registers where appropriate, and variant rubrics cited in the notes (registers 427, 131, 1015, 265, 304).

[32] On Emīr Yūnus (d. 791/1389) who erected this *khān* see references in Mantran and Sauvaget, *Règlements fiscaux Ottomans*, p. 8, n. 2.

[33] It seems that the scribes were not positive about the exact reading of the term, which appears once even as دبركه (register 265). Cf. above, p. 55, n. 33.

[34] An official representative of the treasury charged with the collection of taxes to be transferred later to the treasury (Heyd, *Ottoman Documents*, p. 93, n. 4; Lewis, "Emīn", *EI*[2], vol. II, pp. 695–6.

[35] Although this term does not occur in the following sentences, it should be applied to all other categories of revenue enumerated in this entry.

[36] Lit.: "who come."

[37] The quotation ends with the word "correct" (*ṣaḥḥ*) written three times, serving both to indicate that it was correctly copied from the "old register" and to avoid any unauthorized addition.

[38] At this early date it is specifically pointed out that the toll was collected only in *Khān* Yūnus. Cf. *Ḳānūnnāme-i Şam: "Mekke-i muşerrefeden bahar ve akmişe geldikte Hacc-i Gazze kurbinde Han-i Yunus nâm yerde alırır"* (Barkan, *Kanunlar*, p. 221). The rates were identical with the above-mentioned, but the mention of "both white and black" slaves indicates that at this period the former were also sold there.

[39] This is the earliest date on which the above-mentioned fact of withholding this revenue from the *emīns* is noted. On the replacement of the *emīn* by the tax-farmer see Bistra Cvetkova, *Rocznik Orientalistyczny*, vol. XXVII (1964), p. 111 ff.

[40] "This toll is collected whenever the Ḥajj [caravan] leaves on the Gaza road; if not, it should be levied near Damascus at a village named Ksūra [= Kisve]." The latter was known to be the first halting-place on the Ḥajj route south of Damascus (for further details cf. Gaudefroy-Demombynes, *La Syrie*, p. 49, n. 9. See also *Ḳānūnnāme-i Vilāyet-i Şām*, Barkan, *Kanunlar*, pp. 221, 370).

[41] "In accordance with 'the old register'."

[42] "Above 10,000 [aspers] in the whole *liwāʾ* of Gaza. As for the treasury revenues of male and female slaves and the other *Ghulāms* of the Sultan, it is entirely Imperial Domain". See Inalcık "Ghulām," *EI*[2], vol. II, pp. 1085–91.

[43] See above, p. 48.

[44] In the whole *liwāʾ* of Gaza both sheep and goat tax (Reg. 131).

[45] For a later definition of the term see Shams el-Dīn Sāmī, p. 616. *Dellāliye resmi* was a small duty collected in the silk-markets (Dalsar, *Bursada ipekçilik*, p. 242). For a *dallāllık* tax in Istanbul and Galata see Anhegger and Inalcık, *Kannunname-i Sultani*, pp. 57–9. For *dellāliye* in Damascus, see Barkan, *Kanunlar*, pp. 221–2.

	932/1525–6	*ca.* 945/1538–9	955/1548–9	964/1556–7	1005/1596–7
10. Scales for cotton (*mizān-i ḳuṭn*)[47] ID.					
per year			400	500	1,000
11. Revenue of scales (*ḳapan*) of the city of Gaza					
per year	300[48]	1,000 AG			
12. Tax on baskets (*kharāj-i ḳawāṣir*).[49] ID.					
per year			400	400	600
13. Tithe (ᶜ*ushr*) on the vineyards, both waqf and *mülk*, in the city of Gaza, with orchards (*bāgh* and *bustān*) and *kharāj*. *Maḳṭūᶜ*. ID.					
per year	4,455[50]	10,000[51]	12,112	15,500	20,000 + 4,500 (addition in accordance with the "new register")
14. Revenue of the chief of the night-watches (*ser-i ᶜasesān*) in the city of Gaza. AG.					
per year	8,000	10,000	5,000	5,000	5,000
15. Revenue of the inspection of the markets (*iḥtisāb*)[52] in the city of Gaza together with the scales (*ḳapan*), market for pickles and sweets (*sūḳ al-ḥumḍ wa-l-khamis*)[53] and *dār al-wakāla wa-l-ḍamān*, the market of spinning and dyeing (*sūḳ al-ghazl wa-l-ṣibāgha*).[54] AG.					
per year	18,000 (*iḥtisāb* only)	27,000 (*iḥtisāb* only)	63,000	63,000	65,000
16. Revenue of the *Dār al-wakāla* in the Khān-i Shajjāᶜiyya. AG.					
per year	2,000[55]	3,000			
17. Occasional revenues (*bād-i havā*), fines and penalties (*cürm-i cināyet*) and bride-tax (*resm-i ᶜarūsāne*) and the house of the prison (*dār al-ḥabs*)[56] in the city of Gaza. AG.					
per year	50,000 (*bād-i havā* of the whole *liwā*ᵓ of Gaza)	10,000	24,128	24,134	28,134

Taxes and Revenues (contd.)

	932/1525–6	*ca.* 945/1538–9	955/1548–9	964/1556–7	1005/1596–7
18. Occasional revenues, fines and penalties and bride-tax of the city of Ramle, with half the occasional revenues and the bride-tax on the district (*nāḥiye*) of Gaza and Ramle apart from Imperial Domain and free *ziʿāmets* and waqfs of the two Holy Cities. AG. per year		8,800 (All the revenue of these taxes pertaining to Ramle and the two districts)	57,724	57,724	59,724
				—	

Muḥiṭ al-Muḥiṭ, part I, p. 580). Two other possible readings, neither of them very likely, are: (1) A distorted form of *ḫalāʾiḳ*, female slaves (Cf. *ḫalāʾik bāzārı dellālları*" in Anhegger and Inalcık, *Kanunname-i Sultani*, p. 59). (2) Reading جلاديه for حلاعه, mentioned as an old Mamluk tax in an inscription in the great Mosque of Sarmin, dating 1369: مكس دلالة الجلد (Sauvaget, *Bulletin d'études orientales*, tom XII [1948], p. 38).

47 According to ʿĀrif (p. 269) this is a "light" scales which consists of two "hands" made of copper, as distinct from the "heavy" one, on which merchandise is put.

48 "But has been included in the *iḥtisāb* since old time."

49 From *ḳawṣara*. Cf. Dozy (*Supplément*, vol. II, p. 419) who does not mention that it was originally used for dates (Bustāni, *Muḥiṭ al-muḥiṭ*, vol. II, p. 1774, *ḳawṣarra*). Cf. *resm-i sepet* ("basket money") on vineyards (Kaldy-Nagy, *Acta Orientalia*, vol. XXI [1968], pp. 200–1).

50 Added up from a long and very detailed list of the above-mentioned with their respective revenues.

51 "Apart from the waqfs of the two Holy Cities" and "apart from the plots of land registered at the bottom of the list."

52 On the collection of this as well as other market-tolls in Gaza in the Mamluk period cf. Sauvaget, *Bulletin d'études orientales*, vol. XI (1948), p. 33.

53 The reading of this term is fairly clear and more or less identical in the registers, but unpointed. The first word appears to be *ḥumd*, meaning pickles or sour things; the second word looks like *Khamis*, and the term "Thursday market" is common enough, but it is difficult to see the logic of combining the names of a commodity and a day in a single expression. Other possible readings, neither of them very convincing, are *jumayz*, "sycamore" (a product plentifully available and not normally sold in the market), and *khamīs*, referring to the special market in Nabulus in which *ḥelva*, a sweetmeat was sold.,

54 In a firman dated Muḥarrem 987/March 1579 a newly built covered market (*bezzāstān*) is referred to, as having been erected as a result of a petition of local merchants, mainly cloth merchants (Heyd, *Ottoman Documents*, p. 135). It may well have been related to this open market.

55 Register 131 includes in this sum the revenues of *Sūḳ al-khayl wa-'l-dawwāb*, which is listed under a separate heading in register 427 (cf. entry no. 6).

56 The term lends itself to several possible readings, of which this one seems the most likely. It may have been Dār al-ḥashīsh; cf. Bayt al-ḥashīsh wa al-ḳimār in Damascus, Bakhīt, *Ottoman Province of Damascus*, p. 282; for *Ḥashish khāne* as a separate *muḳāṭaʿa* in Hamat in the same period cf. ʿAbd al-Wadūd Muhammad Yūsuf Barghūth. *Liwāʾ Hamāt*. p. 52.

	932/1525–6	*ca.* 945/1538–9	955/1548–9	964/1556–7	1005/1596–7
19. Revenue of the measuring-tax (*keyyāliye*) of the city of Gaza with the brokerage of corn (*simsāriye-i ğilāl*) in the city of Gaza. AG.					
per year	6,000[5]	6,000	10,000	10,000	10,000
20. Revenue of the dyehouse in the city of Gaza.					
per year		2,000 ID	2,000 Waqf of *Bīmāristān* of Gaza. Entirely		
21. Revenue of the Poll-tax (*jizya*) on Christians, Jews and Samaritans.					
per year	21,180 (60 each person)	31,040 (80 each person)	38,000 (80 each person calculated)	35,440 (80 each person calculated)	34,380 (80 each person calculated)
22. Bedouin-tax (*ʿādet-i ʿurbāniye*)[58] of the tribes (*ṭāʾife*) of Banī ʿAṭiyya.[59] AG.					
per year	5,000 14 tribes ID	15,000 14 tribes	15,000 14 tribes	15,000 14 tribes	15,000 14 tribes
23. Bedouin-tax of Banī ʿAṭāʾ. AG.					
per year	5,000	12,500 9 tribes	15,000 9 tribes	15,000 9 tribes	15,000 9 tribes
24. Bedouin-tax of Banī Haytham, Malāliḥa. AG.[60]					
		8,000	6,000	6,000	6,000
25. Bedouin-tax of Banī Sawālima.[61] AG.					
		12,500 9 tribes	15,000 9 tribes	15,000 9 tribes	15,000 9 tribes

	932/1525–6	*ca.* 945/1538–9	955/1548–9	964/1556–7	1005/1596–7
26. Bedouin-tax of *cürüm.*[62] AG.					
	20,000	15,000 + 10,000	5,000	5,000	5,000
		9 tribes + 3 tribes[63]	8 tribes	8 tribes	8 tribes

[57] "*Samsarat al-ghilāl*", i.e., *bāzār-i ghille*.

[58] Also called *ʿādet-i ʿurbān*, levied annually for their right of pasturage (*ḥaḳḳ-i marʿā*).

[59] Mentioned in a firman dated 1001/1593 as being, together with Banī ʿAṭāʾ, "in a state of permanent rebellion" (Heyd, *Ottoman Documents*, p. 85). For further details on these tribes see Oppenheim, *Die Beduinen*, vol. II, pp. 277–8, 287–8.

[60] "If Banī ʿAṭāʾ and Banī ʿAṭiyya do not come then the Sawālima bedouins come and consequently this tax is collected from them."

[61] Also called ʿArab Sawālim (Ḥaci Ḫalīfe, *Cihān nüma*, p. 554).

[62] The earliest register supplies us with a possible clue to the name of the tribe: ʿUrbān Amīr Jürüm. Ḥaci Ḫalīfe refers to this tribe (*ḳabile*) as Banū Jürüm ibn Thaʿlaba, forming a part of the Ṭay (Ḥaci Ḫalīfe, *Cihān nüma*, p. 554).

[63] Duʿaym, Bazzāzīn, Banī Jamīl, three tribes which are mentioned only here.

• 7 •

RAMLE رمله

1. QUARTERS AND INHABITANTS[1]

REGISTER 427 OF 932/1525–6

Quarter of:

Miṣriyyīn[2] مصريين 1 imam, 38 households, 2 bachelors

Bāshkardī[3] باشقردى 1 imam, 28 households, 2 bachelors

Jāmiʿ al-Abyaḍ[4] جامع الابيض 30 households, 3 bachelors

[1] For details on the origin of the name and further information cf. Gaudefroy-Demombynes, *La Syrie*, pp. 56–9. Marmardji, *Textes géographiques*, pp. 81–6; Le Strange, *Palestine under the Moslems*, pp. 303–8. Toward the end of the Mamluk period it was described by Mujīr al-Dīn: "No trace has remained in our time of all that had been described in Ramla. Its old walls and markets have disappeared . . . [Only] one third to one fourth of the city is left . . . and the buildings which have still remained in the city are mostly ruined" (*Al-Uns al-jālil*, vol. II, p. 417). A couple of years before the Ottoman occupation it was described by a Franciscan priest as follows: "Round and has a circumference of three miles, without walls and almost in ruins and unpeopled . . . This city supplies the cities of Gaza and Jerusalem with an abundance of fruit and garden products" (Francesco Suriano, *Publications of the Studium Biblicum Franciscanum*, vol. VIII [1949], p. 39). A similar picture emerges from a description by a traveller in 1532: "Rama est une grande ville destruite en laquelle y a plusieurs belles tours carrées et rondes" (L. Possot, *Le voyage de la Terre Sainte*, p. 158). And again in 1575, as described by Dr. Rauwloff: "Town Rama . . . is pretty large, but very open like unto a village, very pityfully built" (Ray, *Collection of travels*, vol. I, p. 270).

[2] "The Egyptians", also called Ḥawsh al-Miṣrī. Local tradition relates the name to an Egyptian element which settled there (cf. Map 5).

[3] The most probable interpretation is "Bashkirs" (see above, p. 34). According to Mujīr al-Dīn (*Al-Uns al-jalil*, vol. II, p. 419), the tomb of Shaykh Muḥammad al-Baṭāʾiḥī was in this quarter. In the southern part of the city, within the Bashāwiyya quarter (cf. Map 5), there is a tomb of al-Shaykh ʿAbd Allah Maḥmūd al-Baṭāʾiḥī, probably the same monument. It is most likely that both names of the quarter were confused; they are very similar in writing (و can easily be taken for قر). Local tradition identifies the two and provides a popular etymology, explaining that it was called al-Bāshāwiyya (in colloqual Arabic, pertaining to the Pashas) as a result of the affluent and respectable families who lived there.

[4] "The White Mosque." An Umayyad mosque, originally erected by Sülaymān ibn ʿAbd al-Malik, later improved and reconstructed by Nāṣir ibn Ḳalāʾūn, Ṣalāḥ al-Dīn and Baybars. Toward the end of the Mamluk period, i.e., shortly before the

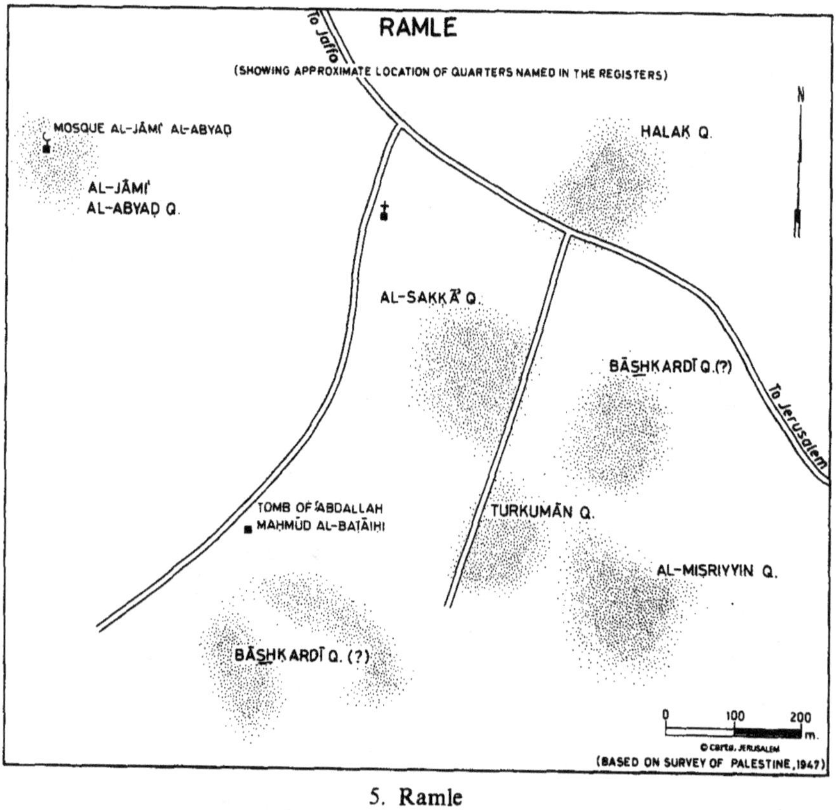
RAMLE
(SHOWING APPROXIMATE LOCATION OF QUARTERS NAMED IN THE REGISTERS)
To Jaffa
MOSQUE AL-JĀMI' AL-ABYAḌ
AL-JĀMI'
AL-ABYAḌ Q.
HALAḲ Q.
N
AL-SAḲḲĀ' Q.
BĀSHKARDĪ Q.(?)
To Jerusalem
TOMB OF 'ABDALLAH
MAḤMŪD AL-BAṬĀIḤI
TURKUMĀN Q.
AL-MIṢRIYYIN Q.
BĀSHKARDĪ Q. (?)
0
100
200
m.
© carta, JERUSALEM
(BASED ON SURVEY OF PALESTINE, 1947)

5. Ramle

Ḥalaḳ (?)[5] حلق 2 imams, 102 households, 4 bachelors

Al-Shaḳā[6] الشقى 2 imams, 58 households, 2 bachelors

Turkumān[7] بركمان 2 imams and *khaṭībs*, 54 households, 3 bachelors

Community of Christians, 26 households

REGISTER 1015 OF *ca* 945/1538-9

Quarter of:

Jāmiʿ al-Abyaḍ جامع الابيض 40 households, 6 bachelors, 1 imam

Al-Shaḳā الشقى 73 households, 7 bachelors, 2 imams

Community of Christians in the above-mentioned quarter, 33 households

Al-Miṣriyyīn المصرين 59 households, 3 bachelors, 2 imams, 12 *sharīfs*

Bāshḳārdī باشقاردى 33 households, 2 imams

Al-Turkumān التركمان 62 households, 7 bachelors, 2 imams, 1 *sharīf*

Khalaf خلف 115 households, 5 imams [122 names listed]

preparation of our register, it was described by Mujīr al-Dīn as having once been considered one of the most famous buildings, to become ruined in his own days. "Of [all] the old buildings nothing is left around the . . . mosque except for a quarter [lying] to its north, which is considered as a village (*ḥukmuhā ḥukm al-ḳurā*). The city has thus become separated from the mosque" (Mujīr al-Dīn, *Al-Uns al-jalīl*, vol. II, pp. 417–18). This tallies with the information of the different *taḥrīrs*, which show this quarter to be the smallest of all through most of the century. In spite of all this, the white mosque was still very conspicuous even at a later date, as described by Pīrī Reis: "The [distinguishing] mark of the above-mentioned Ramle from the sea is that a white sanctuary is visible [there]" (Heyd, *Israel Exploration Journal*, vol. VI (1956), p. 208; Pīrī Reis, *Kitabı Bahriye*, p. 724). In spite of Heyd's doubt based on the "yellowish and reddish stone" of the tower, the reference in Pīrī Reis cannot possibly be to any other building). For photographs of this mosque cf. Mayer and Pinkerfeld, *Muslim Religious Buildings*, plates 19–21. For early references see Marmardji, *Textes géographiques*, p. 85; Condor and Kitchener, *The Survey of Palestine*, vol. II, pp. 270–5).

5 According to dubious local tradition the inhabitants of this quarter (cf. Map 5) were known to be the less important and venerated element of the city. Perhaps *ḥalḳ* in the Turkish sense—the common people.

6 A distorted form of al-Saḳḳāʾ, "The water-carrier" (cf. Map 5).

7 Cf. Map 5.

REGISTER 265 OF 955/1548–9

Quarter of:

Jāmiᶜ Abyaḍ[8] جامع ابيض 56 households, 10 bachelors

Turkumān تركمان 117 households, 19 bachelors [126 names listed]

Bās͟hk̤ārdī باشقردى 74 households, 7 bachelors [71 households, 1 s͟harīf, 7 bachelors listed]

Ḥalḳ حلق 92 households, 15 bachelors, 2 imams, 1 muezzin

Miṣriyyīn مصريين 114 households, 9 bachelors, 1 imam [1 imam, 9 bachelors, 13 s͟harīfs, 102 households listed]

Al-Saḳā السقى 87 households,[9] 3 bachelors

Community of Christians in the above-mentioned quarter, 57 households, 7 bachelors, 2 blind men [65 names listed]

Community of Rīmāwıyyīn[10] who came from the village of Bayt Rīmā, a waqf of the Rock in the *liwāʾ* of Jerusalem, and became resident here. It has been decreed by a noble command that their *jawālī*[11] will be collected for the waqf of the Noble Rock, and it has duly been entered into "the new register." At present the *jawālī* of twenty-five persons are collected from the above-mentioned village, 25 persons. *Jizya* at 80 [totals] 2000

REGISTER 304 OF 964/1556–7

Quarter of:

Miṣriyyīn مصريين 105 households, 11 bachelors, 13 *s͟harīfs*, 1 blind man

Ḥalḳ حلق 92 households, 15 bachelors, 4 imams and muezzins

[8] One of the inhabitants listed was S͟hayk͟h Muḥammad al-Imām Ṭarablusī, "Sojourner (*mujāwir*) within the minaret of the white mosque."

[9] Three of them are designated "son of the Jew."

[10] The explusion or departure of most of the Christian inhabitants of this village (Bayt Rīmā) must have occurred not very long after, if not during, the Ottoman occupation. Whereas the earliest register, dated 932/1525–6 does not mention any Christian population at all in this village, one can trace a slow influx of Christians to Bayt Rīmā recorded in 945/1538–9 (6 households listed) and in 961/1553–4 (11 households listed). Whatever be the origin of these newcomers, those Christians who were or "had previously lived in" Bayt Rīmā had left it at an earlier date and probably settled in the nearby city of Ramle between the years 1538–48.

[11] *Jizya* payments. Cf. Cl. Cahen, "Djawālī," *EI*², vol. II, p. 490.

Bāshkārdī باشقاردى 65 households, 22 bachelors, 1 *sharīf*, 1 imam, 2 blind men [87 names listed]

Al-Shakā الشقى 85 households, 6 bachelors, 5 *jundī-i ḥalka*, 1 madman

Community of Christians in the above-mentioned quarter, 41 households

Community of Christians from Rīmā (*Rīmāwiyyīn*), waqf of the Noble Rock, 29 households

Turkumān تركمانن 101 households, 22 bachelors, 2 imams and muezzins, 8 *sharīfs*, 1 blind man, 1 madman [136 names listed]

Community of Christians in the above-mentioned quarter, 5 households (these are the peasants (*fellāḥ*) of Hebron; their *jizya* should be paid to the waqf)

Jāmiʿ al-Abyaḍ جامع الابيض 54 households, 12 bachelors

REGISTER 546 YEAR 1005/1596–7

Quarter of:

Miṣriyyīn مصريين 1 imam, 2 muezzins, 56 households, 11 bachelors

Ḥalk حلق 2 *khaṭībs* and imams, 34 households, 4 bachelors

Bāshkārdī باشقاردى 1 imam, 1 muezzin, 18 households, 3 bachelors

Al-Shafā الشفى 29 households

Community of Christians in the above-mentioned quarter, 42 households

Community of Christians from Rīmā (*Rīmāwiyyīn*), waqf of the Noble Rock, 35 households.

Turkumān تركمانن 2 imams and muezzins, 52 households, 5 bachelors, 1 blind man

Community of Christians in the above-mentioned quarter, 5 households (they are peasants of Hebron; their *jizya* should be paid to the waqf)

Jāmiʿ al-Abyaḍ جامع الابيض 2 muezzins, 12 households

TABLE 4
Quarters and Population of Ramle

	932/1525–6				*ca.* 945/1538–9				955/1548–9				964/1556–7				1005/1596–7			
	h.	b.	r.	d.	h.	b.	r.	d.	h.	b.	r.	d.	h.	b.	r.	d.	h.	b.	r.	d.
									Muslims											
Miṣriyyīn	38	2	1	—	59	3	14	—	102	9	14	—	105	11	13	1	56	11	3	—
Bāshḳardī	28	2	1	—	33	—	2	—	74	7	—	—	65	22	2	2	18	3	2	—
Jāmiʿ al-Abyaḍ	30	3	—	—	40	6	1	—	56	10	—	—	54	12	—	—	12	—	2	—
Halḳ (Khalaf?)	102	4	2	—	117	—	5	—	92	15	3	—	92	15	4	—	34	4	2	—
Al-Saḳḳāʾ	58	2	2	—	73	7	2	—	87	3	—	—	85	6	—	1	29	—	—	—
Jundīs	—	—	—	—	—	—	—	—	—	—	—	—	5	—	—	—	—	—	—	—
Turkumān	54	3	2	—	62	7	3	—	117	19	—	—	101	22	10	2	52	5	2	1
Total	310	16	8	—	384	23	27	—	528	63	17	—	507	88	29	6	201	23	11	1
									Christians											
Al-Saḳḳāʾ	26	—	—	—	33	—	—	—	57	7	—	2	41	—	—	—	42	—	—	—
Christians from Bayt Rīmā	—	—	—	—	—	—	—	—	25	—	—	—	29	—	—	—	35	—	—	—
Christians from Hebron	—	—	—	—	—	—	—	—	—	—	—	—	5	—	—	—	5	—	—	—
Total	26	—	—	—	33	—	—	—	82	7	—	2	75	—	—	—	82	—	—	—
Total	336	16	8	—	417	23	27	—	610	70	17	2	582	88	29	6	283	23	11	1

2. TAXES AND REVENUES[12]

	932/1525–6	*ca.* 945/1538–9	955/1548–9	964/1556–7	1005/1596–7
1. Revenue of *Dār al-wakāla*[13] in Ramle. Rice, dates, henna, grape juice, dried onion and garlic which arrive by sea and by land, are gathered to the appointed place where they are sold. The rate is half a *raṭl*[14] from each load of merchandise arriving by land, 1 1/3[15] asper on each load arriving by sea. As for *ḳaliye*,[16] it is sold by package (*kise*), 2 aspers are to be collected from each half-load (*denk*).[17] ID.					
per year	3,200				
2. Revenue of the inspection of the market (*iḥtisāb*) in the city of Ramle with butchers'-tax (*ḳaṣṣāb*).					
per year	1,500	2,000 (*ihtisāb* only) AG	1,280 (*ḳaṣṣābiye* only) ID	1,500 (*ḳaṣṣābiye* only)	2,000 (*ḳaṣṣābiye* only)
3. Revenue of scales (*ḳapan*) of Ramle: 3 aspers are to be collected from any item weighed. ID.					
per year	1,200	2,000 (+ *dār al-wakāla* and *dār al-khuḍar*).[18] AG	6,200 (+ *dār al-wakāla* and *iḥtisāb*). AG	6,200 (+ *dār al-wakāla* and *iḥtisāb*). AG	8,000 (+ *dār al-wakāla* and *iḥtisāb*). AG
4. Revenue of the vegetable-market (*sūḳ al-khuḍar, al-khuḍrawāt*) in Ramle: 3 aspers are to be collected from each hundred aspers worth of vegetables sold. ID.					
per year	1,200	1,200 AG			
5. Revenue of wheat [and] [or: grain of] sesame (*hınṭa-i sımsım*) for the making of *ḳaliye* is as follows: from each load of *ḳaliye* sold to a townsman in the town 4 aspers are to be collected. This is the due collected on what is sold here by land. What is collected in *Dār al-wakāla* is the tax due on what is sold by sea. ID.					
per year	1,500	1,500 AG	1,500 AG	2,000 AG of Jerusalem	2,000 AG
6. Toll on the corn-market (*bāc-i bāzār-i ğille*[19]) in the city of Ramle. ID.					
per year	350	720 AG			

Taxes and Revenues (contd.)

	932/1525–6	*ca.* 945/1538–9	955/1548–9	964/1556–7	1005/1596–7
7. Occasional revenues (*bād-i havā*), fines and penalties (*cürüm ve cināyet*), property of absent and missing persons (*māl-i ğā'ib* and *māl-i mefḳūd*), stray cattle and treasury revenues (*bayt al-māl*) of the *Ḳazā'* of Ramle with the market for riding and pack animals (*dābba*).					
per year	8,000[20]				
8. Revenue of road-toll (*bāc-i rāh*) to be collected [at the following rates]: 4 aspers per camel-load, 2 aspers per horse and mule-load, 1/2 asper per donkey-load, 10 aspers per black or white, both male and female slaves, brought for sale. However, nothing will be levied on loads of spices (*bahār*) arriving from Mecca the Ennobled. ID.					
per year	8,000	30,000	46,740	50,000 (donkey-load 1 asper, oxen and water-buffaloes 3 aspers)	55,000 (donkey-load 1 asper, oxen and water-buffaloes 3 aspers)
9. Tithe (ʿ*ushr*) on plots of land, orchards and vineyards, both *mülk* and waqf, in the lands of Ramle					
per year		2,000 AG	2,500		

[12] Compiled from the following registers: 427, 131, 1015, 265, 304, 546. The order followed was, basically, that of registers 427 and 1015.

[13] For a photograph of a building which served a similar function in Nabulus cf. J.-A. Jaussen, *Naplouse*, plate III 2. This term, which is an Egyptian expression for the more common *khān*, appears only in the two southern cities of Palestine, Ramle and Gaza, which entertained close links with Cairo (see Sauvaget, *Bulletin d'études islamiques*, tom. XII (1948), p. 30, n. 5).

[14] A *raṭl* in Ramle = 2,321 kg (Hinz, *Islamische Masse und Gewichte*, p. 30).

[15] *"yükünden bir akçe ve birer üç nesne alınır"*.

[16] "Graines grillées, puis mouillées sur le feu" (Barthélemy, *Dictionnaire Arabe Française*, p. 680).

[17] A common Ottoman term indicating half the load carried by an animal, i.e., the contents of one of the two paniers. Cf. *denk akçesi* levied at an identical rate in some Balkan ports (Cvetkova, *La vie économique de villes balkaniques*, p. 229).

[18] Cf. ʿ*Adet-i dār al-hudar* in Damascus (Barkan, *Kanunlar*, p. 223). For the same institution in Damascus in the Mamluk period see Sauvaget, *Bulletin d'études islamiques*, vol. II (1932), p. 40.

[19] In Erzurum the same *bāc* was levied at the rate of 2 1/2% (1/2 *müdd* from each *kile*) of wheat, barley and other cereals (Barkan, *Kanunlar*, p. 69).

[20] *Bād-i Havā* of the districts (*nāḥiye*) of Ramle only was 3,000 aspers in the same year (Register 131).

	932/1525–6	*ca.* 945/1538–9	955/1548–9	964/1556–7	1005/1596–7
10. Revenue of the scales of spun and raw cotton (*mīzān-i ğazl ve-ḳuṭn*). AG.					
per year		1,500	3,560 (+ *bāc-i bāzār-i ğille, sūḳ al-khuḍrawāt, sūḳ al-ḥamīr wa-l-baḳar, bāc-i siyāh*)	3,560 (idem.)	3,560 (idem.)
11. Revenue of toll on oil (*bāc-i zeyt*). AG.					
per year		1,000	2,070 (one *baṭmān*[21] from each village)[22]	3,470 (one *baṭmān* from each load)	3,470 (one *men* from each load)[23]
12. Revenue of the donkey-market (*sūḳ al-ḥamīr*). AG.					
per year		115			
13. Revenue of the cattle-market (*sūḳ al-baḳar*). AG.					
per year		25			
14. Tax on goats and sheep (*resm-i maʿze ve ghanam*) of the inhabitants of the city of Ramle. AG.					
per year		500	3,087 (+ *resm-i naḥl*)	3,500 (+ *resm-i naḥl*) (AG of Jerusalem)	3,500 (+ *resm-i naḥl*)
15. Tax on bees (*resm-i naḥl*). AG.					
per year		1,000			
16. Poll-tax (*jizya*) on Christians in the city of Ramle. ID.					
per year	1,560 (60 per person)	2,640 (80 per person)	7,280	6,000	6,560[24]

Taxes and Revenues (contd.)

	932/1525–6	*ca.* 945/1538–9	955/1548–9	964/1556–7	1005/1596–7
17. Revenue of property of missing and absent people, stray animals and *bayt al-māl* of the city of Ramle, above 10,000, with *bayt al-māl* of male and female slaves of the ʿ*askeris*[25] and *bayt al-māl* of the *gulāms* of the Sultan and berāt holders (*arbāb-i berāt*)		4,000 (up to 10,000 AG)	10,000 (belonging entirely to the *bayt al-māl*)	10,000 (idem.)	12,000 (idem.)
18. Revenues of baskets (*ḳawṣara*) in the city of Ramle. ID. per year			100	150 (*maḳṭū*ʿ held by [*der* ʿ*uhde*] Sīdī Yūsuf Khalīl and *mu*ʿ*allim* Shaʿbān, who are *mu*ʿ*allims* in the city of Ramle)	200
19. Revenue of orchards (*bustān*), i.e., guard-tax (ʿ*ādet-i deştbānī*)[27] of Ramle per year			400 (*Kharāj*)	500 (AG of Jerusalem)	500 AG

[21] One *batmān* in Syria in the twelfth century = 819 gr. (Hinz, *Masse und Gewichte*, p. 16).

[22] This seems to be a mistake of the scribe who read: كوي (*köy*) instead of يوك (*yük*).

[23] One menn = one *batmān* (Hinz, *Masse und Gewichte*, p. 11).

[24] The last three figures are calculated at the rate of 80 aspers.

[25] A term used of the military official class as a whole, including "slaves of the Porte," feudal cavalry etc.

[26] The readings of this last term vary in the registers. The earliest appears to read *erbāb-i berāt*, i.e., "holders of a berat"; in the later registers the corresponding passage can be read *veledān bā berāt*. The reference is presumably to holders of a *timār* worth 6,000 aspers or more, and therefore requiring a certificate, *teẕkere*, issued by the Sultan in the form of a *berāt*.

[27] The scribe does not seem to have been positive on the meaning, let alone spelling, of this term. From recurring references to this tax in the *ḳānunnāmes* (Barkan, *Kanunlar*, pp. 34, 134, 286, 539, etc.) it emerges as a fine which was collected from owners of sheep, goats etc., which caused damage to cultivated lands (see also Beldiceanu, *JESHO*, vol. XI (1968), pp. 37–8; Halası-Kun, *Belleten*, vol. XXVIII (1964), p. 24 where it appears together with *Bad-i Hava*, *Resm-i Arusane*, etc.). See also Heyd, *Studies*, pp. 124, n. 12, 280.

· 8 ·

NABULUS نابلس

1. QUARTERS AND INHABITANTS[1]

REGISTER 1038 OF *ca.* 945/1538–9

Quarter of:

Al-Ḳaysāriyya[2] القصاريه 97 households, 3 bachelors, 2 imams, 2 madmen

ʿAḳaba[3] عقبه 102 households, 2 bachelors, 2 imams

Al-Dabbūra الدبوره 92 households, 2 bachelors, 2 imams, 1 madman, 1 blind man

Jews in the above-mentioned quarter 32 households

G̲h̲arb[4] غرب 251 households, 20 bachelors, 4 imams, 1 blind man

[1] The accepted reading is Nābulus, as mentioned by many Arab historiographers (cf. Ḳalkas̲h̲andī, *Ṣubḥ al-Aʿs̲h̲ā*, vol. IV, p. 103; Yāḳūt, cited by S. al-Dahhān, *Taʾrīk̲h̲ Lubnān*, p. 243). Colloquially pronounced as Nāblus cf. a Jewish traveller's account (Bassola) dated 1521: "Napleys" in Yaʿari, *Massaʿōt*, p. 162). See also Marmardji, *Textes géographiques*, pp. 198–200; Le Strange, *Palestine under the Muslims*, pp. 511–14; Pantaleão de Aveiro, *Itinerario*, pp. 449–56.

[2] See Map 6, XI (when compared with an earlier one sketched by Kitchener in the 1870's only few differences can be traced with regard to the location of quarters). Jaussen found in 1923 that the city consisted of 12 quarters, 6 of which had kept their original names mentioned in the sixteenth century registers. All of the quarters mentioned in the early Ottoman registers were situated on the lower slopes of Mount Gerizim. In response to questions about the etymology of the name of this quarter (called both "al-Qaṣṣariyah" and "al-Qayṣariyah" Jaussen was told (p. 5) of two "big buildings" (*ḳaṣr*), erected by the governor Tuḳâby, which had formerly stood in that part of the city. Kitchener's map of *ca.* 1880 mentions only "Keisariyeh," obviously from the classical Arabic *ḳaysariya*, which in Syria was used as the equivalent of *K̲h̲ān* (cf. Sauvaget, *Bulletin d'études Islamiques*, tom. XII, (1948), p. 30, n. 5).

[3] Cf. Map 6, IX. "The quarter of the steep-mountain road," lying south of the Great Mosque, on the mountainside.

[4] See Map 6, V, "[The] West[ern]," extending along the western extremity of the city. Jaussen mentions (*Naplouse*, p. 5) that it had two different names: "al-Gharby" and "Ḥârat al-Fawâk̲h̲ir." In this quarter a Christian community existed at the time of the *tahrir*, most probably Greek Orthodox, in the vicinity of the convent of this congregation, which outlived the Ottoman regime. Kitchener's map depicts this quarter as stretching further north to include what in Jaussen's time became "al-Musk."

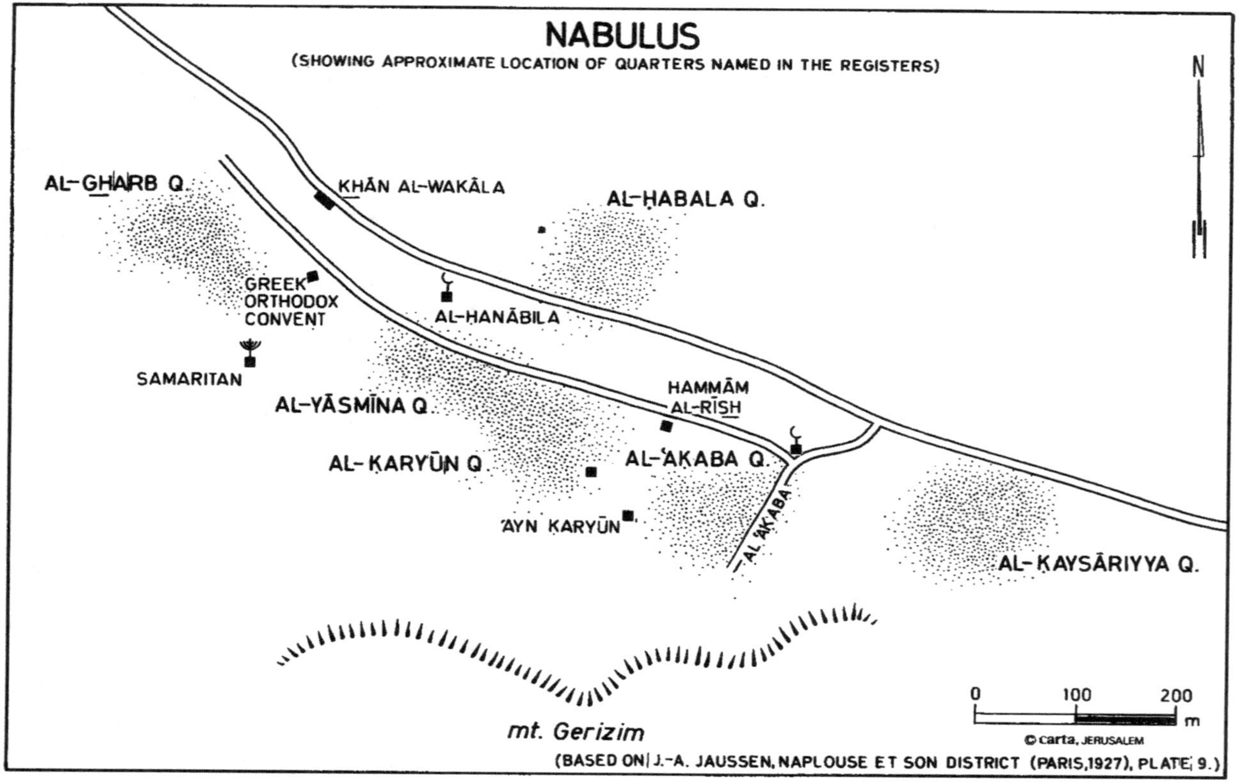
NABULUS
(SHOWING APPROXIMATE LOCATION OF QUARTERS NAMED IN THE REGISTERS)
N
AL-GHARB Q.
KHĀN AL-WAKĀLA
AL-ḤABALA Q.
GREEK ORTHODOX CONVENT
AL-ḤANĀBILA
SAMARITAN
AL-YĀSMĪNA Q.
ḤAMMĀM AL-RĪSH
AL-ḲARYŪN Q.
AL-'AḲABA Q.
'AYN ḲARYŪN
AL 'AḲABA
AL-ḲAYSĀRIYYA Q.
0
100
200
m
mt. Gerizim
© carta, JERUSALEM
(BASED ON J.-A. JAUSSEN, NAPLOUSE ET SON DISTRICT (PARIS, 1927), PLATE 9.)

6. Nabulus

Christians [in this quarter], 7 households

Yāsmīn[5] ياسمين 155 households, 2 bachelors, 2 *sharīfs*, 3 imams [161 names listed]

Christians in the above-mentioned quarter, 8 households

Ḥabala[6] حبلة 287 households, 14 bachelors, 5 imams

Community of Mustaʿrib[7] Jews, 34 households

[Community of] Frankish (*ifranj*) Jews, 5 households

Community of Samaritans (*Sāmiriyyān*)[8] in Nabulus, 29 households, 4 bachelors

REGISTER 258 OF 955/1548–9

Quarter of:

Gharb غرب 94 households, 56 bachelors,[9] 1 *khaṭīb*, 2 imams, 2 muezzins, 1 cripple, 4 blind men [names listed: 266 households 56 bachelors, 1 *khaṭīb*, 2 muezzins, 4 blind men, 1 cripple]

[5] See Map 6, VII, "Yasmînah," according to Jaussen, deriving its name from the flower Jasmine. In the sixteenth century this quarter included a Samaritan community. By Jaussen's time this community was classified as a separate "quarter of the Samaritans" (*Naplouse*, p. 5).

[6] Exceptionally, the various registers differ on the spelling of this name. The earliest register, often deficient in diacritical points, reads Ḥabala, i.e., the name is unpointed. The latest register, usually more accurate and reliable reads Jabala. To complicate matters, Jaussen mentions both a Ḥabala and al-Djabaliyah quarter. The earlier version seems preferable in this case for the following reasons: (1) According to Jaussen (*Naplouse*, pp. 4–5) Djabaliyah was mainly inhabited by foreign population which came in from the Ḥawrān or Judean mountains (hence its name, "mountain-people") and settled at the beginning of the nineteenth century. (2) Our registers show a substantial Jewish element in this quarter. Jewish families also lived in Ḳalyūn and ʿAḳaba. It seems very unlikely that the Jewish population of Nabulus would have been scattered among the different parts of the city. As elsewhere (Jerusalem, Safed), they would almost certainly have preferred to live close to one another, hence in (Jaussen's) Ḥabala, which is adjacent to the other two quarters with Jewish inhabitants (cf. Map 6, III).

[7] Three were named *al-Maghribi*; one, *al-Kurdi*.

[8] Toward the end of the Mamluk period there are said to have been about 2,500 Samaritans in Syria and Egypt. In Palestine they were usually town-dwellers (Jaffa, Gaza and Safed in addition to Nabulus), but also lived in some villages (Ben Zvi, *Eretz Israel*, p. 420). Mujīr al-Dīn (*Al-Uns al-jalil*, vol. II, pp. 42–3) mentions "many Samaritans" in Nabulus (on their importance in this town see Gaudefroy-Demombynes, *La Syrie*, p. 63 and n. 3). Although distinct in certain respects, they were still regarded by the Ottoman officials as people "who belong to the Jews" (Heyd, *Ottoman Documents*, p. 172 and n. 3).

[9] In this register the bachelors are listed together at the end of the section devoted to each quarter and not scattered among the married men as usual.

Community of Christians in the above-mentioned quarter, 6 households, 1 bachelor

Yāsmīn ياسمين 124 households, 18 bachelors, 1 *khaṭīb* [names listed: 179 households, 18 bachelors, 1 imam]

Ḳalyūn[10] also called: Dabbūra(قليون (دبوره 2 imams,[11] 8 muezzins, 110 households, 13 bachelors [names listed: 111 households, 13 bachelors, 2 imams, 7 muezzins]

Ḥabala حبله 1 imam, 349 households, 2 muezzins, 22 bachelors, 1 cripple [names listed: 347 households, 22 bachelors, 1 imam, 3 muezzins, 1 cripple]

Community of Christians in the quarter of Yāsmīn, 10 households, 1 bachelor

Community of Samaritans in the quarter of Yāsmīn, 34 households, 1 bachelor

Community of Jews in the quarter of Ḳalyūn, 21 households, 1 bachelor

Community of Jews in the quarter of Ḥabala, 12 households, 3 bachelors

Community of Jews in the quarter of ʿAḳaba, 3 households, 1 bachelor

REGISTER 549 (100) OF 1005/1596–7

Quarter of:

Yāsmīn ياسمين 137 households, 9 bachelors

Community of Christians in the above-mentioned quarter, 12 households (being *reʿāyā*[12] of Hebron, they pay their poll-tax to its waqf)

Community of Samaritans in the above-mentioned quarter, 20 households

Gharb غرب 213 households, 1 bachelor

[10] "Ḥārat al-Ḳâriyûn" (cf. Map 6, VIII) at the beginning of the present century. The local inhabitants told Jaussen (*Naplouse,* p. 5) without any possible explanation that their quarter, like the fountain of Ḳâriûn, derives its name from an old Roman building.

[11] Imams are sometimes listed at the beginning of each quarter, especially in this register. See p. 38.

[12] See above, p. 124, n. 28.

Community of Christians in the above-mentioned quarter, 6 households

Jabala جبله 164 households

Community of Jews in the above-mentioned quarter, 1 household

Ḳaysāriyya قيساريه 77 households

ʿAḳaba عقبه 89 households

Community of Jews in the above-mentioned quarter, 1 household

Ḳalyūn (also called: Dabbūra) (ديوره) قليون 116 households

Community of Jews in the above-mentioned quarter, 13 households

TABLE 5
Quarters and Population of Nabulus

	ca. 945/1538–9				955/1548–9				1005/1596–7			
	h.	b.	r.	d.	h.	b.	r.	d.	h.	b.	r.	d.
					Muslims							
l-Kaysāriyya	97	3	2	2	—	—	—	—	77	—	—	—
Aḳaba	102	2	2	—	—	—	—	—	89	—	—	—
.alyūn or Dabbūra (Duyyura?)	92	2	2	2	110[111]	13	10[9]	—	116	—	—	—
ḥarb	251	20	4	1	94[266]	56	5[3]	5	213	1	—	—
'āsmīn	155	2	5	—	124[179]	18	1	—	137	9	—	—
Jabala	287	14	5	—	349[347]	22	3[4]	1	164	—	—	—
Total	984	43	20	5	677[903]	109	19[17]	6	796	10	—	—
					Jews							
.alyūn	32	—	—	—	21	1	—	—	13	—	—	—
Jabala (Mustaʿrib)	34	—	—	—	12	3	—	—	1	—	—	—
(Frankish)	5	—	—	—	—	—	—	—	—	—	—	—
Aḳaba	—	—	—	—	3	1	—	—	1	—	—	—
Total	71	—	—	—	36	5	—	—	15	—	—	—
					Samaritans							
'āsmīn	29	4	—	—	34	1	—	—	20	—	—	—
					Christians[a]							
ḥarb	7	—	—	—	6	1	—	—	6	—	—	—
'āsmīn	8	—	—	—	10	1	—	—	12	—	—	—
Total	15	—	—	—	16	2	—	—	18	—	—	—
Total	1,099	47	20	5	763[989]	117	19[17]	6	849	10	—	—

[a] Evliya Çelebi (*Seyāḥatnāme*, vol. IX, p. 458) also mentions a Christian element of the population.

2. TAXES AND REVENUES [13]

	ca. 945/1538–9	955/1548–9	1005/1596–7
1. Revenue of the inspection of the markets (*iḥtisāb*) with the scales (*ḳapan*) in the city of Nabulus. ID. per year	20,000	32,400 (*iḥtisāb* only)	33,000 (*iḥtisāb* only)
2. Revenue of the scales (*kapan*) in the city of Nabulus. ID.		600	1,000
3. Revenue of toll on cloth (*bāc al-ḳumāsh*) in the city of Nabulus. 40 aspers to be levied on each load. ID. per year	12,000	16,400	18,000
4. Revenue of the beaters of cloth (*daḳḳāḳin-i ḳumāsh*)[14] in the city of Nabulus. ID. per year	2,400	2,500	3,000
5. Revenue of the dyehouse (*maṣbagha*) in the city of Nabulus. ID. per year	200	240	1,000
6. Revenue of the tannery (*dabbāghkhāne*) in the city of Nabulus. ID. per year	960	1,100	1,500
7. Revenue of toll on corn (*bāc al-ğilāl, bāc-i ğilāl*) in the city of Nabulus. ID. per year	500	1,000	1,500
8. Revenue of the market for riding and pack animals (*sūk al-dawwāb*) in the city of Nabulus. ID. per year	400	1,000	1,200

[13] The order follows basically that of Register 1038, supplemented by registers 258 and 549.

[14] "Beaters" from *daḳḳa*—"he beat it; namely a garment or the like; in washing and whitening" (Lane, *Arabic-English Lexicon,* book I, part 3, p. 895). See also Barthélemy, p. 245; Barkan, *Kanunlar,* p. 593, who translates it *boyaci* ("dyer"). Mantran, *JESHO,* vol. X (1967), p. 257, n. 2, ventures another explanation: "celui qui écrase et réduit en poudre les produits tintoriaux." Cf. Sauvaget, *Bulletin d'études Islamiques,* tom. II (1932), p. 35, n. 3.

[15] "Rūm" means the old Ottoman territories in Anatolia and Rumelia (cf. Heyd, *Ottoman Documents,* p. 68, n. 1). "Sā'ir vilāyet" means other countries—both other provinces of the Ottoman Empire and foreign countries. Though the normal route for foreign pilgrims was by sea to Jaffa and thence to Jerusalem, some came overland via Damascus. In the *ḳānūnnāme* for Jerusalem (Barkan, *Kanunlar,* p. 219) a similar distinction is drawn between Rūm and other provinces of the Ottoman Empire. An almost identical reference dating back to the eleventh century A.D. was made with regard to Christian and Jewish pilgrims to Jerusalem from "des pays des *Rūms*" (though this may mean Christendom). (Marmardji, *Textes géographiques,* p. 29, citing Nāṣir-i Khusraw, *Safarnâma*). See also Heyd, *Ottoman Documents,* p. 50, n. 2.

Taxes and Revenues (contd.)

	ca. 945/1538–9	955/1548–9	1005/1596–7
9. Revenue of the toll on Christians, Jews and other unbelievers (*bāc al-naṣārā wa-l-yahūd waghayrihim min al-kefere*) who come as pilgrims from Rūm[15] and other lands (*sā'ir vilāyet*)[16] to Jerusalem. They shall pay 16 aspers upon arrival and departure. ID.			
per year	20,000	22,000	23,000
10. Tax on sweet-sellers (*resm-i ḥelvāciyān*) to be collected from those among them who sell sweets (*ḥelva*)[17] in their market which they call "Thursday" (*khamis*)[18] and which they hold for one or two days in every year. ID.			
per year	1,000	1,000	1,200
11. Tax on girth-straps (*resm-i ṣeddādiye*) levied on every load from the merchants who bind them. ID.			
per year	240	338	500
12. Tithe (*ʿushr*) on plots of land, [vegetable] gardens (*junayna*)[19] and orchards (*bustān*). ID.			
per year	15,000	18,000	20,000[20]

[16] This is the original version as it appears in register 1038. Later on (registers 258, 549) a more simplified version is given: "who come as pilgrims from the [different] parts [of the Empire?]" (*eṭrāfdan*).

[17] A special sweet-paste made of carob-fruit, for which Nabulus was famous in the fourteenth century. Ibn Baṭṭūṭa describes it as follows: "At Nabulus there is manufactured also the carob-sweet, and it too is carried to Damascus and elsewhere. The method of making it is as follows. The carobs are cooked and then pressed, the juice that runs out of them is gathered and the sweet is manufactured from it. The juice itself is also exported to Egypt and other parts of Syria" (Gibb, *The Travels of Ibn Baṭṭūṭa*, vol. I, p. 82). For further references to *Ḥelvacı* cf. Barkan, *Kanunlar*, pp. 123–4; Muḥammad Ghālib, *Tarih-i Osmanı Encümeni Mecmuası*, vol. II (1327), p. 644.

[18] Most probably coined in this way after the day on which it was originally held, i.e., "Thursday" (*yawm al-khamis*). For the custom of fixing a special day for this purpose in Palestine see Heyd, *Ottoman Documents*, pp. 115, 143, n. 6. This tax should not be confused with the *khamisiyya* which was collected weekly in Jerusalem and other cities as another unauthorized *ḥisba* (see Sauvaget, *Bulletin d'études Islamiques*, tom. XII [1948], p. 35).

[19] This is not a technical term, and does not occur in any of the other registers for Palestine in the descriptions of the cities.

[20] The last two figures are qualified as follows: "Tithe (*ʿushr*) on plots of land, orchards and vegetable gardens (*ḥākūra*), both waqf and *mülk*, with the tax on the vineyards (*kharāj-i bāğāt*) of Wādī Ṣur (?) and Ṣūr (?), part of the *qism* revenues of lands of the Mīrī and orchards in the city of Nabulus, together with half the revenues of Roman olives (*zeytūn-i Rūmānī*)." A distinction is made throughout all the Syrian *ḳānūnnāmes* between Islamic olives (*zeytūn-i Islāmī*) and infidel or Roman olives (*kāfirī, Rūmānī*). This distinction which practically meant different rates of taxation,

Taxes and Revenues (contd.)

	ca. 945/1538–9	955/1548–9	1005/1596–7
13. Tax (*kharāj*) on vineyards in Wadi Ṣūr and another [place called] Ṣūr.[21] ID.			
per year	5,000		
14. Tax (*resm*) on the goats of the same city. ID.			
per year	500	1,000 (goats and bees)	1,500 (goats and bees)
15. The tribe (*ṭā'ife*)[22] of Banī Naᶜja bedouins. ID.			
per year	4,000		
16. The tribe of Naᶜīm bedouins. ID.			
per year	6,000		
17. The tribe of Banī Shākir bedouins. ID.			
per year	6,000		
18. The clan (*cemāᶜat*) of Banī Ḳurāyna (?) ID.			
per year	10,000		
19. The tribe of Ḥamīda bedouins. ID.			
per year	5,000		
20. Revenue of [tax on] the wine-shop (*khammāra*) in the city of Nabulus. AG.			
per year	1,000	1,000	
21. Revenue of the head of the night-watches (*ser-i ᶜasesān*) in the city of Nabulus. AG.			
per year	2,000	2,000	6,000
22. Occasional revenues (*bād-i havā*), fines and penalties (*cürm-i cināyet*) and bride-tax (*resm-i ᶜarūsāne*) of the city of Nabulus. AG.			
per year	5,000	26,500 (of the city and half of the districts [*nāḥiye*] of Jabal	40,000

was apparently preserved from the Arab conquest, referring to the original owners of the plot of land in question. In any case, all available evidence, and the *sijill* of Jerusalem in particular, indicates no other practical differentiation in the sixteenth century apart from the above-mentioned. Register 296 which gives identical information from the same year does not mention the word "half."

[21] About two miles southeast of Nabulus.

[22] For a similar distinction between *ṭā'ife* and *cemāᶜat* among the Turkoman nomad population in Anatolia and Northern Syria in the sixteenth century see: F. Sümer, *Istanbul üniversitesi iktisat fakültesi mecmuası*, vol. II (1950), p. 498.

Taxes and Revenues (contd.)

	ca. 945/1538–9	955/1548–9	1005/1596–7
		Shāmī, Ḳiblī, Banī Ṣaᶜb and Ḳāḳūn apart from ID and *ziᶜāmets* and free tīmārs)	(idem.)
23. Occasional revenues, fines and penalties and bride-tax of the district (*nāḥiye*) of Jabal Ḳiblī and Shāmī, apart from ID, *ziᶜāmets* and free tīmārs. AG. per year	30,000		
24. Revenue of mills (*ṭāhūn*), *mülk* and waqf, in the above-mentioned city, 26 stones, on each stone sixty. ID. per year		960	960 (in accordance with the "old defter")
25. Revenue of shops in the city of Nabulus. 3 doors. ID. per year		488	500
26. Revenue of the bathhouse of Rīsh[23] in the city of Nabulus. ID. per year		360 (Share of *Mīrī* 9 *ḳirāṭ* 135 share of waqf 15 *ḳirāṭ* 225)	360 (idem.)
27. Treasury revenues (*bayt al-māl*) and property of absent and missing persons and runaway slaves and stray cattle in the city of Nabulus and its districts (*nāḥiye*). ID. per year		6,000	6,500
28. Revenue of houses in the street (*shāriᶜ*) of al-ᶜĀkiba[24] in the above-mentioned city.		Share of the *Mīrī* 16 *ḳirāṭ*	Share of the *Mīrī* 16 *ḳirāṭ*
29. Community of nomad Kurds who pay a share (*ḳismat*) to the owner of whatever land they cultivate *resm-i ricāliye*.[25] ID. per year	960		

[23] Probably one of the two mentioned by Evliya Çelebi (*Seyāḥātname*, vol. IX, p. 457). Cf. Jaussen (*Naplouse*, p. 7), "ar-Rayš," still operative in 1923 (see Map 6).

[24] Most probably al-ᶜAḳaba of later days (see Map 6).

[25] Twenty-two households, 4 bachelors listed, who pay *ricāliye*, at the rate of 20 and 80 aspers, respectively. *Dirham al-rijāl* is a term which occurs in central and northern Syria as a tax levied in villages known to be Nusayrī, Ismaili etc. This may mean that the Kurds in question belonged to a heretical Muslim sect. See above, p. 18.

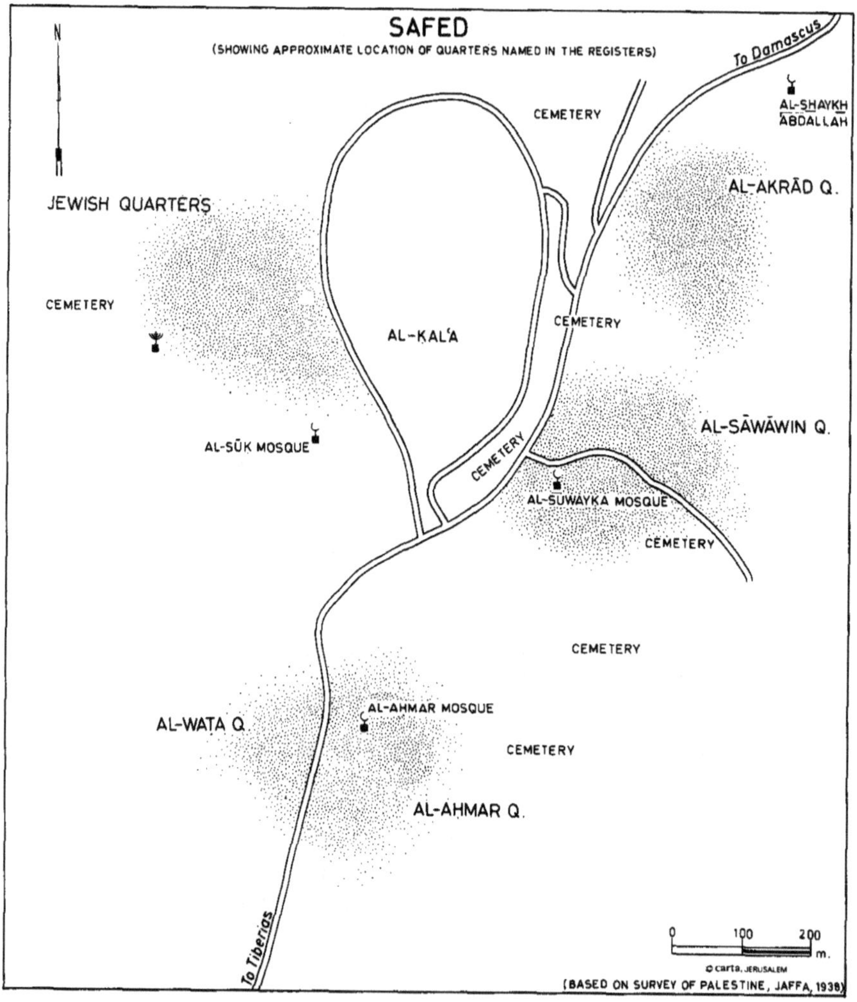
SAFED
(SHOWING APPROXIMATE LOCATION OF QUARTERS NAMED IN THE REGISTERS)
N
To Damascus
AL-SHAYKH ABDALLAH
CEMETERY
AL-AKRĀD Q.
JEWISH QUARTERS
CEMETERY
AL-KAL'A
CEMETERY
AL-SŪK MOSQUE
AL-SĀWĀWIN Q.
CEMETERY
AL-SUWAYKA MOSQUE
CEMETERY
CEMETERY
AL-WATA Q.
AL-AHMAR MOSQUE
CEMETERY
AL-AHMAR Q.
To Tiberias
0 100 200 m.
© carta, JERUSALEM
(BASED ON SURVEY OF PALESTINE, JAFFA, 1938)

7. Safed

• 9 •

SAFED صفد

1. QUARTERS AND INHABITANTS

REGISTER 427[1] OF 932/1525–6

Quarter of:

Akrād[2] اكراد *Sipāhīs* from former times—13 persons, imams and <u>*khaṭībs*</u>—5 persons, 105 households, 26 bachelors

Ṣawāwīn[3] صواوين 6 imams and <u>*khaṭībs*</u>, 174 households, 4 blind men, 7 bachelors

Community of *ajnād-i ḥalḳa*[4] who used to be *sipāhs*[5] in former times, 20 households

Al-Waṭā[6] الوطا Imams and <u>*khaṭībs*</u>—6 persons, 135 households, 7 bachelors, 3 blind men [only 141 names listed]

Community of *ajnād-i ḥalḳa* who used to be *sipāhs* in former times, 6 households

Ḥiṣwān, known as Jāmiʿ al-Aḥmar[7] (جامع الاحمر) حصوان 5 imams and <u>*khaṭībs*</u>, 136 households, 2 blind men

[1] In this register the name Safed is followed by the formula *al-maḥrūsa* ("the God-guarded"). This does not occur in other registers nor is it applied to any of the other five cities under consideration. For additional information on Safed see also Gaudefroy-Demombynes, pp. 118–19); Marmardji, *Textes géographiques*, pp. 115–17; Le Strange, *Palestine under the Moslems*, pp. 524–5. Pantaleão de Aveiro, *Itinerario*, pp. 478–82; Schweigger (1581), cited by <u>Ish</u>-<u>Sh</u>alōm, *Christian Travels*, p. 304; Radzivill (1583), in <u>Ish</u>-<u>Sh</u>alōm, p. 305.

[2] The Kurdish quarter, in the northeastern part of the city. On the Kurdish population, see p. 34.

[3] The southeastern part of the city, to the south of the Kurdish quarter.

[4] See above, p. 18.

[5] The use of the term *sipāh* instead of the common Ottoman *sipāhī* is significant. The latter is an Ottoman technical term denoting a specifically Ottoman institution. The former is used in a generic sense, to indicate the military order of another society.

[6] The lower quarter, in the southwestern part of the city. *waṭʾ*—*waṭāʾ* meaning "depressed land, low ground between eminences" (Lane, *Arabic-English Lexicon*, book I, p. 2949).

[7] The southern part of the city, where a mosque gave its name to the whole quarter. This pattern of naming a quarter after a mosque, more common in other parts of the Ottoman Empire (cf. Gökbilgın, *Belleten*, vol. XVI (1962), pp. 296–7) is not prevalent

Community of *ajnād-i ḥalḳa* who used to be *sipāhs* in former times, 21 households

Funduḳ[8] فندق 1 imam, 41 households

Sūḳ[9] سوق *Khaṭibs*, imams, and muezzins—3 persons, 42 households

Mustaʿriba[10] Jews[11] يهودان مستعربه 130 households [131 names listed]

Community of Frankish (*ifranjiye*) Jews belonging to the above-mentioned [quarter], 48 households

Community of Portuguese[12] Jews, 21 households

Community of Maghribis,[13] 33 households

in Palestine. The reason for this departure from local custom may be that it was the largest mosque in Safed. Originally built in 674/1275–6, it was reconstructed by the governor of the city, Sāliḥ Bey, in 1082/1671–2 (Evliya, *Seyāḥatnāme*, vol. IX, pp 439–40, for a detailed description of the mosque). For pictures taken of the building as well as inscriptions therein cf. Mayer and Pinkerfeld, *Muslim Religious Buildings*, plates 16, 36, 46–51.

[8] A scribal misreading of Khandak ("moat"), the form given in the other registers. This was most probably the quarter adjoining the citadel. Cf. *ḥārat al-khandaḳ* in Heyd, *Ottoman Documents*, pp. 122–3.

[9] The Market, in the western part of the city, where the el-Suq mosque is mentioned in the map drawn in 1938 Survey of Palestine (cf. Map 7).

[10] Lit. "arabized" or "arabizing." This term is used of the native Arabic-speaking Jews, as distinct from recent immigrants from other countries. Jewish sources refer to them as *Moriscos* (e.g., Bassola in Yaʿari, *Massaʿōt*, p. 138).

[11] The northwestern part of the city, which is named in the *Survey of Palestine* (1938) Map as "The Jewish Quarter" (*Ḥārat al-Yahūd*). In these registers the Jewish part of the city is subdivided into separate "quarters," according to the place of origin of their inhabitants. Some of these communities are so small that they can hardly have constituted separate quarters ("Partout où les Juifs espagnols s'éstablirent, ils ne se mêlèrent point au reste de leur correligionaires, ils formèrent des communautés absolument distinctes de celles de Juifs allemands et indigènes. Ils poussèrent même leurs idées séparatistes au point de se grouper entre eux, en égard à leur pays d'origine, de sorte que tel qui appartenait à la communauté *Aragonaise* n'avait garde de fréquenter la synagogue de la communauté *Cordovane* ou *Barcelonaise*. (Franco, *Essai sur l'histoire des Israelites de l'Empire Ottoman*, p. 40). For a description (dated 1535) by a Jewish merchant see: Yaʿari, *Letters*, pp. 183–7.

[12] سمعاليه is the term used, most probably a deformation of بورتغاليه, Portuguese. This conjectural emendation, suggested in Lewis, *Notes and Documents*, p. 36, n. 3, is confirmed by the later register not available at that time.

[13] North African Jews, coming from the western (*Maghrib*) part of the Arabic-speaking and islamic world.

REGISTER 300 OF 963/1555–6

Quarter of:

Ṣawāwīn صواوين 385 households,[14] 30 bachelors, 8 imams, 8 muezzins, 2 cripples, 2 blind men [only 425 names listed]

Community of Kurds (*Akrād*)[15] within the [above]-mentioned quarter, 14 households, 1 bachelor

Community of *jundiyān-i ḥalḳa* within the [above]-mentioned quarter, 26 households, 3 bachelors

Khandaḳ خندق 27 households, 1 bachelor

Ghirāwiyya[16] غراويه 40 households, 4 bachelors

Jāmiᶜ al-Aḥmar جامع الاحمر 157 households, 39 bachelors, 7 *khaṭibs* and imams, 9 muezzins, 1 cripple, 1 blind man [only 204 names listed]

Community of *ajnād-i ḥalḳa* in the [above]-mentioned quarter, 37 households

Akrād اكراد 153 households, 71 bachelors, 2 imams, 2 muezzins, 1 blind man [only 224 names listed]

Community of *ajnād-i ḥalḳa* in the [above]-mentioned quarter, 12 households

Al-Waṭā الوطا 183 households, 63 bachelors, 7 imams, 5 muezzins, 1 blind man

Community of *ajnād-i ḥalḳa* in the [above]-mentioned quarter, 9 households, 1 bachelor

[14] Four of whom are referred to as "*ibn Shaykh al-balad.* See above, p. 119, n. 16.

[15] It is noteworthy that this Kurdish group, probably recent arrivals in the city since most of them are designated as *Kurdī* or *ibn Kurdī* preferred to settle in close proximity to the original Kurdish quarter. The same tendency can be seen in other minority groups.

[16] In a firman dated 972/1564 Heyd (*Ottoman Documents,* pp. 122–3) read "the Gazan Quarter" (*Ḥārat al-Ghazzāwī*). This may well have been the name of the quarter, the only one for which no local evidence was available in the Mandatory period. As neither of the two registers used has any diacritical sign on the "r," the name is transliterated as given. If Heyd's reading is correct, then this quarter might have derived its name (like similar cases in Palestine) from the Bedouin tribe of Ghazāwiyya, which was roving between ᶜAjlūn and the river Jordan prior to the Ottoman conquest. Some of its families might have reached Safed and settled there. On this tribe see von Oppenheim, *Die Beduinen,* vol. II, pp. 194–6.

Sūḳ سوق 50 households, 9 bachelors, 2 imams, 13 muezzins, 1 madman

Community of Jews[17] in the city of Safed

Quarter of:

Portugal (*Pūrtuḳāl*), 143 households, 18 bachelors

Cordova (*Ḳurṭuba*), 35 households, 7 bachelors

Castile (*Ḳasṭilia*), 181 households, 12 bachelors

Mustaʿriba, 98 households, 10 bachelors

Maghāriba, 38 households, 7 bachelors

Aragon with Catalan (*Arāghūn maʿa Ḳatalān*), 51 households, 3 bachelors

Hungarian (*Macār*), 12 households

Apulia (*Pūlya*), 21 households, 1 bachelor

Calabria (*Ḳalāvriya*), 24 households

Seville (*Sabīliya*), 67 households, 4 bachelors

Italian (*Ṭalīyān*), 29 households

German (*Alāmān*), 20 households, 1 bachelor

Total: Households of the Muslims of the city of Safed—1,099 households, 217 bachelors, 16 imams and *khaṭībs*, 37 muezzins, 2 cripples, 6 blind men

Households of Jews 1175

The said Jewish community (*Yahūdā ṭāʾifesī*) used to pay *kharāj*[18] to the *mīrī*[19] for 1,075 households, at the rate of 40 paras, according to their status making 1,075 gold pieces. Later, at the time of the *taḥrīr*,[20] they agreed of their own accord to pay for an extra hundred houses. An imperial order was issued accordingly, and an annual payment of 1,175 gold pieces to the *mīrī* entered in the register.

[17] The figures which follow were obtained by adding the names listed for each quarter. No totals are given in the register.

[18] Used as a synonym for *jizya* (cf. "Djizya," *EI*², vol. II, p. 562; B. S. Nedkoff, *Die Ǧizya*, p. 23). See above, pp. 70–72

[19] The *Bayt al-māl* (Lewis, *Notes and Documents*, p. 36, n. 6; Lewis, "Bayt al-Māl," *EI*², vol. I, pp. 1147–8.

[20] I.e., when this register was compiled.

REGISTER 17738[21] OF *ca* 975/1567–8

Quarter of:

Sūḳ سوق 59 households, 12 bachelors [3 muezzins listed]

Community of *ajnād-i ḥalḳa,* 6 households

Akrād اكراد 155 households, 59 bachelors, 5 muezzins, 1 imam [only 4 muezzins listed, one of which is muezzin of the *zāwiya* 1 imam of the *zāwiya,* 1 blind man, 1 madman listed]

Community of *ajnād-i ḥalḳa,* 6 households, 4 bachelors

Khandaḳ خندق 19 households, 11 bachelors [2 *sharīfs* listed]

Ghirāwiyya غراويه 29 households, 15 bachelors, 1 muezzin

Jāmiᶜ al-Aḥmar جامع الاحمر 160 households, 27 bachelors, 2 imams, 2 *khaṭībs,* 8 muezzins [28 bachelors, 8 muezzins, 2 *faḳīhs,* 2 imams, 2 *khaṭībs,* 157 households listed]

Community of *ajnād-i ḥalḳa* in the above-mentioned quarter, 31 households, 4 bachelors

Al-Waṭā الوطا 198 households, 31 bachelors, 2 imams, 3 muezzins [1 *faqīh,* 1 blind man listed]

Community of *ajnād-i ḥalḳa* in the quarter of al-Waṭā, 11 households

Ṣawāwīn صواوين 287 households, 143 bachelors, 4 imams, 9 muezzins [281 households, 138 bachelors, 4 imams, 9 muezzins,[22] 3 *sharīfs,* 1 blind man listed]

Community of *ajnād-i ḥalḳa,* 28 households, 3 bachelors

Community of Kurds, 8 households

Community of Jews in the city of Safed

[21] Although no date is given the register is clearly later than Süleyman the Magnificent, who is referred to as "the late" (*marḥūm*) in connection with waqfs bearing his name. The use of *al-marḥūm* instead of *ṭāba thurāhu* or any of the other formulae normally used of earlier Sultans, may mean that the death of Süleymān was recent. In this register, unlike the others, an introductory page was inserted headed: "a list of the quarters of the city of Safed." The various quarters are transcribed in a very clear hand; an attempt has obviously been made to punctuate them as fully as possible, and all of them are grouped as either "the quarters of the Muslims" (*maḥallāt-i Muslimin*) or "the quarters of the Jews" (*maḥallāt-i Yahūdāyān*).

[22] Two of whom are also listed as bachelors.

Quarter of:

Portugal (*Pūrtughāl*), 200 households

Castile (*Ḳasṭīla*), 200 households

German with Hungarian (*Alāmān maʿa Mācar*), 50 households [43 households, 7 bachelors listed]

Aragon (*Araghūn*), 72 households [only 57 names listed]

Maghribis (*Maghāriba*), 55 households [3 bachelors listed]

Calabria (*Ḳalāvrīya*), 20 households

Mustaʿriba (*Mustaʿriba*), 70 households [only 45 names listed]

Italian (*Ṭālīyā*), 35 households

Seville (*Sūbīliyya*), 120 households [160 names listed]

Cordova (*Ḳurṭuba*), 55 households [2 bachelors listed]

Apulia (*Pūlia*), 25 households

Hungarian (*Macār*), 15 households

Households of Muslims in the city of Safed—988 households, 2 *khaṭībs*, 9 imams, 26 muezzins, 314 bachelors

Households of Jews in the above-mentioned city—957. *Jizya* of the above-mentioned with the additional tax [decreed on the occasion] of the Imperial accession (*cülūs-i hümāyūn*) as fixed (*ber vech-i maḳṭūʿ*) in the possession of the said persons, annually 160,600.

TABLE 6
Quarters and Population of Safed

	932/1525–6				964/1555–6				*ca.* 975/1567–8			
	h.	b.	r.	d.	h.	b.	r.	d.	h.	b.	r.	d.
					Muslims							
Akrād	105	26	5	—	153	71	4	1	155	57	5	3
Jundīs	13	—	—	—	12	—	—	—	6	4	—	—
Ṣawāwīn	174	7	6	4	385	30	16	4	284	136	13	1
Jundīs	20	—	—	—	26	3	—	—	28	3	—	—
Kurds	—	—	—	—	14	1	—	—	8	5	—	—
Al-Waṭā	135	7	6	3	183	63	12	1	196	31	6	1
Jundīs	6	—	—	—	9	1	—	—	11	—	—	—
Jāmiʿ al-Aḥmar or Ḥiṣwān	136	—	5	2	157	39	16	2	157	28	14	—
Jundīs	21	—	—	—	37	—	—	—	31	4	—	—
Khandaḳ	41	—	1	—	27	1	—	—	19	11	—	—
Sūḳ	42	—	3	—	50	9	15	1	56	12	3	—
Jundīs	—	—	—	—	—	—	—	—	6	—	—	—
Ghirāwiyya	—	—	—	—	40	4	—	—	29	15	1	—
Total	693	40	26	9	1,093	222	63	9	986	306	42	5
					Jews							
Mustaʿriba	131	—	—	—	98	10	—	—	70	—	—	—
Frankish (Ifranjiye)	48	—	—	—	—	—	—	—	—	—	—	—
Portuguese (Pūrtuḳāl)	21	—	—	—	143	18	—	—	200	—	—	—
Maghribis (Maghāriba)	33	—	—	—	38	7	—	—	52	3	—	—
Cordova (Kurṭuba)	—	—	—	—	35	7	—	—	53	2	—	—
Castile (Kastilia)	—	—	—	—	181	12	—	—	200	—	—	—
Aragon with Catalan (Araghūn maʿa Ḳatalān)	—	—	—	—	51	3	—	—	72	—	—	—
Hungarian (Macār)	—	—	—	—	12	—	—	—	15	—	—	—
Apulia (Pūlya)	—	—	—	—	21	1	—	—	25	—	—	—
Calabria (Kalāwriya)	—	—	—	—	24	—	—	—	20	—	—	—
Seville (Sabīliya)	—	—	—	—	67	4	—	—	160	—	—	—
Italian (Ṭāliyān)	—	—	—	—	29	—	—	—	35	—	—	—
German (Alāmān)	—	—	—	—	20	1	—	—	43	7	—	—
Total	233	—	—	—	719	63	—	—	945	12	—	—
	926	40	26	9	1,812	285	63	9	1,931	318	42	5

2. TAXES AND REVENUES[23]

	932/1525–6	*ca.* 945/1538–9	963/1555–6	*ca.* 975/1567–8
1. *Muḳāṭaʿa*[24] of the inspection of the markets (*iḥtisāb*)[25] of the city of Safed in accordance with the *sijill.*[26] ID.				
per year	7,200 (AG)	15,000 (AG)	80,000	84,500
2. *Muḳāṭaʿa* of the scales [tax] (*Ḳapan*) in the city of Safed in accordance with the *sijill.* ID.				
per year		1,200	20,000	22.500
3. Revenue of the slaughtering-tax of the Jews (*naḥirat al-Yahūd*)[27] in the city of Safed in accordance with the *sijill*. ID.				
per year	1,200	6,600 (in 11 months)[28]	15,500	17,500
4. Revenue of the brokerage of fruit (*simsāriyyat al-fawākih*). ID.				
per year			830	1,000
5. Revenue of a half-stone[29] mill in Jubayla, with a half [stone] mill in Umm al-Tūt, with a half-stone mill in ʿInab, with a half-stone mill in شو سطه, with a half-stone				

[23] The order followed was basically that of register 300, with additional information from registers 427, 132, 1038, 17738.

[24] A fiscal unit (sometimes a fiscal region) which has been farmed out by the state to an individual for a specific period, so as both to assure and expedite the remittance of these revenues to the treasury. The collection of various dues could be assigned as *muḳāṭaʿa*, e.g., *bāc ʿushri, niyābet* (Inalcık, *Defter-i sancak-i Arvanid*, pp. xxxiv–xxxv), customs (Beldiceanu, *JESHO*, vol. XI (1968), p. 41, n. 1), as well as *iḥtisāb* (Cvetkova, *Rocznik Orientalistyczny*, vol. XXVII, [1959], p. 114). For a further description of the system see pp. 113–15; Fekete, *Die Siyāqat-Schrift*, vol. I, p. 85; A. Cohen, *Palestine in the 18th Century*, p. 180. It is interesting to note that this term does not occur in any city of Palestine in the sixteenth century other than Safed (and even here, only in the later registers dating from the second half of the century).

[25] This involved not only weights and measures, but the collection of many taxes (cf. *EI*², vol. III, pp. 489–90; Gibb and Bowen, *Islamic Society and the West*, vol. II, pp. 7–9). For very similar figures for the first half of the century in Mardin see Göyünç, p. 143. A firman dated 987/1579 mentions a complaint by the inhabitants of Safed that the *muḥtesib* and the tax-farmer secretly buy the provisions that come to the town and force the shopkeepers to buy them (Heyd, *Ottoman Documents*, pp. 82–3). This is a long-standing problem well known to Muslim jurisprudence.

[26] The registers of the religious court, where copies of Imperial orders and nominations, judicial reports and verdicts, as well as listed of prices of all the principal commodities issued by the *muḥtesib* were kept.

[27] Cf. Lewis, *Notes and Documents*, pp. 12–13.

[28] It seems as if they were officially forbidden from slaughtering during the holy month, Muḥarram. Cf. entry no. 30 and note.

[29] Half-stone is to be understood as a term of accountancy and not as a description of the size of the stone. Its probable meaning is that the mill worked effectively for only half the year, because of the lack of water in the summer. The term is in common use in Palestine and elsewhere in the Ottoman Empire (Kaldy-Nagy, *Acta Orientalia*, vol. XXI [1968], p. 212). Cf. in the province of Qaraman: "Le droit de moulin est . . . de 30 *aspers* par moulin qui ne peut fonctionner que pendant 6 mois" (Beldiceanu, *JESHO*, vol. XI [1968], p. 51).

Taxes and Revenues (contd.)

	932/1525–6	*ca.* 945/1538–9	963/1555–6	*ca.* 975/1567–8
mill in Judayda, with a half-stone mill in اعسر, with a half-stone mill in حلمه in Wadi Dilbāy,[30] apart from duties. In accordance with the *sijill*. ID.			5,840 (Mill-tax (*resm-i ṭavāḥīn*) 240 [at the rate of] 30 [aspers] for each half-stone)	10,800[31]
6. Revenues of the mill of صو السميط and the mill of بطيطه in Wadi Dilbāy, apart from dues (*resm*), in accordance with a *sijill*. ID. per year			3,280	5,800
7. Revenue of the *ḥammām* al-Sulṭān in the city of Safed. ID. per year		2,000	1,200 In accordance with a fixed payment (*maķṭūᶜ*). Whereas when the said bathhouse was formerly in use and every year 1,600 aspers were paid by the *mīrī*[32] as lease-money (*icāre*) and whereas it has for a long time been in ruin, and not a single asper or penny has accrued to the *mīrī*, and in the event of its restoration by the *mīrī* much money would be required, therefore it has been agreed that the sipāhīs Kātib Aḥmad and Naṣṣūḥ from the	1,200 Lease (*ḥikr*) *maķṭūᶜ*, held by (*der ᶜuhde*) Kātib Aḥmad and Khalīl

[30] According to al-Dimashkī, writing in the early fourteenth century, it was known as Wādī Dalība, near Mayrūn, where some watermills already existed (in *Nukhbat al-dahr fī ᶜajāʾib al-barr wa-al-baḥr*, p. 118 cited in Marmardji, *Textes géographiques*, p. 203). Al-ᶜUthmānī, who used the above-mentioned source extensively, refers to it as Wādī Dilbayya (B. Lewis, *Bulletin of the School of Oriental and African Studies*, vol. XV [1953], p. 481). It has not been possible to identify the other names mentioned under this heading.

[31] Register 17738 reads also: "mill-tax (*resm-ı ṭawāḥin*) 30 [aspers] for every half [stone] [total] 120. Its details were copied in the relevant place of the district (*nāḥiye*)".

[32] The Imperial Public Treasury (*Bayt al-Māl-ı ᶜĀmme*).

Taxes and Revenues (contd.)

	932/1525–6	*ca.* 945/1538–9	963/1555–6	*ca.* 975/1567–8
			city of Safed, in partnership having reconstructed it at their own expense, shall pay 1,200 aspers a year as bounty (*bi-ṭariḳ al-khayr*) to the *mīrī* on condition that it be not given to any offering to pay more. This has been entered in the register	
8. Revenue of the tax of spice-merchants (*ʿaṭṭār*) with measuring-tax (*keyyāliye*) and tax of slave market (*bāc-i bāzār-i esārā*)[33] in the city of Safed in accordance with the *sijill.* ID.				
per year		1,000 (with tax on fruits without tax on slave-market)	5,700	8,300
9. Revenue of the *muḳāṭaʿa* of dye-house (*maṣbagha, bōyakhāne*)[34] of broad-cloth (*çoḳa*)[35] with the dye-house of cloth (*ḳumāş*)[36] in accordance with the *sijill.* ID.				
			4 doors[37]	4 doors
per year	300 + 300 (*ziʿāmet* of ʿIsā, Alay Bey of Safed)	1,000	2,236 (dye-house of *çoḳa* 1,000 per year; dye-house of cloth 1,236 per year)	2,250

[33] Cf. *ʿAdet-i bazar-i esir* in Barkan, *Kanunlar*, p. 223; *Bac-ı bazarı esarı* in Mantran and Sauvaget, *Règlements fiscaux Ottomans*, p. 112, n. 2. On the import of black slaves from Egypt either to or through Safed see Heyd, *Ottoman Documents*, pp. 123–4. On *bāc* see above, p. 103, n. 34.

[34] Here as elsewhere, Arabic terms are progressively rep'aced by their Turkish equivalents. In this case Arabic terms are used in the registers compiled in the first half of the century. Turkish terms are used exclusively from 1555–6 onward. The same process occurs with other terms.

[35] See above p. 55, n. 43.

[36] "Occurs also in the customs registers without any qualifier, it may have referred to the tissues [sic] that could not be easily identified" (Kaldy-Nagy, *Acta Orientalia*, vol. XVIII [1965], pp. 303–4).

[37] I.e., dye-houses.

Taxes and Revenues (contd.)

	932/1525–6	*ca.* 945/1538–9	963/1555–6	*ca.* 975/1567–8
10. Treasury revenues (*bayt al-māl*) and property of absent and missing persons (*māl-i ğā'ib* and *māl-i mefḳūd*) and stray cattle and runaway slaves in the city of Safed and its dependencies.[38] ID.				
per year			10,000	10,000
11. Revenue of tithe (*ʿushr*) of [pieces of] land, orchards (*bustān*),[39] vineyards (*karm*) [held as] waqf and *mülk*, with *kism* [revenues] of *mīrī* lands and tax on the vineyards and other trees (*kharāj al-kurūm ve-ashjār-i sā'ire*) in the vicinity of the city of Safed. ID.				
per year		2,000	2,500	2,500
12. Toll-post (*bāc-i aghfār*)[40] in the village of Minya.[41] *ʿĀdet:* 2 aspers from a camel-load,[42] 1 asper from a horse or mule load, 1/2 asper from a donkey-load, 8 aspers from Christian pilgrims to Jerusalem, 6[43] aspers from Jewish pilgrims to Jerusalem. ID.				
per year	6,000		23,000	23,000
13. Toll-post in Jisr Yaʿḳūb.[44] *ʿĀdet:* 2 aspers from a camel-load, 1 asper from horse				

[38] I.e., the districts (*nāḥiye*) of which the sanjak of Safed consists.

[39] Kaldy-Nagy mentions a wider variety of interpretations of the term: "fieldgarden . . . vegetable garden . . . a melon field by the river or at the end of the village, or even among the arable lands of the village" (*Acta Orientalia*, vol. XXI [1968], pp. 203–4).

[40] Lit : "Toll [collected at] toll-posts." In early periods, in the Ilkhānid dominions, *bāc*, according to Köprülü, when referred to "must be the *rāhdārī* (traveller's protection tax) levied. . in return for maintaining peace and security on caravan routes and lakes" (*EI*², vol. I, pp. 860–1). The term was more prevalent in its singular form *ğafar* or *ğafer* (cf. Heyd, *Ottoman Documents*, firman dated Rebīʿ I 968/November 1560, pp. 123–4). In a variety of forms the term is frequently mentioned by western travellers.

[41] On the northwestern shore of Lake Tiberias (cf. Heyd, *Ottoman Documents*, p. 127, n. 6; Evliya, *Seyāḥatnāme*, vol. IX, p. 520; Ahmad Ferīdūn Bey, *Munsha'āt al-Salāṭin*, vol. I, p. 400 misreads Maymana, but p. 403 Minya). A Franciscan traveller from the sixteenth century refers to "Elimini [where] is paid, even today, a certain tax or maritime customs duty" (H. C. Luke, *Franciscan's Narrative*, p. 19). Sanderson, who travelled in 1601 between Damascus and Jerusalem, mentions Almenia, which lay to the north of Tiberias, near the shore, and the river Jordan, and a *khān* which was near (Foster, *Travels of Sanderson*, p. 114).

[42] Although the actual term used is the Turkish *yük*, it is apparently similar to its Arabic equivalent *ḥiml*. A camel-load was approximately 250 kg (Hinz, *Masse und Gewichte*, p. 13).

[43] The scribe of register 17738 appears to have misread the Turkish *altışar;* ("six each") for *ikişer* ("two each"). There is no evidence of any such change in practice. One should note that in 4 check points, the rate of *ğafar* tax levied on Jews is 25 % lower than Christians, and in the remaining 2 it is equal. This may indicate an attempt on behalf of the Ottoman government to encourage Jewish traders; in any case this can not be justified on purely religious grounds, as they both figure as *Dhimmis*.

[44] For further references cf. Ferīdūn, vol. I, p. 400; Evliya, *Seyāḥatnāme*, vol. IX, p. 525; Heyd, *Ottoman Documents*, p. 127 and n. 5. "The Bridge of Jacob . . . close by the bridge is a certain Can, where a toll is levied on those crossing the bridge" (Luke, *Franciscan's Narrative*, p. 18).

Taxes and Revenues (contd.)

	932/1525–6	*ca.* 945/1538–9	963/1555–6	*ca.* 975/1567–8

or mule loads, 10 aspers from a black or white slave, 8 aspers from Christian pilgrims to Jerusalem, 6 aspers from Jewish pilgrims to Jerusalem, 1 beast from each flock of sheep on their way to be sold.[45] ID.

per year	6,000		25,000	25,000

14. Toll-post in the village of Jibb Yūsuf: 4 aspers from a camel-load, 2 aspers from a horse or mule-load, 1/2 asper from a donkey-load, 10 aspers from either a white or a black slave, 8 aspers from Christian merchants (*bāzirkān-i kāfir*), 6 aspers from Jewish, 1 beast from each flock of sheep travelling for sale, 8 aspers from Christian pilgrims to Jerusalem, 6 aspers from Jewish pilgrims to Jerusalem. ID.

per year	6,000		13,000	13,000

15. Toll-post in the village of Ṣaᶜṣaᶜa[46] dependent on Shaḳīf in accordance with the *sijill.* Old *ḳānūn:* 4 aspers from each camel-load, 2 aspers from a horse or a mule-load, 1/2 asper from a donkey-load, 10 aspers from Christian merchants, 6 aspers from Jewish, 10 aspers from white and black, both male and female slaves. ID.

per year	5,700	6,000	21,500	21,500

16. Toll-post in ᶜUyūn Tujjār:[47] 4 aspers from each camel-load, 2 aspers from a horse or mule-load, 1/2 asper from a donkey-load, 8 aspers from the Christian merchants, 6 aspers from the Jewish, the same rate [respectively] from Christian and Jewish pilgrims [travelling] to and from Jerusalem, 10 aspers from white and black, both male and female slaves, 1 beast from each flock of sheep that passes. ID.

per year	6,000[48]	7,000	11,500	11,500

A Jewish traveller from 1521 gave the following details: "The Jordan is crossed over a stone bridge called 'the bridge of Jacob' . . . Between the Jordan and Damascus . . . there are four *khāns;* i.e., a place where the caravans stay overnight. These are like a closed city. There are six miles from one another. Three *Ḳafar* are paid: 15 dirhams on the bridge, 10 dirhams on each of the two other [posts]" (Bassola in Yaᶜari, *Massaᶜōt*, pp. 150–1). At the present time the place is known as "the bridge of the daughters of Jacob" (*Benōt Yaᶜkōv*, Heb., *Banāt Yaᶜḳub*, Ar.).

[45] Cf. "To the town of Safed sheep [used to] come from Damascus. Thus when sheep did not come, the poor [inhabitants of Safed complained] saying, 'We suffer considerable hardship from [lack of] meat" (Heyd, *Ottoman Documents*, p. 134, firman dated 990/1582). See above, p. 58.

[46] The scribe misread it سوسسه; the proper form is سعسع. For further references cf. Heyd, *Ottoman Documents*, pp. 101, n. 1, 126, n. 4; Evliya, *Seyāḥatnāme*, vol. IX, pp. 527–8; Ferīdūn, *Munshaʾāt al-Salāṭin*, vol. I, p. 400 reading Shaᶜshaᶜa and p. 430 Saᶜs. A Franciscan traveller (H. C. Luke, *A Franciscan narrative*, p. 17) called it Sasia, "where is paid by the Frank Christians a certain tax". Heyd (*Ottoman Documents*, p. 101, as suggested by a firman dated 989/1581) says "a village is to be established at Saᶜsaᶜa, an isolated halting-place." Whereas our register mentions specifically the term "village" at an earlier date. This might possibly mean that the village which had existed there in 963/1555–6 was deserted by its inhabitants at a later date (as a result of bedouin incursions?) and it had to be resettled about twenty years later.

[47] For further references see Ferīdūn, vol. I, p. 400; Evliya Çelebi, *Seyāḥatnāme*, vol. IX, pp. 449–450; Heyd, *Ottoman Documents*, pp. 111–113.

[48] Six thousand or more aspers in Khān Lajjūn, which do not appear in any other register.

Taxes and Revenues (contd.)

	932/1525–6	*ca.* 945/1538–9	963/1555–6	*ca.* 975/1567–8
17. Toll-post on the road of Sūr[49] (Raʾs Sūr?) dependent on Acre: 2 aspers from each camel-load, 1 asper from a mule-load, 1/2 asper from a donkey-load, 8 aspers from the Christian merchants and similarly from the Jewish, the same rate from both Christian and Jewish pilgrims [travelling] to and from Jerusalem, 10 aspers from white and black both male and female slaves, 1 beast from each flock of sheep that passes. ID.				
per year	1,720 30,000 *bāc-i* *ghafāre* in the *liwāʾ* of Safed.	1,400	6,000	6,000
18. Revenue of taxes on certain persons (*muʿayyenān*) in the city of Safed and its dependencies apart from armourers (*cebeciyyān*)[50] and blacksmiths (*ḥaddādīn*). ID.				
per year			1,000	3,000
19. Revenue of fisheries in the district (*nāḥiye*) of Minya and Tiberias. ID.				
per year			3,300[51]	3,300[52]
20. Revenue of fisheries in the above-mentioned district in the Baḥr Ḳadas (*Ḥūle*). ID.				
per year			1,700	1,700[53]
21. Revenue of fisheries at Ḳāsimiyya[54] and near the Salt Sea [or: lake] (*baḥr-i mālīḥ*)				

[49] Possibly another name for Raʾs Naḳūra. Pıri Reʾis mentions "a place ten miles from the above-mentioned Acre, there is a big point of land; that point is called Reʾs-i Beyâz . . . On the above-mentioned point of land there is a tower" (Heyd, *Israel Exploration Journal*, vol. VI [1956], pp. 213–14 n. 63: Pīrī Reis, *Kitabı Bahriye*, p. 728.

[50] The scribes themselves were clearly uncertain as to the meaning of the word since in contrast to the following word, *ḥaddādin*, which is clear and standard, this one appears deliberately vague and varies from register to register. The likeliest reading is *cebeciyān* ("armourers"). This is corroborated by Fekete, *Siyāqat-Schrift*, vol. I, p. 96): "Als nächste Truppengattung pflegte in grösseren Garnisonen unter dem Namen *müteferriqa*, 'verschiedene [Berufsangehörige]' eine Truppe aufezahlt zu werden, die keinen eigentlichen Waffendienst versah, wobei in dieser Gruppe auch einige beim Militär dienende Handwerker usw. erwähnt werden: . . . *ğebeği*, Waffenschmied, *ḥaddād*, schmied . . . Alle diese kommen nur in viel kleinerer Zahl und mit einem viel kleineren sold". There are, however, several other possible readings and emendations of the word, which looks like صرمصان. These include: صرمصر "envelopper. . .empaqueter" (Berthélemy, *Dictionnaire Arabe Français*, p. 430), and جرجي "mauvais ouvrier" (*ibid.*, p. 135) or "pedlar" (Redhouse, *Turkish-English Lexicon*, s.v.), neither of which seems very plausible in this context. جرخجي, knife-grinder would be much more probable, but involves a more substantial emendation. Another possibility which may be considered is that these are the names of tribes in the area.

[51] A firman dated 967/1560 says: "The *emin* of Safed collects . . . 15,000 aspers for the fish [caught] in the lake [of Tiberias]" (Heyd, *Ottoman Documents*, p. 141).

[52] "Waqf of the ʿ*imāret* of Sultan Süleymān in Damascus."

[53] "Waqf of the ʿ*imāret* of the late Sultan Süleymān."

[54] Situated about five miles north of Tyre.

Taxes and Revenues (contd.)

	932/1525–6	*ca.* 945/1538–9	963/1555–6	*ca.* 975/1567–8
with the revenues of the port of Tyre within the district of Tibnīn. ID.				
per year			4,000 (2,000 per year from the revenue of the port; 1,000 per year from the revenues of the fisheries of Ḳāsimiyya; 1,000 per year from the revenues of the fisheries in Baḥr Māliḥ)	4,000 (idem.)
22. Revenues of the port of Acre and fisheries and Nahr al-Nuᶜaymān and brokerage of measuring-tax (*keyyāliye*) in Acre. ID.				
per year			11,000 (10,000 per year revenues of the port; 500 per year revenues of pole-net (*ṭālyān*)[55] fishing; 500 per year revenues of brokerage of measuring-tax)	11,000 (idem.)
23. Revenue of the *muḳāṭaᶜa* of the stamp-duty (*tamġā*) for the *çoḳas* of Safed. It has been decreed by Noble Command that a stamp duty be collected at the rate of 1 para from each pastav of kersey (*ḳarziye*)[56] and 2 paras from each pastav of broad *çoḳa*. This has also been duly entered into the "new register". ID.				
per year			12,000	12,000
24. Revenue of the *muḳāṭaᶜa* of fisheries near the *mezraᶜa*[57] of Shutayra(?) and the *mezraᶜa* of ᶜUbaydiyya[58] dependent on the district of Tiberias, known as قتيل (?). *Maḳṭuᶜ*. Held by (*der ᶜuhde*) Shaykh Aḥmad ibn Nāfiᶜ and Ḥājj Muḥammad Maṭbūḥa of the city of Safed.				

[55] See above, p. 67, n. 70.

[56] See above, p. 60.

[57] Lit.: "a cultivated place, plot of land". In the sixteenth century it signified an uninhabited, cultivated place, very often in the vicinity of village (*ḳarye*). Previously inhabited villages when deserted by their inhabitants were specifically reduced to the level of *mezraᶜa* (*ḫāli ez raᶜiyyet* (*ᶜan reᶜāyā*) *mezraᶜa dir*). Conversely a place listed as a *mezraᶜa* in an earlier register may be transformed into a *ḳarye* in a later edition by the addition of some names. See also above, p. 24.

[58] Most probably ᶜAbeydiyya, situated about 2 miles south of the lake on river Jordan.

Taxes and Revenues (contd.)

	932/1525–6	*ca.* 945/1538–9	963/1555–6	*ca.* 975/1567–8
per year			800	1,200
25. ʿ*Ādet* of taxes on winter pasturage (ʿ*ādet-i rusūm-i ḳishlāḳ*)[59] of the tribes (*ṭāʾife*) of Banī Dāʾūd and Banī Jallās and ʿAnza[60] and the tribe of Banī Sākir and the other bedouin tribes of Syria together with pasturage rights (*ḥaḳḳ-i merʿā*). ID. per year			4,000	4,000
26. From the revenues of the head of the night-watches (*ser-i* ʿ*asesān*) in the city of Safed. AG. per year			7,000	7,000
27. From the revenues from the market for riding and pack animals (*sūk al-dawwāb*) in the city of Safed. AG. per year			300	300
28. From the occasional revenues (*bād-i havā*), fines and penalties (*cürm-i cināyet*) and bride-tax (*resm-i* ʿ*arūsāne*) of the city of Safed. AG. per year	30,000 (in the *liwāʾ* of Safed[61] except of ID)	10,000	16,500	20,000
29. ʿ*Ādet* of taxes on winter pasturage (ʿ*ādet-i rusūm-i kishlāḳ*) of the bedouins (ʿ*urbān, aʿrāb*) of the Biḳāʿ. AG. per year			10,000	10,000
30. Revenue of the wine shop (*khammāra*) in the city of Safed except during the forbidden months (*ashhur-i ḥarām*).[62] ID. per year	6,000	6,000		
31. Poll-tax (*jizya*) of Christians in the *liwāʾ* of Safed. ID. per year	31,310			
32. Poll-tax of Jews in the city of Safed. ID. per year			94,000	160,600
33. Tax on water-buffalo (*resm-i jawāmis*) in the *liwāʾ* of Safed. ID.	11,880 (990 beasts at the rate of 12)			

[59] "If sheep come in a *timār* from elsewhere in order to winter-pasture, a beast is to be taken from a "heavy" [probably cows] flock, six aspers from a "light" [sheep and goats] flock, nothing else is to be taken" (*Kānunnāme-i Al-i Osmān*, p. 43). See above, p. 17.

[60] See Gräf, "ʿAnaza," *EI*², vol. I, pp. 482–3.

[61] The correct version is given in the *icmāl* of Register 132, while it was mistakenly copied as "the *liwāʾ* of Damascus" in Register 427.

[62] This term in pre-Islamic times meant the four following months: Dhuʾl-Ḳaʿda, Dhūʾl-Hijja, Muḥarram, Rajab. This is unlikely to be the meaning here, and it seems probable that *ashhur* (اشهر), months, is an error for *al-shahr* (الشهر), the month; i.e., "the forbidden month," *Muḥarram*. Cf. the limitation of the Jewish slaughtering to 11 months (p. 161).

CONCLUSION

THE foregoing study of six towns in Palestine in the sixteenth century is based primarily on one series of documents—that contained in the *tapu* registers in Istanbul and Ankara. Other documentary and literary evidence from sixteenth century Palestine has been used, as well as from other times and places, when required for comparative purposes. But it was employed to interpet and clarify the information contained in the *tapu* registers, rather than to construct a general picture. This is a task which must wait for the future.

This study has been concerned basically with two themes—population and revenue. Under the first we have considered the numbers, composition, and distribution of the population, topographically and in other respects within the city. Under the second we have tried to establish the different headings of revenue, the manner of assessment, and, as far as possible, collection, the yield, and the destination of the money collected. On these two subjects the *tapu* registers are far and away the richest source of information, and it is likely that any future study on these subjects will have to rest primarily on the information which they provide.

The picture that emerges from these registers is of a well-organized, well-articulated and efficiently functioning bureaucracy, dealing with a wide range of affairs, and rapidly increasing its range and effectiveness in the decades that followed the Conquest.

Clearly, the Ottomans brought considerable changes, though these are difficult to measure. It is dangerous to argue from silence. We have no comparable evidence from the pre-Ottoman period, though from various indications it seems likely that the Mamluk administration maintained a system of registers. Another impediment to comparisons is that some important matters are not mentioned in the *taḥrīr* registers at all, since they were not relevant to the function and purpose for which these registers were compiled. Thus, for example, the headman of the urban quarter appears only at the beginning of the period, and not thereafter. On the evidence of registers alone, this might indicate that the office fell into desuetude; it might equally mean however that some change in administrative arrangements had made it no longer relevant to the work of the *taḥrīr* commissions. A parallel and a warning may be seen in the absence from the *taḥrīr* registers of the kadi and of the *ḳażā*, his area of jurisdiction. The importance of these in the Ottoman provincial administration is well known from other sources, and indeed in the registers of waqfs, which involve questions of religion and law, they take their proper place. They do not appear in the *taḥrīrs,* since the kadis were not concerned with matters covered in them.

The Ottoman registers for Syria and Palestine are basically of the same type as those already compiled in earlier times for the Ottoman provinces in Anatolia and Rumelia, and become more so; i.e., the new rulers gradually applied to the newly acquired provinces the system which they had already developed elsewhere.

To what extent this system was modified in its application by pre-existing usage is difficult to say in the absence of precise information. Ottoman rule was however in general conservative, and tended to maintain, at least for a while, the existing order. Some indications appear in the registers, and especially in the *ḳānūnnāmes;* some can be inferred from other sources. The evidence of the Ottoman registers, taken together with material from earlier periods, may impose some reconsideration of the situation under the late Mamluks.

Even within the limitations of topic and area which we set ourselves, we have very far from exhausted the information which the *tapu* registers offer. Each description of a city or town in the registers begins with an enumeration of the quarters and their inhabitants, followed by a list of taxes and of the yields obtained from them.

It is on the lists of quarters and taxes that our monograph is based. But this does not end the description of the city, or the information which can be extracted or deduced from it. For each quarter in the cities, as for each village in the countryside, there is a list of the names of the adult male inhabitants, indicating family relationships. An intensive study of these, for the whole period, might well yield further demographic data.

In most *taḥrīr* registers, the description of the city is followed by a list of holdings, principally of two categories: *mülk* and waqf. The first of these consists of lands in private freehold ownership; the second of pious foundations, sometimes for a genuine pious purpose, sometimes for the benefit of the family and descendants of the founder of the waqf, with some religious or charitable beneficiary as residuary legatee, if the line of family heirs is extinguished. *Mülk*—the nearst equivalent to freehold or fee-simple in Islamic law—is to be found primarily in cities and their immediate environs, and it is only from *mülk* that private individuals can establish waqfs. For this reason, private waqf too is to be found mainly in and around cities; royal waqfs could of course be consecrated from any crown property or revenue, in town or countryside.

The registers contain long lists of such holdings, both *mülk* and waqf, and, indeed, in addition to the descriptions contained in the *Mufaṣṣal taḥrīr* registers, there are also separate registers devoted exclusively to *mülk* and/or waqf, containing much fuller details. These holdings are listed, the entry normally giving their names, the names of the owner (for *mülk*) or founder and beneficiary (for waqf), some indication of their whereabouts and topographical limits, frequently some statement of the purpose for which they are used, and, of course, of the revenue which they produce. The waqf registers usually give fuller details—a copy of the foundation deed, and a detailed statement of the income of the waqf, indicating the source and yield of each item; for charitable waqfs this is sometimes followed by a summary of the expenditure of the waqf, itemized and detailed. Many of the waqfs date back to Mamluk or even to Ayyubid times. From these lists it is clear that apart from sites occupied by private or public buildings, the great majority of such holdings were used as vineyards, vegetable gardens and fruit gardens. The next task, it would seem, is to undertake a detailed study of descriptions of *mülk* and waqf in and about the cities of Palestine. Such a study should yield valuable information on urban and more generally economic development.

After the city, there is the countryside, and the detailed descriptions, village by village, of the four sanjaks into which Palestine was divided. Some of this material was used in articles which we have published elsewhere, and which are listed in the bibliography.

All this again is limited to one particular series of registers. There are many others, and notably the *sijill,* the records of the kadi's courts, in which a vast range of local public and private business is recorded, and the *mühimme,* the register of important affairs in Istanbul, parts of which were studied by Heyd. There are special series dealing with such matters as the status of the non-Muslim communities and the taxes paid by them, appointments, transfers, and promotions in the military organization, customs, supplies, and numerous others illustrating the manifold bureaucratic activities of a great empire.

Most of these still await the attention of scholars. It is to be hoped that in this study in depth of one series of documents on one aspect of the history of Palestine, we will have given to scholars and searchers some indication of what can be accomplished and of what remains to be done.

BIBLIOGRAPHY

UNPUBLISHED SOURCES

Istanbul, Office of the Prime Minister's Archives (Başbakanlık Arşivi)

Mufaṣṣal No. 427 of Sanjaks of Jerusalem, Safed and Gaza
Mufaṣṣal No. 1038 of Sanjaks of Safed and Nabulus
Mufaṣṣal No. 300 of Sanjak of Safed
Mufaṣṣal No. 1015 of Sanjaks of Gaza and Jerusalem
Mufaṣṣal No. 289 of Sanjak of Jerusalem
Mufaṣṣal No. 342 of Sanjak of Jerusalem
Icmāl No. 346 of Sanjak of Jerusalem
Mufaṣṣal No. 265 of Sanjak of Gaza
Mufaṣṣal No. 304 of Sanjak of Gaza
Mufaṣṣal No. 258 of Sanjak of Nabulus
Mufaṣṣal No. 17738 (*Maliyeden müdevver*) of Sanjak of Safed

Ankara, Tapu ve Kadastro müdürlüğü Archives

Mufaṣṣal No. 515 (178) of Sanjak of Jerusalem
Mufaṣṣal No. 516 (112) of Sanjak of Jerusalem
Mufaṣṣal No. 549 (100) of Sanjak of Nabulus
Mufaṣṣal No. 546 (192) of Sanjak of Gaza

Jerusalem S͟harʿī court (al-maḥkama al-s͟harʿiyya) Archives

Sijill volumes Nos. 1–83

Rome, Vatican Library

Manuscript No. 286 Vat. Arabo (an arabic description of the churches of Jerusalem)

London, British Museum

Celāl-zāde Muṣṭafā Çelebī, *Maʾāṣiri-i Selīm Ḫānī* Ms. Add. 7848.

BOOKS

Affagart, G. *Relation de Terre Sainte* (1533–1534) (Paris, 1902).
Anhegger, R. and Inalcık, H. *Ḳānūnnāme-i Sulṭāni ber mūcebi-i ᶜorf-i ᶜOsmānī* (Ankara, 1956).
Antreassian, A. *Jerusalem and the Armenians* (Jerusalem, 1969).
ᶜĀrif al-ᶜĀrif, *Taʾrikh Ghazza* (Jerusalem, 1943).
Aveiro, Fr. Pantaleão de. *Itinerario de Terra Sancta* (Coimbra, 1927).
Bakhīt, M. *The Ottoman Province of Damascus in the Sixteenth Century* (unpublished Ph.D. thesis, London, 1972).
Barghūt, ʿAbd al-Wadūd Muḥammad, *Liwāʾ Ḥamāt fi al-qarn al-sādis ᶜashar* (unpublished M. A. thesis, ᶜAyn Shams, 1970).
Barkan, Ö. L. *XV ve XVI inci asırlarda Osmanlı Imparatorluğunda zirai ekonominin hukukî ve malî esasları*, vol. I, *Kanunlar* (Istanbul, 1943).
Barthélemy, A. *Dictionnaire Arabe Français* (Paris, 1935).
Beldiceanu, N. *Les actes des premiers Sultans conservés dans les manuscrits turcs de la Bibliothèque Nationale à Paris* (Paris, 1960).
Ben Zvi, I. *Eretz Yisraʾel ve-yishūvah biyyemê ha-shilṭōn ha-ᶜOttomanī* (Palestine and Its [Jewish] Community in the Period of Ottoman Rule) (Jerusalem, 1953).
Braslavski, J. *LʾHeḳer Artzenu* (Studies in our Country, its past and remains) (Tel Aviv, 1954).
Braudel, F. *La méditerranée et le monde méditerranéen à l'époque de Philippe II* (Paris, 1966).
al-Bustānī, Buṭrus. *Muḥīṭ al-Muḥīṭ* (Beyrut, 1867–1870).
Cerulli, E. *Etiopi in Palestina* (Rome, 1943).
Cohen, A. *Palestine in the 18th Century—Patterns of Government and Administration* (Jerusalem, 1973).
Cohen, A. *Yehūde Yerūshalayim ba-meʾah ha-shesh ᶜesreh* (Ottoman Documents on the Jewish Community of Jerusalem in the Sixteenth Century) (Jerusalem, 1976).
Condor, C. R. and Kitchener, H. H., *The Survey of Palestine, Samaria,* vol. 2 (London, 1882).
Cook, M. A. *Population Pressure in Rural Anatolia, 1450–1600* (London, 1972).
Cvetkova, B. A. *Vie économique de villes et ports Balkaniques aux XVᵉ et XVIᵉ siècles* (Paris, 1971).
al-Dabbāgh, Muṣṭafā. *Bilādunā Filasṭīn* (Beirut, 1972).
al-Dahhān, Sāmī. *Taʾrikh Lubnān waʾal-Urdun wa-Filasṭīn* (Damascus, 1962).

Dalsar, F. *Türk Sanayi ve ticaret tarihinde Bursada ipekçilik* (Istanbul, 1960).
Dozy, R. *Supplément aux dictionnaires arabes* (Leiden, 1967).
Dudon, R. *St. Ignatius of Loyola* (Milwaukee, 1949).
Eisenstein, J. D. (ed.) *Ozar Massaoth: A Collection of Itineraries by Jewish Travellers to Palestine, Syria, Egypt and Other Countries* (in Hebrew) (New York, 1926).
The *Encyclopaedia of Islam*, rev. ed. (Leiden, 1960–).
Evliya Çelebi. *Seyāḥatnāme*, vol. IX (Istanbul, 1935).
Fekete, L. *Die Siyāqat-Schrift in der türkischen Finanzverwaltung* (Budapest, 1955).
Fekete, L. and Káldy-Nagy, Gy. *Rechnungsbücher türkischer Finanzstellen in Buda (Ofen) 1550–1580* (Budapest, 1962).
Ferīdūn Bey, Aḥmed. *Munshaʾāt al-Salāṭīn* (Istanbul, 1849).
Foster, W. (ed.) *The Travels of John Sanderson in the Levant, 1584–1602* (London, 1931).
Franco, M. *Essai sur l'histoire des Israelites de l'Empire Ottoman* (Paris, 1897).
Gaudefroy-Demombynes, M. *La Syrie à l'époque des Mamelouks* (Paris, 1923).
Gibb, H. A. R. *The Travels of Ibn Baṭṭūṭa*, vol. I (Cambridge, 1958).
Gibb, H. A. R. and Bowen, H. *Islamic Society and the West*, vol. I (London, 1950 and 1957).
Gökbilgin, M. T. *XV–XVI asırlarda Edirne ve Paşa livası* (Istanbul, 1952).
Göyünç, N. *XVI Yüzyılda Mardin Sancağı* (Istanbul, 1969).
Guérin, V. *La Terre Sainte* (Paris, 1884).
al-Ḥalabī, Ibrāhīm b. Muḥammad. *Multaḳā al-Abḥur* (Cairo, n.d.)
de Hammer, J. *Histoire de l'empire Ottoman*, vol. VI (Paris, 1836).
von Hammer, J. *Des Osmanischen Reichs Staatsverfassung und Staatsverwaltung* (Vienna, 1815).
Hault, N. de. *Le voyage de Hierusalem* (Paris, 1601).
Heyd, U. *Ottoman Documents on Palestine, 1552–1615* (Oxford, 1960).
———. (V. L. Ménage, ed.). *Studies in Old Ottoman Criminal Law* (Oxford, 1973).
Hinz, W. *Islamische Masse und Gewichte* (Leiden, 1955).
d'Ohsson, M. *Tableau général de l'Empire Ottoman* (Paris, 1824).
Ibn Iyās, Muḥammad ibn Aḥmad al-Ḥanafī, *Badāʾiʿ al-zuhūr fī waḳāʾiʿ al-duhūr*, vol. V (Istanbul, 1932).
Ibn Ṭūlūn, Shams al-Dīn Muḥammad. *Mufākahat al-khillān fī ḥawādith al-zamān*, vol. II (Cairo, 1964).

Inalcık, H. *Hicrî 835 tarihli sûret-i defter-i sancak-i Arvanid* (Ankara, 1954).
Ish-Shalōm, M. *Masʿe nōtzrīm le-Eretz Yisraʾel* (Christian Travels in the Holy Land) (Tel-Aviv, 1965).
Jaussen, J.-A. *Naplouse et son district* (Paris, 1927).
Jikyā, S. *Defter-i mufaṣṣal-i vilayet-i Gurjistan* (Tbilisi, 1947).
Kahane, H. R. and Tietze, A. *The Lingua Franca in the Levant* (Leiden, 1958).
al-Kalkashandī, Aḥmad Abūʾl-ʿAbbās. *Ṣubḥ al-Aʿshā* (Cairo, 1331/1913–1338/1920).
Kâtib Çelebi, also known as Ḥacci Ḫalīfe. *Cihān Nüma* (Istanbul, 1145).
Khitrowo, B. *Itinéraires Russes en Orient* (Geneva, 1889).
Lane, E. W. *An Arabic-English Lexicon* (London, 1867).
Lapidus, I. M. *Muslim Cities in the Later Middle Ages* (Cambridge, Mass., 1967).
Le Strange, G. *Palestine Under the Moslems* (London, 1890).
Lewis, B. *Notes and Documents from the Turkish Archives* (Jerusalem, 1952).
Luke, H. C. *Anatolica* (London, 1924).
———. *A Spanish Franciscan's Narrative of a Journey to the Holy Land* (London, 1927).
Luṭfī Paşa, *Āṣaf-nāme* ed. and trans. G. Jacob, Türkische Bibliothek (Berlin, 1910).
al-Maḳrīzī, Taḳī al-Dīn. *Kitāb al-mawāʿiẓ waʾl-iʿtibār bi-dhikr al-Khiṭaṭ waʾl-āthār* (Cairo, 1911).
Mantran, R. and Sauvaget, J. *Règlements fiscaux Ottomans, les provinces syriennes* (Beirut, 1951).
Marmardji, A. S. *Textes géographiques arabes sur la Palestine* (Paris, 1951).
Mayer, L. A. and Pinkerfeld, J. *Some Principal Muslim Religious Buildings in Israel* (Jerusalem, 1950).
Moore, E. A. *The Ancient Churches of Old Jerusalem* (Beirut, 1961).
Mujīr al-Dīn al-Ḥanbalī, *Al-Uns al-Jalīl bi-Taʾrīkh al-Ḳuds waʾl-Khalīl* (Cairo, 1283).
Nedkoff, B. S. *Die Ǧizya (Kopfsteuer) im Osmanischen Reich* (Leipzig, 1942).
al-Nimr, I. *Taʾrīkh Jabal Nābulūs waʾl-Balḳāʾ*, vol. II (Nabulus, 1961).
Nūrī, Muṣṭafā. *Netāʾic ül-Vuḳūʿāt* (Istanbul, 1877–9).
Nūrī, ʿOṣmān. *Mecelle-i umūr-i belediye* (Istanbul, 1922).
von Oppenheim, M. F. *Die Bedouinen* (Leipzig, 1943).

Pakalın, M. Z. *Osmanlı tarih deyimleri ve terimleri sözlüğü* (Istanbul, 1946–1955).

Papadopoullos, T. *Social and Historical Data on Population (1570–1881)*, (Cyprus Research Center, *Texts and Studies on History of Cyprus*, vol. I) (Nicosia, 1965).

Pīrī Reis, *Kitabi Baḥriye* (Istanbul, 1935).

Poliak, A. N. *Feudalism in Egypt, Syria, Palestine and the Lebanon, 1250–1900* (London, 1939).

Possot, L. *Le voyage de la Terre Sainte* (Paris, 1890).

Rabie, H. *The Financial System of Egypt A. H. 564–741/A.D. 1169–1341* (London, 1972).

Rāfiḳ, ᶜAbd al-Karīm. *Bilād al-S̲h̲ām wa-Miṣr min al-fatḥ al-ᶜUt̲h̲mānī ilā ḥamlat Nābulyūn Būnabart (1517–1798)* (Damascus, 1968).

———. *Al-ᶜArab waʾl-ᶜUt̲h̲māniyyūn 1516–1916* (Damascus, 1974).

Ray, J. *A Collection of Curious Travels and Voyages* (London, 1963).

Redhouse, J. W. *A Turkish and English Lexicon* (Constantinople, 1921).

Refik, Ahmed. *Hicri on birinci asırda Istanbul hayatı* (Istanbul, 1931).

S̲h̲ams al-Dīn Sāmī, *Ḳāmūs al-aᶜlām*, 6 vols. (Istanbul, 1306–1316).

Sanjian, A. K. *The Armenian Communities in Syria under Ottoman Dominion* (Cambridge, Mass., 1965).

Sauvaire, H. (tr.), *Histoire de Jérusalem et d'Hebron* (Paris, 1876).

Schefer, Ch. *Le voyage de la sainte cyté de Hierusalem* (Paris, 1882).

Shaw, S. J. *Financial and Administrative Organization and Development of Ottoman Egypt* (Princeton, 1958).

———. *Ottoman Egypt in the Age of the French Revolution* (Cambridge, Mass., 1964).

S̲h̲ūs̲h̲terī, Muḥammad ᶜAlī. *Farhang-i Važahā-i Fārisī dar zabān-i ᶜArabī* (Teheran, 1347s).

Strauss, E. (As̲h̲tōr). *Tōledōt̲h̲ ha-Yehūdīm be-Miṣrayyim ve-Sūriyā taḥat s̲h̲ilṭōn ha-Mamlūkīm* (History of the Jews in Egypt and Syria under the Rule of the Mamluks) (Jerusalem, 1970).

Tritton, A. S. *Materials on Muslim Education in the Middle Ages* (London, 1957).

Tveritinova, A. *Agrarny stroy Osmanskoy imperii XV–VII & VV: dokumenty i materialy* (Moscow, 1963).

Tunçer, H. *Osmanlı Imparatorluğunda toprak hukuku, arazi kanunları ve kanun açıklamaları* (Ankara, 1962).

Uzunçarşılı, I. H. *Osmanlı devletinin merkez ve bahriye teşkilatı* (Ankara, 1948).

Vefīḳ Bey, ᶜAbd al-Raḥmān. *Tekālif ḳavāᶜidi* (Istanbul, 1328).

Wilson, C. W. *Ordnance Survey of Jerusalem*, 1864–5 (Great

Britain Ordnance Survey, London 1865).
Wright, W. L. *Ottoman Statecraft* (London, 1935).
Yaʿarī, A. (ed.), *Massaʿōt Eretz Yisraʾel* (Travels in Palestine by Jewish Travellers) (Jerusalem, 1946).
———. *Iggerōt Eretz Yisraʾel* (Letters from the Land of Israel) (Givʿatayim, 1971).
Zuallart, J. *Le très dévot voyage de Jerusalem* (Antwerp, 1608).

ARTICLES

Ashtōr, E. "Yerushalayim biyyemê ha-beynayyim ha-meʾukharim" (Jerusalem in the Late Middle Ages). *Yerushalayim*, vol. II (1955), pp. 71–116.
———. "L'administration urbaine en Syrie médiévale." *Rivista degli Studi Orientali*, vol. XXXI (1956) pp. 73–128; vol. XXXIII–XXXIV (1958–9), pp. 181–209.
Avītzūr, S. "Tzefat—merkaz le-arīgê tzemer ba-meʾah ha-ṭêt vāv." (Safed—Center of the Manufacture of Woven Woolens in the Fifteenth Century), in I. Ben Zvi and M. Benayahu (eds.), *Studies and Texts on the History of the Jewish Community in Safed, Sefunot*, vol. VI (Jerusalem, 1962), pp. 43–59.
Ayalon, D. "The Wafidiya in the Mamluk Kingdom." *Islamic Culture*, vol. XXV (1951), pp. 89–104.
———. "Studies on the Structure of the Mamluk Army." *Bulletin of the School of Oriental and African Studies (BSOAS)*, vol. XV (1953), pp. 203–28, 448–76.
Barkan, Ömer Lutfi. "Türkiyede Imparatorluk devirlerinin büyük nüfus ve arazi tahrirleri ve Hâkana mahsus istatistik defterleri." *Istanbul Üniversitesi, Iktisat Fakültesi Mecmuası* (IFM) (1941), vol. II, pp. 1–40, 20–38, 214–28, 242–47.
———. "Tarihi Demografi" araştırmaları ve Osmanlı tarihi." *Türkiyat Mecmuası*, vol. X (Istanbul, 1953), pp. 1–26.
———. "Quelques observations sur l'organisation économique et sociale des villes ottomanes des XVᵉ et XVIIᵉ siècles," in *Recueils de la société Jean Bodin, La Ville* (Brussels, 1955), pp. 289–311.
———. "Essai sur les données statistiques des régistres de recensement dans l'empire Ottoman aux XVᵉ et XVIᵉ siècles." *Journal of Economic and Social History of the Orient (JEHSO)* vol. I (Leiden, 1958), pp. 9–36.
———. "894 (1488/1489) yılı cizyesinin tahsilâtına ait muhasebe bilançoları." *Belgeler*, vol. I (1964), pp. 1–117.
———. "The Social Consequences of Economic Crisis in later

Sixteenth Century Turkey." *Social Aspects of Economic Developments* (Istanbul, 1964), pp. 17–36.

———. "XVI asrın ikinci yarısında Türkiyede fiyat hareketleri." *Belleten,* vol. XXXIV (Ankara, 1970), pp. 557–607.

———. "The Price Revolution of the Sixteenth Century: A Turning Point in the Economic History of the Near East." *International Journal of Middle East Studies,* vol. VI (1975), pp. 3–28.

Beckingham, C. F. "Pantaleão de Aveiro and the Ethiopian Community in Jerusalem." *Journal of Semitic Studies,* vol. VII (1962), pp. 325–338.

Beldiceanu, N. and Beldiceanu-Steinherr, "Recherches sur la province de Qaraman au XVIe siècle." *JESHO,* vol. XI (1968), pp. 1–29.

Bosworth, C. E. "Abū ʿAbdallāh al-Khwārazmī on the Technical Terms of the Secretary's Art." *JESHO,* vol. XII (1969), pp. 113–164.

Çağatay, Neşʾet. "Osmanlı Imparatorluğunda reayadan alınan vergi ve resimler." *Ankara Üniversitesi Dil ve tarih-coğrafya fakültesi dergisi,* vol. V (1947), pp. 483–511.

Canard, M. "La destruction de l'Eglise de la Résurrection par le calife Hakim." *Byzantion,* vol. XXXV (1965), pp. 16–43.

Cvetkova, B. "Recherches sur le système d'affermage (*iltizām*) dans l'empire Ottoman au cours du XVIe–XVIIIes. par rapport aux contrées Bulgares." *Rocznik Orientalistyczny,* T. XXVII (1959), pp. 111–32.

———. "L'évolution du régime féodal turc de la fin du XVIe siécle jusqu'au milieu du XVIIIe siécle." *Etudes historiques,* vol. I (1960), pp. 171–206.

Fekete, L. "Türk vergi tahrirleri." *Belleten,* vol. XI (1947), pp. 299–328.

Ghālib, Muḥammad. "Iḥtisāb Ağālığı," in *Tārīh-i ʿOṣmānī Encümeni Mecmuası,* vol. II (Istanbul, 1327), pp. 569–84, 640–8.

Gökbilgin, M. Tayyib. "Kanuni Sultan Süleyman devri başlarında Rumeli eyaleti, livaları, şehir ve kasabaları." *Belleten,* vol. XX (1956), pp. 247–94.

———. "XVI Yüzyil başlarında Trabzon livası ve doğu Karadeniz bölgesi." *Belleten,* vol. XXVI (1962), pp. 293–337.

Golvin, L. "Quelques notes sur le sūq al-Qaṭṭānīn et ses annexes à Jérusalem." *Bulletin d'études orientales,* tom. XX (1967), pp. pp. 101–17.

Halasi Kun, T. "Avrupadaki Osmanlı yer adlari üzerinde Araştırmalar." *Türk Dili ve Tarihi hakkında Araştırmalar* (1952), pp. 63–104.

———. "Sixteenth Century Turkish Settlements in Southern Hungary." *Belleten*, vol. XXVIII (1964), pp. 1–72.

Hamilton, J. and Beldiceanu, N. "Recherches autour de *Qars*, nom d'une étoffe de poil." *BSOAS*, vol. XXXI (1968) pp. 303–46.

Heyd, U. "Yehūdê Eretz-Yisraᵓel be-sôf ha-meᵓah ha-yôd zayin" (The Jews of Palestine at the End of the Seventeenth Century). *Yerushalayim*, vol. IV (1952), pp. 173–84.

———. "A Turkish Description of the Coast of Palestine in the Early Sixteenth Century." *Israel Exploration Journal*, vol. VI (1956), pp. 201–16.

Hoexter, M. "The Role of the Qays and Yaman Factions in Local Political Division." *Asian and African Studies*, vol. IX (1974), pp. 249–311.

Inalcık, H. Osmanlı Imparatorluğunun Kuruluş ve inkişafi devrinde Türkiyenin iktisadi vaziyeti." *Belleten*, vol. XV (1951), pp. 629–84.

———. "Osmanlılarda Raiyyet rüsumu." *Belleten*, vol. XXIII (1959) pp. 575–610.

———. "Adaletnameler." *Belgeler*, vol. II (1967), pp. 49–142.

———. "The Heyday and Decline of the Ottoman Empire," in *The Cambridge History of Islam*, vol. I (Cambridge, 1970), pp. 324–53.

Issawi, C. "Comment on Professor Barkan's Estimate of the Population of the Ottoman Empire in 1520–30." *JESHO*, vol. I (1957–8), pp. 329–31.

Kaldy-Nagy, J. "Two Sultanic *Hāṣṣ* Estates in Hungary during the XVIth and XVIIth Centuries." *Acta Orientalia Academiae Scientiarum Hungaricae*, vol. XIII (1961), pp. 31–62.

———. "Names of Merchandise in a Mediterranean Turkish Customs Register." *Acta Orientalia Academiae Scientiarum Hungaricae*, vol. XVIII (1965), pp. 299–304.

———. "The Administration of the *Sanjāq* Registration in Hungary." *Acta Orientalia Academiae Scientiarum Hungaricae*, vol. XXI (1968), pp. 181–223.

Ḳānūnnāme-i Āl-i ᶜOṣmān, in *Tārīh-i ᶜOṣmānī Encümeni mecmuası ilavesi* (supplement) (Istanbul, 1330), pp. 1–72.

Kenaᶜanī, Y. "Ha-ḥayyim ha-kalkaliyyim bi-Tsfat uvisevivoteha ba-meᵓah ha-shesh ᶜesrêh va-ḥatsi ha-meᵓah ha-shevaᶜ ᶜesrêh" (Economic Life in Safed and its Environment in the Sixteenth and First Half of the Seventeenth Centuries). *Zion*, vol. VI (1934), pp. 172–217.

Lapidus, I. M. "Muslim Urban Society in Mamluk Syria," in Hourani, A. H. and Stern, S. M. (eds.), *The Islamic City, A Colloquium* (Oxford, 1970), pp. 195–205.

Lemerle, P. and Wittek, P. "Recherches sur l'histoire et le status des monastères athonites sous la domination turque." *Archives d'histoire du droit oriental,* vol. III (1948), pp. 411–72.
Lewis, B. "The Ottoman Archives as a Source for the History of the Arab Lands." *Journal of the Royal Asiatic Society (JRAS),* (1951), pp. 139–55.
———. "An Arabic Account of the Province of Safed." *BSOAS,* vol. XV (1953), pp. 477–88.
———. "Studies in the Ottoman Archives—I." *BSOAS,* vol. XVI (1954), pp. 469–501.
———. "ʿArê Eretz Yisraʾel ba-meʾah ha-ṭet zayin ʿal-pī teʿūdōt me-ha-arkiyyōn ha-ʿothmānī." *Yerūshalayim* (Jerusalem) vol. II/5 (1956), pp. 117–27.
———. "Registers on Iran and Adharbayjan in the Ottoman Defter-i Khaqani," in *Mélanges Massé* (Teheran, 1963), pp. 259–63.
———. "Nazareth in the Sixteenth Century, according to the Ottoman *Tapu* Registers," in George Makdisi (ed.), *Arabic & Islamic Studies in Honor of Hamilton A. R. Gibb* (Leiden, 1965), pp. 416–25.
———. "Jaffa in the Sixteenth Century, according to the Ottoman *Taḥrīr* Registers," in *Necati Lugal Armağanı* (1968), pp. 435–46.
Mandaville, J. E. "The Ottoman Court Records of Syria and Jordan." *Journal of the American Oriental Society,* vol. 86, pp. 311–19.
Mantran, R. "Règlements fiscaux ottomans. La province de Bassora." *JESHO,* vol. X (Leiden, 1967), pp. 224–77.
Mayer, L. A. "Arabic Inscriptions of Gaza." *Journal of the Palestine Oriental Society,* vol. XI (1931), pp. 144–51.
McGowan, B. "Food Supply and Taxation on the Middle Danube (1568–1579)." *Archivum Ottomanicum,* vol. I (1969), pp. 138–96.
Ménage, V. L. Review of G. Clauson, "An Etymological Dictionary of Pre-thirteenth-Century Turkish." *BSOAS,* vol. XXXVI (1973), pp. 658–9.
Miquel, A. "Jérusalem Arabe." *Bulletin d'études Orientales,* tom. XVI (1961), pp. 7–13.
Peradze, G. "An Account of the Georgian Monks and Monastaries in Palestine." *Georgica,* nos. 4–5 (London, 1937), pp. 181–246.
Perényi, J. "Villes Hongroises sous la domination Ottomane aux XVIᵉ–XVIIᵉs., les chefs-lieux de l'administration Ottomane," in N. Todorov (ed.), *Studia Balcanica, III, La Ville Balkanique XVᵉ–XIXᵉ* ss. (Sofia, 1970), pp. 25–31.
Qip'shidze, D. A. "Zhitie Prokhora, much. Luki i much. Nikolaya

Dvali." *Izvestiya Kavkazskogo Istoriko-Arkheologicheskogo Instituta.* tom. II (Leningrad, 1927), pp. 31–68.

ᶜAbdul-Karim Rafeq, "Les registres des tribunaux de Damas comme source pour l'histoire de la Syrie." *Bulletin d'études Orientales,* tom. XXVI (1973), pp. 219–26.

Russel, J. C. "Late Medieval Balkan and Asia Minor Population." *JESHO,* vol. III (1960), pp. 265–74.

Sauvaget, J. "Décrets Mamelouks de Syrie." *Bulletin d'études Orientales,* tom. II (1931), pp. 1–52; tom. XII (1948), pp. 1–60.

Schechter, S. "Safed in the Sixteenth Century," in *Studies in Judaism,* vol. II (Philadelphia, 1908), pp. 202–85.

Stoianovich, T. "Model and Mirror of the Premodern Balkan City," in N. Todorov (ed.), *Studia Balcanica, III, La Ville Balkanique XVᵉ–XIXᵉ ss.* (Sofia, 1970), pp. 83–110.

Sümer, F. "XVI asırda Anadolu, Suriye ve Irakta yaşayan türk aşterlerine umumi bir bakış." *Istanbul Üniversitesi, Iktisat Fakültesi Mecmuası,* vol. II (Istanbul, 1950), pp. 509–23.

———. "Osmanlı devrinde Anadoluda yaşayan bazı Üçoklu Oğuz boylarına mensup teşekküller." *Istanbul Üniversitesi Iktisat Fakültesi Mecmuası,* vol. II (Istanbul, 1950), pp. 437–508.

———. "Döğerlere dair." *Türkiyat mecmuası,* vol. X (Istanbul, 1953), pp. 139–58.

Suriano, Francesco. *Treatise on the Holy Land* (Jerusalem, 1949).

Togan, Z. V. "Bas͟hdjirt," *EI*², vol. 1, pp. 1075–77.

Wansbrough, J. "Africa and the Arab Geographers," in D. Dalby (ed.), *Language and History in Africa* (London, 1970), pp. 89–101.

Yūsuf, ᶜAbd al-Wadūd Muḥammad. "Ṭawāʾif al-ḥiraf waʾl-ṣināᶜāt aw ṭawāʾif al-aṣnāf fī Ḥamā fiʾl-ḳarn al-sādis ᶜas͟har." *Majallat al-ḥawliyyāt al-at͟hariyya,* vol. XIX (1969), pp. 85–102.

APPENDIX

Text of Revenues of the City of Jerusalem, 961/1553–4
(Register 289, pp. 45–6)

محصولات نفس قدس شريف

محصول
رسم دار القمامة در قدس شريف
وقف حضرة پادشاه عالم پناه خلد الله
ملكه على قراء الاجزاء في صخرة
الشريف
في سنة
١٢٠٠٠٠

محصول
رسم كيالية المغل هر دوه يوكندن بر
عثماني وقاتر يوكندن ومركب يوكندن
بچقر عثماني النور رسم كياليه وقف
صخرة الله بر موجب حكم شريف
في سنه
٨٠٠٠

محصول
رسم قبان در خان الوكاله ودار
الخضر در نفس قدس شريف وقف
صخرة الله تماما
في سنه
١٢٢٠٠

محصول
دكاكين در نفس قدس شريف وقف
صخرة الله

خراب	المعمور
باب	باب
١٤٧	٢٠٣

في سنه
١٣٦٣٧

محصول
مخازن دقاقين در نفس قدس شريف
وقف صخرة الله در محلهء يهود تماما
في سنه
٦٠٠

محصول
مغل در قرب حرم شريف وقف صخرة
الله تماما
في سنه
٧٢٠

محصول
عن طائفهء افرنج كه بدار القمامه آيند بر موجب عادت قديمه بجهه وقف صخره الله
بهر نفر في ٥٠
في سنه
٣٠٠٠

محصول
رسم احمال صابون كه از نفس قدس شريف بمصر ميروند وقف صخره الله وخليل الرحمن تماما
بهر حمل سير
في ١٦ عثماني
في سنه
١١٠٥٦
منها
حصه وقف صخره الله — حصه وقف حضرت خليل الرحمن عليه السلام
ثلث ٣٦٨٥ — ثلثان ٧٣٧٠

محصول
حمام القدس در نفس قدس شريف المشهور بحمام العمود وقف صخرة الله تماما
في سنه
٣٤٧

محصول
طاحون در نفس قدس شريف در محلهء يهود وقف صخره الله تماما
في سنه
٤٨٠

محصول
مخلفات طائفهء مجاورين حرم شريف وقف صخره الله بر موجب حكم شريف تماما
في سنه
٥٠٠
١٦٠٠٠

محصول
احكار در نفس قدس شريف وقف صخره الله تماما
باب ١١
في سنه
٤٠٠

محصول
حمام العين در نفس قدس شريف در باب قطانين وقف صخره الله
حصه وقف صخره الله ١٢ ط — حصه وقف دكيزيه ١٢ ط
في سنه ٨٠٠٠ — في سنه ٨٠٠٠

محصول
جزيهء كبران وسريانيان وقبطيان ويهوديان در قدس شريف غير از نصاراء بيت لحم وبيت جالا كه در نفس قدس شريف متمكنند
نفرا
٧٩١
بهر نفر في ٨٠ مبلغ ٦٣٢٨٠
منها
حصه صخره الله بر وجه مقطوع
نفرا
١٤٢

تتمهء
وقف صخره الله

عن جماعت
يهوديان در نفس
قدس مقطوع نفرا ٨٥
بهر نفر في ٨٠
مبلغ
٦٨٠٠

عن جماعت
ارمنيان در نفس
قدس مقطوع
نفرا ١٥ في ٨٠
مبلغ
١٢٠٠

عن جماعت
نصاراء روم
ملكيه در نفس قدس
مقطوع نفرا ١٥
في ٨٠
مبلغ
١٢٠٠

عن جماعت
قبطيان در نفس
قدس مقطوع
نفرا ١٠ في ٨٠
مبلغ
٨٠٠

عن جماعت
نصاراء ريما
در نفس مزبور نفرا ١٣
في ٨٠
مبلغ
١٠٤٠

عن جماعت
نصاراء خليليين
در نفس مزبور نفرا ٤
بهر نفر ٨٠
مبلغ
٣٢٠

الباقي
غيراز حصهء وقف صخره الله شريف
خاص شاهى
نفرا
٦٤٩
بهر نفر في ٨٠
مبلغ
٥١٩٢٠

محصول
بيت المال ومال غائب ومال مفقود كه
اون بيكدن زياده اوله مع بيت المال
سپاهيان ومستحفظان وغلمان
پادشاهى عالم پناه وعبد وجوارى
سپاهيان وغلمان پادشاهى
ومستحفظان غير از يوه واوابق
تيمارهاء سربست واوقاف حرمين
وصخره الله وحضرت خليل الرحمن
في سنه خاص
١٥٠٠٠

محصول
قبان القطن في سوق القطانين هر دوه
يوكندن رسم قبان بر پاره النور اما
ات وقاتر ومركب يوكندن تمام پاره
النميوب دوه يوكنه بر پاره اولمق
حسابى اوزرنه النور
في سنه خاص
١٥٠٠

محصول
حمر كه بيلده بر دفعه درياى لوطدن
چيقوب كناره دكولور شمديه دكين
خارجدن ضبط اولنور ايمش
خاص خارج از دفتر
في سنه
١٠٠٠٠

المعصرات
در نفس مدينهء قدس شريف
باب
١٥
خارج
حصل خاص
٩٣٠

محصول
باج بازار سیاه که تفصیلی قانون
نامه ده یازلمشدر خاص میرلوا
في سنه
۲۰۰۰

محصول
باج بازار اسب وجمل وبغل وحمار
وبقر که دوه صاتندن اون اقچه وات
قاتر صاتندن دردر اقچـــه ومرکب
وصغر صاتندن اکی شر اقچه النور
وقیون وکجی صاتندن اوچنه بر اقچه
النور خاص میرلوا
في سنه
۲۰۰۰

محصول
رسم قبان زیت هر ظرفنه بر اقچـــه
رسم النور اما ظرف بیوك اولوب
درد ظرفی بر دوه یوکی اولدغـــی
تقدیرجه ظرف کوچك اولیجاق بر دوه
یوکنه درد اقچه النمق اوزره حساب
اولنوب رسم النه خاص میر لوا
في سنه
۵۰۰۰

محصول
بیت المال ومال غائب ومال مفقود
ویوه وقاچقون قول وجاریه ودواب
قسمندن اولا در نفس قدس شریف
وخلیل الرحمن اون بیکدن وارنجـــه
اوله غیر از حصهء اوابق تیمارهاء
سربست واوقاف حرمین وصخره الله
وخلیل الرحمن وغیر از مجاوران حرم
شریف
خاص میرلوا
في سنه
۱۲۰۰۰

محصول
احتساب نفس قدس شریف کـــــه
تفصیلی قانون نامهده مقید در کلیا
موزونات احتسابه
راجعدر خاص میرلوا
في سنه
۲۳۰۰۰

محصول
رسم عســـان ومحبس عسسیه دیو
هر دکاندن که مغفل اولا اندن بر اقچه
النور وحبس اولان کمسنه دن اطلاق
اولدغی محلده اکثر
پاره النور خاص میرلوا
في سنه
۲۰۰۰

محصول
قصابان نفس قدس شریف اکی قیونه
واکی کجیه بر اقچه النور وجاموســه
اکی پاره قره صغره بر پاره النـــور
بوغازلندغی تقدیرجه خاص میرلوا
في سنه
۳۰۰۰

محصول
باد هوا ورسم عروسانهء قـــدس
شریف وخلیل الرحمن مع نصف نیابت
ورسم عروسانهء ناحیهء قدس شریف
وخلیل الرحمن
غیر از سربستها خاص میرلوا
في سنه
۳۳۰۰۰

محصول
رسم اغنام نفس قدس شريف اكـــى
قيونه بر اقچه النور وسوريه بر پاره
قوزنيك داخى اكسنه بر اقچه النور
خاص ميرلوا
في سنه
٥٠٠

محصول
حمام في باب الاسباط في قدس شري
وقف صلاح الدين يوسف بن ايو
على مدرسته بالقدس الشريف تما
في سنه
١٤٠٠٠

اسواق
الشرقي والغربي وقف خانقاه
حمديه دكاكين
باب
٦ معمور خراب
١ ٥
في سنه
١٠٠

INDEX*

Acre, 12, 30, 67, 167, 168.
ʿādet-i ağnām waʾl-miʿze, 103, 129, *see also: resm-i aghnām*.
ʿādet-i bāc-i rāh-i Mişr, 55, 129. *See also: bāc-i rāh*
ʿādet-i deştbāni, 67, 144.
ʿādet-i ḳaşşābān, 114.
ʿādet-i ḳishlāḳ, 66.
ʿādet-i rusūm-i ḳishlāḳ, 169.
ʿādet-i ʿurbāniye, 133, 134 n. 58.
Affagart, G., 59 n. 42, 107 n. 1, 117 n. 1.
aghnām, see: sheep.
agriculture, 64–65.
aḥkār (sing. *ḥikr*), 97, 104, 113, 163.
Aḥmad ibn kātib al-Wilāya, 117 n.3.
Aḥmed III, 5.
Ahmet Rasim, 5 n. 16.
ʿAjlūn, 4 n. 8, 157 n. 16.
al-ʿAḳaba (quarter in Hebron), 108, 109, 111.
ʿAḳaba (quarter in Nabulus), 145, 147 n. 6, 148, 149, 153.
ʿAkabat al-Sitt (quarter in Jerusalem), 81, 82 n. 7, 84, 85, 89, 91, 92.
akçe, see · asper.
Akrād (quarter in Gaza), *see*: Shajjāʿiyyat al-Akrād.
Akrād (quarter in Safed), 155, 157, 159, 161.
Akrād Ḳaysī (quarter in Hebron), 108, 109, 110, 111.
ʿAlam(quarter in Jerusalem), *see*: al-Sharaf.
ʿAlam al-Dārī al-Anṣārī, waqf of (in Hebron), 115.
ʿAlam al-Dīn Sulaymān, 82 n. 8.
Alay Bey, ziʿāmet of, 60.
Aleppo, 20, 21, 26.
animals, 53–54, 58, 73, 95, 100, 129, 142, 143, 150, 165, 169.
Ankara, Cadastral Office, 4.
Antreassian, A., 84 n. 20.
Appanage of the governor, *see*: *Ḫāṣṣ-i Mīr-i Livāʾ*.
ʿĀrif al-ʿĀrif, 117 n. 2, n. 3, n. 4, 119 n. 7, 132 n. 47.
ʿArif al-ḥāra, 38.
ʿarūs resmi, see: resm-i ʿarūsāne.
ʿasesān, 69. *See also resm-i ʿasesan, ser-ı ʿasesān*.
Ashtōr (Strauss), E., 38 n. 56, 40 n. 62, 70 n. 80, 87 n. 34.
aşl, 8.
asper (akçe, akçe-i ʿosmāni), 11 n. 40, 28, 43, 44, 71, 72, 73, 95, 100, 101, 103, 109, 125, 129, 141, 142, 151, 163, 164, 165, 166.
asses (*ḥamīr*), 51 n. 22, 53, 95, 100, 129, 142, 143, 150, 165, 166, 167.
ʿavārizḫāne, 70.
Aveiro, Fr. Pantaleão de., 59 n. 42, 83 n. 15, 145 n. 1, 155 n. 1.
Avitzur, S., 60 n. 47, 61 n. 48.
awlād al-nās, 18.
Ayalon, D., 18 n. 62, 34 n. 46.
Aʿyān, 38 and passim.
Ayyūbiye, community of, 85, 89, 91.

Bāb al-ʿAmūd (quarter in Jerusalem), 18, 81 n. 3, 82, 83, 85, 89, 91, 92.
Bāb al-Asbāt (quarter in Jerusalem), 82 n. 11, 95 n. 53, 102, 103.
Bāb al-Ḥiṭṭa (quarter in Jerusalem), 39, 81, 84, 85, 89, 91, 92, 93.
Bāb al-Kaṭṭānīn (quarter in Jerusalem), 81, 83, 85, 89, 91, 92, 97.
bāc-i aghfār, 165, 167. *See also: ğafare*.
bāc-i bahār-i ḥacc-i şerīf, 55, 129.
bāc-i bāzār, 114.
bāc-i bāzār-i esārā, 164.
bāc-i bāzār-i ğille, 141, 142.
bāc-i bāzār siyāh, 60 n. 44, 62, 100, 101 n. 72, 113, 143.

*prepared by Irıt Blay

bāc-i dirin, 55 n. 33, 129.
bāc al-ġilāl, 150.
bāc al-ḳumāş, 62, 150.
bāc al-naṣārā wa-l-yahūd, 151.
bāc-i rāh, 55, 56, 142. *See also*: *ʿādet-i bāc-i rāh-i Miṣr*.
bāc-ı zeyt, 143. *See also*: *resm-i kapan-i zeyt*.
bād-i havā, 73, 74, 75, 102, 116, 131, 142, 152, 169.
bağçe or *bustān*, *see*. orchards.
Baḥr Kadas (Hūle), 67, 167.
baḳar, *see* · cattle.
Bakhīt, M., 20, 50 n. 21, 132 n. 56.
Banī ʿAṭāʾ, bedouins of, 17, 133, 134 n. 59.
Banū ʿAṭiyya, bedouins of, 17, 133.
Banī Dāʾud, bedouins of, 16a.
Banī Ḥamīda, bedouins of, 152.
Banī Ḥārith (quarter ın Jerusalem), 36, 40, 81, 83, 92.
Banī Haytham and Malāliḥa, bedouins of, 17, 133.
Banī Jallās and ʿAnza, bedouins of, 169
Banī Jürüm b. Thaʿlaba, bedouins of, (or Cürüm), 133, 134 n. 62.
Banī Kurāyna, clan of, 152.
Banī Naʿīm, bedouins of, 152.
Banī Naʿja, bedouins of, 152.
Banī Saʿd (quarter in Jerusalem), 81 n. 3
Banū Sawālima, bedouins of, 17, 133.
Banī Shākir, bedouins of, 152, 169.
Banī Zayd (quarter in Jerusalem), 18, 36, 40, 82, 84, 92.
Bar Yohay, tomb of, 30.
Barghūt, ʿAbd al-Wadūd Muhammad, *Liwāʾ Hamāt fi al-qarn al-sādıs ʿashar* 39 n. 57, 55 n. 31, 60 n. 47, 132 n 56.
Barkan, O. L., 3 n. 3, 5–6, 7, 10, 11 n. 37, n. 38, 14 n. 48, 15 n. 49, 18 n. 60, 19, 20, 21, 22, 24 n. 15, 26, 27 n. 24, n. 25, 44 n. 2, 47 n. 14, 62 n. 52, 72 n. 85, 95 n. 54, 101 n. 72, 103 n. 78, 130 n. 38, n. 40, n. 45, 142 n. 18, n. 19, 144 n. 27, 150 n. 14, n. 15, 151 n. 17.
Barthélemy, A., 142 n. 16, 150 n. 14, 167 n. 50.
Bāshkardī (quarter in Ramle), 34, 135, 137, 138, 139, 140.
bathhouse, *see*. *ḥammām*.
baṭmān, 143, 144 n. 21, n. 23.
bawwāb, 15 and passım.
Baybars, 135 n. 4.
Bayt Jālā, 32, 86, 90, 93, 98.
Bayt Jibrīn, 32, 119 n. 13.
bayt al-māl, 73, 74, 99, 116, 129, 142, 144, 153, 158 n. 19, 163 n. 32, 165.
Bayt Rīmā, 32, 33, 89, 93, 98, 120 n. 14, 121 n. 19, 138, 139, 140.
bāzār-i esb, 100.
bāzār-ı esārā, 59.
Beckingham, C. F., 83 n. 15, 86 n. 31.
bedouins (nomads), 17–18, 23, 24, 35, 36, 66, 81 n. 3, 82, n. 11, 109 n 3, 152, 157 n. 16, 169.
See also · *ʿādet-i ʿurbāniye*.
bees, 66, 112, 143, 152.
Beldiceanu, N., 15 n. 49, 47 n. 10, 56 n. 34, 60 n. 45, 66 n. 67, 67 n. 69, 70 n. 78, 75 n. 91, 101 n. 72, 103 n. 78, 114 n. 26, 144 n. 27, 162 n. 24 , n. 29.
Beldiceanu-Steinherr, 15 n. 49.
Ben Zvı, I., 109 n. 12, 120 n. 15, 147 n. 8.
Berber tribes, 119 n. 6.
Bethlehem or Bayt Laḥm, 12, 32, 86, 90, 93, 98, 121 n. 18.
Bikāʿ, bedouıns of, 17, 66.
Bīmāristān of Gaza, waqf of, 133
bitumen (al-Kafr al-Yahūdī or *ḥummar*), 59, 100.
Bosworth, C. E., 8 n. 33.
Bowen, H., 122 n. 21.
Braslavski, J., 28 n. 37, 120 n. 15.
Braudel, F., 22, 26, 27 n 29, 28 n. 35, 56 n. 37.
bride *see*: *resm-i ʿarūsāne*
Burjulıyya (quarter ın Gaza), 117, 120, 122, 124, 125, 127.
al-Bustānī, B. *Muḥiṭ al-Muḥiṭ*, 130 n. 46.

Çağatay, Neşʾet, 17 n. 59, 70 n. 78.
Cahen, Cl., 138 n. 11.
Cairo, 13, 33, 56, 59, 121, 123, 128.
camels, 53, 54, 58, 100, 129, 142, 165, 166, 167.

Canard, M., 87 n. 33.
cattle (*bakar*), 51 n 22, 53, 57, 58, 67, 73, 129.
Cave of Machpela, 73.
cebeciyān, 167.
Cerulli, E., 86 n. 31.
Christians, 11 n. 40, 14, 15 n. 51, 16, 22, 30–31, 32, 33, 36, 68, 71, 72, 81 n. 3, 82 n. 7, 83, 84, 87–91, 93, 94, 95 n. 54, 98, 109, 111, 119, 121, 123, 125, 126, 128, 133, 137, 138, 139, 140, 143, 145 n. 4, 147, 148, 149, 150 n. 15, 151, 165, 166, 169.
  Armenians, 14, 81 n. 4, 84 n. 20, 86, 90, 93, 98.
  Copts, 14, 84, 85, 90, 93, 98, 120, 121. 123, 128.
  Ethiopian Christians, 86, 91.
  Frankish Christians, 83, 87, 88, 90, 96.
  Georgian Christians, 88, 90.
  Greek Christians (Rūmīyan), 14, 86 n 31, 87, 88 n 38, 90, 119 n. 9.
  Jacobite Christians, 83, 93.
  Latin Christians, 14.
  Maronite Christians, 89 n. 47.
  Melkite Christians, 83, 84, 85, 89, 90, 91, 93, 98.
  Syrian (Suryān) Christians, 83, 84, 85, 90, 93, 98
çift resmi velevāḥiki, 75 n. 91
cloth (*ḳumāş*), 59–62, 164. *See also*. *ḳarziye, çoka, daḳḳākin-i kumāş, bāc al-ḳumāş*.
Cohen, A., 7 n. 7, 17, 57, 30 n. 39, 44 n. 3, 70 n. 77, 73 n. 88, 162 n. 24.
çoka (*čoḫa*), 60, 164, 168.
convents:
  Dayr ʿAmūd (Jerusalem), 88 n. 36, 90.
  Dayr Andreas (Jerusalem), 84, 86, 90.
  Dayr (Ḥiẓr (Jerusalem), 87.
  Dayr Kumāma (Jerusalem), 87, 90.
  Dayr Lahm (Jerusalem), 88, 90
  Dayr Mār Eliās (Jerusalem), 91.
  Dayr Mār Yaʿḳūb(Jerusalem), 84, 86, 90
  Dayr Mayda (?) (Jerusalem), 91.
  Dayr Minda (Jerusalem), 86.
  Dayr Muṣallaba (the Monastery of the Cross) (Jerusalem), 88, 90.
  Dayr Sahyūn (Jerusalem), 87.
  Dayr Sīk or Mār Sāba (Jerusalem), 87, 90.
  Dayr Sirb (of the Serbs) (Jerusalem), 87.
  Dayr Zaytūn (Jerusalem), 83, 86, 90.
Condor, C. R., 137 n. 4.
Cook, M. A., 7, 15 n. 50.
Copts *see*: Christians.
cotton, 51 n. 22, 54, 100. *See also*: *kapan-i ḳuṭn, mizān-i ḳuṭn, mizān-i ğazl ve-ḳuṭn*.
Crusaders, 119 n. 8.
curm-i cināyet, 131, 142, 169.
Cvetkova, B., 44 n. 2, 47 n. 10, 56 n. 34, 67 n. 70, 130 n. 39, 142 n. 17, 162 n. 24.

Dabbāgh, M., 119 n. 8.
Dabbāgha (quarter in Gaza), 37, 117 n. 4, 127.
al-Dahhān, S., 145 n. 1.
daḳḳākin-i ḳumāş, 61, 150
Dalsar, F., 101 n. 72, 130 n. 45.
al-Dabbūra (quarter in Nabulus), 145.
Damascus, 9, 10, 11, 20, 21, 22, 39, 57, 58, 59.
Damascus, sanjak of, 26.
dār al-ḥabs, 131
dār al-ḥashīsh, 132 n. 56.
Dār al-Khuḍar, 37, 38, 47 n. 11, 52, 95, 112, 141 (or *sūk al-Khudar*).
Dār al-Khudar (quarter in Gaza), 117, 120, 122, 123, 124, 126, 127.
Dār al-wakāla, 46 n. 6, 47 n 13, 48–49, 52, 53 n. 27, 55, 95, 131, 141.
dār al-wakāla waʾl ḍamān, 49, 131.
dates, 55, 141.
Dayr Zaytūn (quarter in Jerusalem), 83
Dayr al-Dārūm, village of, 19.
Dead Sea, 59, 100.
Defter-i der dest, 4.
Defter-i Ḫāḳānī, 3.
Defter-i Icmāl, 3, 12 n. 41 and passim.
Defter-i Mufaṣṣal, 3 and passim.
Defter-ı Rūznāmçe, 4.
Defterḫāne, 4, 11.

dellāliye, 46, 130.
Deniz, amir or: Amīr Tankız al-Nāṣirī, 97.
denk, 141.
Dhimmis, 70–72.
Dhū al-Rām, 115
Dimashkī, *Nukhbat al-dahr fī ʿajāʾib al-barr wa-l-baḥr*, 163 n. 30.
dibs, *see*. molasses.
dimūs, 63 n. 53.
dirham al-rijāl, 18 n. 60.
Döger Turcomans, 18, 35, 83, 84, 85, 92.
Dome of the Rock (or Noble Rock), Saḥrā-i Şerīfe, Temple Mount, Rock), 81 n. 1, 120 n. 14, 121, 123, 125, 126, 128, 138, 139.
Dome of the Rock, waqf of, 63, 72, 74, 95, 96, 97, 98, 99, 103, 104.
Dozy, R., 97 n. 61, 122 n. 21, 132 n. 49.
Dudon, R., 95 n 54.
dukkān, *see* · shop.
dyeing, 59–62, 133, 150, 164

Egyptians *see*: Mıṣriyyin.
emīn, 44, 56, 67, 68, 129.
erbāb-i berāt, 144.
erbāb-ı veẓāʾif, 73, 97, 113.
Ethiopians *see*: Christians.
Evlıya Çelebi, *Seyāḥatnāme*, 97 n. 58, n. 62, 104 n. 80, 107 n. 1, n. 2, 153 n. 23, 156 n. 7, 165 n. 41, n. 44, 166 n. 46, n. 47.

farrāsh, 15.
Fekete, L, 3 n. 2, n. 3, 4 n. 5, 11 n. 39, 13 n. 42, 101 n. 72, 103 n. 78, 162 n. 24, 167 n. 50.
Ferīdūn Bey, Ahmed, *Munshaʾat al-Salāṭin*, 165 n. 41, n. 44, 166 n. 46, n. 47.
Fikr Tuffāḥ (quarter in Gaza) *see* · Ḥıkr Tuffāḥ.
fishery 64, 67–68.
Foster, W. *The Travels of John Sanderson*, 29 n. 38, 165 n. 41.
Franciscans, 88 n. 39, 165 n. 41, 166 n. 46.
Franco, M., 156 n. 11
fruits, 51 n. 24, 52–53, 64, 172.
Fundūk (quarter in Safed), 156.
Furn al-Sūk (in Hebron), 113.
Fustaka (quarter in Hebron), 109, 110, 111

ğafare, 56, 57, 58, 72, 129. *See also*. *bāc-ı aghfār*.
Galilee, district of, 29, 30.
garlic, 52, 55, 141.
Gaudefroy-Demombynes, M., 18 n. 62, 87 n. 33, 107 n. 1, 113 n. 25, 117 n. 1, 130 n. 40, 135 n. 1, 147 n. 8, 155 n. 1
Gaza, 4, 11, 12, 16, 17, 18, 19, 21, 24, 25, 29, 30, 31, 32, 33, 34, 35, 36, 37, 45, 46, 47, 48, 49, 50, 51, 52, 53, 54, 55, 56, 57, 58, 62, 65, 66, 69, 71, 74, 75, 84 n. 20, 85 n. 26, 109 n. 13, 118–134, 147 n. 8.
Gāza, Sanjak of, 6, 9, 10, 12.
Gaza, niyāba of, 18.
Georgians, *see*: Christians.
Gharb (quarter in Nabulus), 145, 147, 148, 149.
ghirāra, 112
Ghālıb, Muḥammad, 151 n. 17.
Ghazāwiyya, bedouins of, 157 n. 16
Ghırāwıyya (quarter ın Safed), 157. 159, 161
Gıbb, H.A.R., 122 n. 21, 151 n. 17, 162 n. 25.
ğille, *ğilāl*, *muğall*, *see*: grain.
Gokbilgin, M. T., 6 n. 23, 13, 36 n. 50, 40 n. 61, 103 n. 78, 155 n. 7.
gold piece, 43, 44, 70, 71, 99 n. 63, 158.
Golvin, L., 97 n. 62, 104 n. 80.
Göyünç, N., 13 n. 43, 15 n. 48, 40 n. 61, 101 n. 72, 162 n. 25
grain (*ğille*, *ğilāl*, *muğall*), 51–52, 54, 96, 112, 114, 141, 142 n. 19. *See also*: *resm-i keyyaliyet al-muğall*, *keyyalıye-i muğall*, *bāc-i bāzār-ı ğılle*, *bāc al-ğılāl*.
grape juıce, 55, 141.
Guérin, V., 107 n. 2, 119 n. 6.

Ḥabābına or· Jabārina (quarter in Hebron), 107
Ḥabala (quarter ın Nabulus), 147, 148, 149.

Ḥaci Ḫalīfe, *Cihān nüma,* 134 n. 61, n. 62.
Ḥāfiẓ al-Dīn (quarter in Hebron), 108, 111.
ḥājı, 15, 83 n. 16, 84 n. 21, n. 22.
ḥākūra, see: vegetable-gardens.
al-Ḥalabī, Ibrāhīm b. Muḥammad, *Multaḳā al-Abḥur,* 16 n. 52.
Ḥalak or Ḥalk (quarter in Ramle), 137, 138, 139, 140.
Halasi Kun, T., 8 n. 32, 40 n. 61, 101 n. 72, 144 n. 27.
Ḥamat, 39, 54 n. 29, 55 n. 31, 60 n. 47.
ḥamir, see asses.
ḥammām (bathhouse), 69–70, 113.
Ḥammām al-ʿAmūd (Jerusalem), 96.
Ḥammān Al-ʿAyn (Jerusalem), 69, 97.
Ḥammām Bāb al-Asbāṭ (Jerusalem), 69.
Ḥammām Dāʾūd (Jerusalem), 69, 104.
Ḥammām Rīsh (Nabulus), 69, 153.
Ḥammām al-Shifāʾ (Jerusalem), 69, 97 n. 62, 104.
Ḥammām al-Sulṭān (Safed), 69, 163.
von Hammer, J., 43, 67 n. 69.
Ḥanafī law, 16.
ḫāne, (household), 14, 15, 20.
Ḥaram al-Sharīf, 34.
Harameyn Muḥāsebesi, 16 n. 53.
Ḥarameyn Muḳāṭaʿası, 16 n. 53.
Harameyn Şarifeyn, 16.
ḥārat al-Maghāriba (quarter in Jerusalem), 82 n. 12.
ḥārat al-Naṣāra (quarter in Hebron), 109 n. 13.
Ḥārat al-Naṣārā (quarter in Jerusalem) 81 n. 3.
ḥāret Deır al-Surīan (quarter ın Jerusalem), 81 n. 4.
Ḫāric ez defter, 101 n. 71.
ḫāṣṣ-i cedid, 101 n. 72, 114.
ḫāṣṣ-i mir-i livāʾ (appanage of the governor), 17, 42, 54, 63, 66–67. 69, 74, 100, 101, 102, 103.
ḫāṣṣ-ı şāhi (Imperial domain), 17, 42, 44, 49, 52, 54, 57, 59, 60, 61, 62, 63, 64, 66, 68, 72 , 74, 99, 100.
de Hault, N. *Le voyage de Hierusalem* 95 n. 54.
Hebron, 12, 13, 16, 17, 21, 24, 25, 28, 29, 30, 32, 34, 36, 37, 43, 45, 46, 47, 49, 50, 52, 53, 56, 63, 64, 65, 66, 68, 69, 70, 71, 72, 73, 74, 75, 86, 90, 93, 96, 99, 102, 106–116, 125, 126, 140, 148.
helva, 151.
henna, 55, 141.
Heyd, U., 8 n. 32, 17 n. 56, 28 n. 30–n. 34, n. 36, 44 n. 2, 50 n. 21, 66 n. 68, 67 n. 71, 69 n. 73–n. 75, 103 n. 78, 107 n. 3, 108 n. 7, 125 n. 28, 130 n. 34, 134 n. 59, 144 n. 27, 147 n. 8, 150 n. 15, 151 n. 18, 156 n. 8, 157 n. 16, 162 n. 25, 165 n. 40, n. 41, n. 44, 166 n. 45, n. 46, 167 n. 49, 172.
Ḥikr Tuffāḥ (quarter ın Gaza), 117, 120, 123, 124, 126, 127.
Ḥinṭa-i Simsim, 51 n. 23, 141.
Hınz, W., 114 n. 26, 142 n. 14, 144 n 21, n. 23, 165 n. 42.
Ḥışwān (quarter ın Safed), *see* Jāmıʿ al-Aḥmar.
Hiẓr, tımār of (in Hebron), 114, 115.
Hoexter, M., 17.
Holy Sepulchre, 72
horses, 53, 58, 100, 129, 142, 165, 166. *See also: bāzār-i esb.*
Ḥūle, *see:* Baḥr Ḳadas.
Hourani, A., 37 n. 51.

Ibn Iyas, Muhammad, *Badāʾiʿ al-zuhūr,* 24, 33.
Ibn Ṭūlūn, Shams al-Dīn Muḥammad, *Mufākahat al-khillān,* 25, 38–39.
Ibrahim Jenki, timār of (in Gaza), 129.
ıḥtisāb, tax of, 46–47, 48, 49, 50, 51, 52, 55, 102, 114, 131, 141, 150, 162.
ıḳtāʿ, 18.
Ilkhanids, 165 n. 40.
iltizām, 44, 45.
Ilyās, timār of (in Hebron), 114.
Imperial Domaın *see: ḫāṣṣ-ı şāhi.*
Inalcık, H., 6, 10, 19 n. 1, 27, 44 n. 2, 56 n. 37, 74 n. 90, n. 91, 99 n. 68, 101

n. 71, 103 n. 78, 130 n. 42, n. 45, 132 n. 46, 162 n. 24.
Ish-Shalōm, M., 83 n. 15, 117 n. 1, 155 n. 1.
Ismailis, 18 n. 60, 153 n. 25.
Issawi, C., 22.
Istanbul, 4, 20.
istikhrāj, 8.

Jabala (quarter in Nabulus), 149.
al-Jabbāra or Jabbārina or Jabbāriyya, community of (in Gaza), 119, 121, 123, 125, 126, 128.
Jacobites *see*: Christians.
Jaffa, 8 n. 31, 12, 147 n. 8, 150 n. 15.
al-Jāmiᶜ al-Abyaḍ (quarter in Ramle), 37, 135, 137, 138, 139, 140.
Jāmiᶜ al-Aḥmar or Ḥiṣwān (quarter in Safed), 37, 155, 157, 159, 161.
Janissaries, 27.
Jaussen, J. A., 142 n. 13, 145 n. 2, 147 n. 5, n. 6, 148 n. 10, 153 n. 23.
jawāli, 138.
Jenin, 9.
Jerusalem, 4, 12, 15 n. 51, 16, 18, 19, 21, 28, 29–30, 31, 32, 33, 34, 35, 36, 37, 38, 39, 40, 43, 45, 46, 47, 48, 49, 50, 51, 52, 53, 54, 55, 60 n. 44, 62, 63, 64, 65, 66, 68, 69, 71, 72, 73, 74, 75, 80, 81–104, 116, 120 n. 14, 121, 123, 124, 125, 126, 143, 147 n. 6, 150 n. 15, 151.
Jerusalem, Sanjaḳ of, 9, 10, 12, 63.
Jews, 11 n. 40, 14, 16, 28–30, 31, 36, 40, 51, 60 n. 47, 61, 68, 71, 72, 83, 84, 88, 90, 94, 98, 108, 109, 111, 120, 121, 122, 125, 126, 128, 133, 145, 148, 149, 150 n. 15, 151, 158, 159, 161, 165, 166, 169.
Aragon, Jews of, 158, 160, 161.
Ashkenazi Jews, 14.
Apulia, Jews of, 158, 160, 161.
Calabria, Jews of, 158, 160, 161.
Castile, Jews of, 158, 160, 161.
Catalan Jews, 158, 161.
Cordova, Jews of, 158, 160, 161.
Frankish Jews (*ifranj*), 120 n. 15, 147, 149, 156, 161.
German Jews, 158, 160, 161.
Hungarian Jews, 158, 160, 161.
Italian Jews, 158, 160, 161.
Kurdish Jews, 147 n. 7.
Maghribi Jews, 120 n. 15, 147 n. 7, 156, 158, 160, 161.
Mustaᶜriba Jews, 31, 147, 149, 156, 158, 160, 161.
Oriental Jews, 14.
Portuguese Jews, 32, 156, 158, 160, 161.
Sefaradic Jews, 14, 120 n. 15.
Seville, Jews of, 158, 160, 161.
Shāmī Jews, 120 n. 15.
Spanish Jews, 32, 61.
Jibb Yusuf, 57, 58, 166.
Jikyā, S., 101 n. 72.
Jisr Yaᶜkūb, 57, 58, 165.
jizya, 11, 44, 70–72, 98, 99 n. 63, 109, 121, 169.
jizya register, 15 n. 49.
Jordan river, 57, 66, 157 n. 16.
Judayda, mill of, 162, 163.
Jundis (Jund al-Ḥalka), 14, 16, 18, 33–34, 35, 85, 91, 92, 94, 122, 123, 124, 125, 126, 127, 140, 155, 156, 157, 159, 161
Jürüm, bedouins of, 17.

Kahane, R., 67 n. 70.
Kaldy-Nagy, J., 5–6, 7, 10 n. 36, 16 n. 54, 60 n. 43, 75 n. 91, 101 n. 72, 103 n. 77, 114 n. 26, 132 n. 49, 162 n. 29, 164 n. 36, 165 n. 39.
al-Ḳalḳashandi, Aḥmad Abūʾl-ᶜAbbās, *Ṣubḥ al-Aᶜshā*, 107 n. 1, 115 n. 28, 145 n. 1.
kaliye, 141.
Kalyūn (quarter in Nabulus) or Dabbūra, 147 n. 6, 148, 149.
kānūnnāme, 11 and passim.
Ḳānūnnāme-i Āl-i ᶜOsmān, 99 n. 67.
ḳapan, tax on, 46, 47–48, 52, 53, 54, 112, 131, 141, 150, 162
kapan-i ḳuṭn (ḳapan of cotton), 48, 100.
ḳapan-i zeyt (ḳapan of oil), 48.
ḳarye, 13.
ḳarziye, 60, 168.
ḳaṣaba, 13, 112 n. 19.
Ḳāsımıya, 67, 167.

ḳaṣṣābiye, tax of, 46 n. 5, n. 7, 47 n. 13, 48, 50, 102, 129, 141
al-Ḳaysariyya (quarter in Nabulus), 37, 145, 149
Kaysī (quarters in Hebron), 17, 36, 107 n. 3, 108.
Ḳayṭūn (quarter in Hebron), 107, 108, 110, 111.
al-Ḳazzāzīn (quarter in Hebron), 37, 108, 109, 110, 111.
Kenaᶜani, Y., 30 n. 40, 50 n. 26.
keyyāliye, 46, 51, 133, 164.
keyyāliye-i muğall, 51.
K͟hālıdī, family of, 82 n. 7.
k͟hādim, 15, 85 and passim.
K͟halaf (quarter in Ramle), 137.
K͟hamisiyya, 151 n. 18.
k͟hammāra see: wine shops.
k͟hān, 48.
K͟hān al-Amīr, 113.
K͟hān al-Faḥm, 68, 103.
K͟hān al-Furn, 68, 112.
K͟hān Sdūd, 56, 129.
K͟hān al-S͟hiᶜārā, 68, 103.
K͟hān Yūnus, 56, 129.
K͟handak (quarter in Safed), 157, 159, 161.
k͟hānḳāh Ḥandiye, waqf of, 103
k͟harāj, 99 n. 63, 158.
k͟harāj-ı bāğāt, 151 n. 20.
k͟harāj ḳawāṣir, 131. *See also resm-i ḳawāṣir*
k͟harāj al-kurūm, 52, 112, 165.
K͟haṭib, 15 and passim.
K͟hawālidī (quarter in Jerusalem), 40, 82, 84, 92.
Kilkis, 115
ḳis͟hlaḳ, 17.
ḳirāṭ, 97, 153.
ḳism, 63, 115.
ḳiṭᶜa-i arż (plot of land), 65 n. 62.
Kitchener, H. H., 137 n. 4, 145 n. 2.
Koprülü, M. F., 56 n. 34, 101 n. 72, 165 n. 40.
ḳumāş see: cloth.
Kurds, 14, 18, 34, 35, 36, 37, 108, 119, 153, 155, 157, 159, 161.
Lane, E. W., 130 n. 46, 155 n. 6.
Lapidus, I. M., 18 n. 62, 23 n. 13, 37, 38 n. 54, 41 n. 64.
Latin Christians *see:* Christians.
Lejjun, 4 n. 8.
Lejjun, Sanjaḳ of, 9.
Lemerle, P., 15 n. 51.
Le Strange, G., 107 n. 1, 117 n 1, 135 n. 1, 145 n. 1, 155 n. 1.
Lewis, B., 3 n. 1, n. 4, 5 n. 18, 8 n. 31, 10 n 34, 35, 26 n. 20, 44 n. 3, 55 n. 32, 63 n. 53, 74 n. 90, n. 91, 95 n. 56, 130, 156 n. 12, 158 n. 19, 162 n. 27. 163 n. 30.
Lidd, 19.
Luke, H. C., 59 n. 42, 87 n. 36, 88 n. 37, n. 38, 95 n. 54, 165 n. 41, n. 44, 166 n 46
Luṭfī Pas͟ha, *Āṣaf-nāme*, 4, 5 n. 9, 6, 10.

madīna, 13, 112 n. 19.
al-Madrasa (quarter in Hebron), 108, 109, 111.
Mag͟hāriba, Mag͟hribīs (North Africans), 34, 35, 37, 82, 84, 85, 89, 91, 92, 97 n. 59.
maḥalle, 13, 14, 41 n. 65.
Maḥmūd I, 5.
Majdal, 19.
al-Maḳrīzī, *K͟hiṭāṭ*, 5 n. 10, 97 n. 61.
maḳṭūᶜ, 98, 99 n. 65, 102, 131, 160, 163, 168.
māl-i ğāʾib or *māl-i mefḳūd*, 99, 116, 129, 142, 165.
Mālikī school, 35.
Maliyeden mudevver, 4, 10 n. 34.
Mamluks, 3, 9, 14, 16, 18, 23, 24, 33, 34, 37, 38, 70, 81 n. 1, 122, 123, 124.
Mantran, R., 62 n. 52, 63 n. 54, 72 n. 85, 95 n. 54, 103 n. 74, 130 n. 32, 164 n. 33.
Marmardji, A. S., 59 n. 42, 84 n. 20, 87 n. 32, n. 33, n. 34, 88 n. 38, 107 n. 1, 115 n. 28, 117 n. 1, 135 n. 1, 137 n. 4, 145 n. 1, 150 n. 15, 155 n. 1, 163 n. 30.
maᶜṣara, 63, 64, 100, 114.
Maslak͟h or al-Wusṭā (quarter in Jerusalem), 36, 84, 88, 90, 94.
Mayer, L. A., 119 n. 8, 137 n. 4, 156 n. 7.

McGowan, B., 8 n. 31, 15 n. 48.
Meḥmed III, 10, 11 n. 37.
Melkites *see:* Christians.
Ménage, V. L., 3 n. 2.
metrūkāt, 99 n. 67 and passim.
mezraʿa, 13, 24, 101 n. 71, 115, 168.
Miliara, Archimandrite Kallistos *Hoi Hagioi Topoi en Palaistine*, 87 n. 34.
miʿmār bashı, 38.
Minya, 57, 58, 67, 165, 167.
mīrī, 99 n 66, 151 n. 20, 153, 158, 163, 164, 165.
Mişriyyın (Egyptians) quarter in Ramle, 34, 37, 135, 137, 138, 139, 140.
Miquel, A., 87 n. 34.
mizān-i ğazl ve-ḳuṭn, 143.
mizān-i ḳuṭn, 131.
molasses (*dıbs*), 63, 114.
Moore, E. A., 87 n. 34, n. 36, 88 n. 39.
Mount Zion, 8 n. 31, 88 n. 36.
muʿāf, 14, 15.
muʿallim, 15, 89 n. 43, 122 n. 21. and passim.
mucerred, (taxpaying bachelors) 15, 20 and passim.
mudd, 73, 114, 142 n 19.
müderris, 15, 89 n. 43 and passim.
Muezzin, 15 and passim.
mufaṣṣal, 3 and passim
Muḥammad b. ʿAbd Allah, timār of (in Hebron), 114, 115.
muḥaṣṣil, 15, 89 n. 43, 122 n. 21.
muhimme defterleri, 8 n. 32, 27, 172.
muḥtesib ḳapanı, 48.
mujāwir, 73, 82, 97, 101, 113.
Mujīr al-Dīn al-Ḥanbalī, *Al-Uns al-jalīl*, 34 n. 45, 81 n. 1, n. 3, n. 4, n. 5, n. 6, 82 n. 8, n. 11, 87 n. 32, n. 34, 107 n. 2, n. 3, n. 6, 108 n. 7, n. 8, 109 n. 13, 113 n. 25, 117 n. 1, 135 n. 1, 137, n. 4, 147 n. 8.
muḳāṭaʿa, 162, 164, 168.
mukhallafāt, 97, 113.
Mülk, 42, 64, 131, 142, 151 n. 20, 153, 165, 171, 172.
Murād III, 5, 11 n. 37.
Muslims, 16, 21, 24, 26, 28, 29, 31, 41, 70, 82 n 7, 92, 94, 111, 127, 140, 149, 158, 160, 161.
mustāḥfiẓ, 74, 99
muteḳāʿid, 34.

Nabulus, 4, 12, 16, 17, 18, 21, 25, 28, 29, 30, 31, 35, 36, 37, 40, 45, 46, 47, 49, 50, 51, 53, 54, 60, 61, 62, 63, 64, 65, 66, 68, 69, 70, 71, 72, 74, 75, 145–153.
Nabulus, Sanjaḳ of, 9, 10.
naḥirat al-Yahūd, tax of, 48, 162.
nāʾib al-ḳalʿa, 15, 38, 82 n. 9, 83 n. 16.
Nasārā (quarter in Gaza), 119, 121, 123, 124, 128.
Nāṣir b. Ḳalāʾun, 135 n. 4.
Nazareth, 12.
nefs-i, 13.
al-Nimr, I., 62 n. 50.
nıyāba, 9.
nıyābet-i cürüm ve cināyet, 102, 103 n. 78.
Noble Rock *see* Dome of the Rock.
nomads *see:* bedouins.
North Africans *see:* Maghāriba.
Nūrī, Muṣṭafā, *Netāʾic ül-vuḳūʿāt*, 5, 7 n. 25, 11 n. 37, 44 n. 2, 97 n. 60.
Nūri Osman, 101 n. 72.
Nuṣayris, 18 n. 60, 153 n. 25.

d'Ohsson, M., 16 n. 52.
Olive oil, 62–63. *See also: resm-ı ḳapan-i zeyt, bāc-i zeyt, kapan-ı zeyt.*
olive trees, 65 n. 56, 104. *See also. zeytūn-i Islāmī, zeytūn-i Rumānī.*
onions, 52, 55, 141.
von Oppenheim, M. F., 134 n. 59, 157 n. 16.
orchards (*bağçe* or *bustān*), 42, 65, 131, 142, 144, 151, 165.

Pakalın, M. Z., 122 n. 21.
para (silver coin), 43, 69, 95 n. 53, 100, 103, 158, 168.
pastav, 60, 168.
Peradze, G., 88 n. 36, n. 38, n. 39.
Perényi, J., 33 n. 43, 38 n. 53.
pilgrims, 150 n. 15, 151, 165, 166.
Pinkerfeld, J., 137 n. 4, 156 n 7.

Pīrī Reis, *Kitabı Bahriye*, 137 n. 4, 167 n. 49.
Poliak, A. N., 34 n. 46.
Portuguese, 23, 27, 28, 56.
Possot, L., 135 n. 1.

Rabie, H., 55 n. 33.
Ramle, 12, 13, 16, 17, 18, 19, 21, 25, 28, 29, 31, 32, 33, 34, 37, 40, 43, 45, 46, 47, 49, 50, 51, 52, 53, 54, 55, 56, 57, 58, 63, 65, 66, 67, 71, 74, 75, 84 n. 20, 109 n. 13, 132, 135–145.
Ra'ʾs Ḳayṭūn (quarter in Hebron), 109.
Raʾs Ṣūr *see*: Tyre.
raṭl, 55, 141.
Ray, J., 95 n. 54, 135 n. 1.
reʿāyā, 6, 16, 125.
Redhouse, J. W., 3 n. 2, 122 n. 25, 167 n. 50.
Refik, A., 47 n. 14.
resm-ı ağnām, 103, 112, 129, 143. *See also*. *ʿādet-i ağnām waʾl-mîʿze*.
resm-i aḥmāl-i ṣābūn, 96.
resm-i ʿarūsāne, *ʿArūs resmi*, *resm-i ʿarūs*, 102, 116, 131, 152, 169.
resm-i ʿasesān, 102.
resm-i cevāmis, 67, 169.
resm-i Dār al-Kumāma, 95.
resm-ı ḥelvāciyān, 151.
resm-i kafe, 72.
resm-i ḳapan, 95, 100.
resm-i ḳapan-i zeyt, 63, 101. *See also*· *bāc-i zeyt*.
resm-i ḳawāṣır, 52. *See also*: *kharāj ḳawāṣir*.
resm-i keyl, 95.
resm-i keyyāliyet al-muğall, 95.
resm-i maʿz ve naḥl, 112.
resm-i naḥl, 130, 143.
resm-i ricāliye, 18, 153.
resm-i ṣeddādiye, 59, 151.
resm-i tamğā ve-iḥtisāb, 101 n. 72.
resm-ı ṭavāḥin, 60, 163.
resm-ı ʿurbān, 17.
rıce, 55, 141.
Rīsha (quarter ın Jerusalem), 36, 81, 84, 85, 88, 89, 90, 91, 92, 93, 94.
Rizk-Allah, community of (ın Gaza), 119, 121, 123, 125, 126, 128.
Russel, J. C., 15 n. 48, 22 n. 12.
Rüstem Pasha, 43.

Sabbāgha (quarter in Gaza), 117.
Safed, 4 n. 8, 12, 16, 17, 18, 21, 25, 28, 29–30, 31, 32, 33, 34, 36, 37, 40, 43, 45, 46, 47, 48, 49, 50, 51, 52, 53, 54, 58, 59, 60, 61, 62, 65, 66, 67, 68, 69, 70, 71, 74, 75, 85 n. 26, 147 n. 6, n. 8, 154–169.
Safed, niyāba of, 9, 18.
Safed, Sanjaḳ of, 6, 9, 10, 12, 57.
Ṣaḥrā-i Şerīfe *see*. Dome of the Rock.
Sakḳāʾ (quarter in Ramle), 37, 138, 140.
Saladın, 34, 82, 135 n. 4.
Ṣalāḥ al-Dīn, Yūsuf b. Ayyūb, waqf of, 103.
Ṣāliḥ Bey, 156.
de Salignac, Bartolomeo, 86 n. 31.
Samaritans, 14, 16, 30, 31, 120, 121, 122, 125, 126, 128, 133, 147, 148, 149.
Sanjian, A. K., 84 n. 20.
Sarı Meḥmed Pasha, 5.
Saʿsaʿ, 57, 58, 166.
Sauvaget, J., 18 n. 60, 62 n. 52, 63 n. 54, 72 n. 85, 95 n. 54, 103 n. 77, 130 n. 32, 132 n. 46, n. 52, 142 n. 13, 145 n. 2, 150 n. 14, 151 n. 18, 164 n. 33.
Sauvaire, H., 34 n. 45, 81 n. 1, n. 3, 113 n. 25.
Ṣawāwīn (quarter ın Safed), 36, 155, 157, 159, 161.
sayyid, 15 and passim.
Schechter, S., 30.
Schefer, Ch., 82 n. 11.
şehir, 13, 112 n. 19.
Selīm I, 24, 33.
Selīm II, 5, 10, 11, 71.
ser-i ʿasesān, 131, 152, 169.
al-Shaʿābina (quarter in Hebron), 108, 110, 111.
Shafāyina (quarter in Hebron), 109.
al-Shafā (quarter in Ramle), 139.
Shajjāʿiyya or Shajjāʿiyyat al-Akrād or Akrād (quarter in Gaza), 37, 49, 119, 120, 122, 124, 125, 127.

al-Shaḳā (quarter in Ramle), 137, 138, 139.
al-Sharaf or ʿAlam (quarter in Jerusalem), 36, 37, 82, 83, 84, 85, 89, 90, 91, 92, 94.
Sharaf al-Dīn Mūsa, 82 n. 8.
sharīʿa court, 4.
Sharif, 15, 82 n. 8, 84 n. 21.
Shaw, S. J., 44 n. 2, 59 n. 41, 70 n. 78.
Shawbak, 32, 121, 123, 124, 125, 126, 128.
Shawābika, community of (in Gaza), 119, 121, 123, 124, 125, 126, 128.
Shaykh Aḥmad Maghribī, community of, 85, 92.
Shaykh ʿAlī Bakkā Yamānī (quarter in Hebron), 37, 107, 108, 109, 110, 111.
Shaykh al-balad, 38, 119 n. 16, 157 n. 14.
Shaykh al-ḥāra, 38–40.
Shaykh al-Yahūd, 88 n. 42.
Shaykh al-zukāḳ, 39.
sheep (*aghnām*, *ghanam*), 53, 58, 66, 67, 100, 103, 112, 129, 143, 152, 166, 167, 169 n. 59.
Shīʿites, 18 n. 60.
shops, 68–69, 96, 112.
Shujāʿ al-Dīn ʿUthmān b. Alakān al-Kurdī, 119 n. 8.
Shūshterī, Muhammad ʿAlī, *Farhang-ı Fārısi*, 47 n. 10.
Shutayra, *mezraʿa* of, 168
Sidon, 30, 60.
sikke-i ḥasane, 71–72.
silver, silver coins, 43, 44, 71.
silver, American, 27.
simāṭ, 73, 113.
simsāriye, 46.
simsāriyat al-fawākih, 52, 162.
simsārıye-ı ğılāl, 51, 133.
Sinān Pasha, 24, 50 n. 21.
Sipāhis, 27, 74, 99
Al-Sitt Tanshaq bint ʿAbd Allah al-Muẓaffariyya, 81 n. 81.
Siyāh see: bāc-i bāzār siyāh.
slaves, 51 n. 25, 58–59, 73, 74, 129, 142, 144, 164, 166, 167. *See also: bac-i bāzār esārā, bāzār-i esārā.*
soap, 55, 62–63, 96, 113. *See also resm-i ahmāl-i ṣabūn.*
spice trade, 23, 28, 51 n. 25, 56, 142, 164.
Stoianovich, Tr., 40 n. 61, 41 n. 65.
stock raising, 64, 65–67.
Sūḳ (quarter in Safed), 37, 156, 158, 159, 161.
Sūk al-ʿAṭṭārīn (Jerusalem), 47.
sūḳ al-dawwāb, 53, 150, 169.
sūḳ al-ghazl waʾl-ṣibāgha, 62, 131.
sūk al-ḥamīr wa-l-baḳar, 143.
sūḳ al-ḥumḍ wa-l-khamīs, 131.
sūk al-khallāʿiyya wa dellālıya, 130.
sūk al-khudrawāt, 143.
Sūḳ Shajjāʿiyya (Gaza), 47.
Sülayman b. ʿAbd al-Mālik, 135 n. 4.
Süleymān the Magnificent, 4, 6 n. 25, 10, 11, 26, 71, 159 n. 21.
Sümer, F., 14 n. 48, 18 n. 61, 36 n. 49, 152 n. 22.
ṣundūḳ al-nudhūr, 73, 104, 114.
Sunnīs, 35.
Sūr (Raʾs Sūr?), 167
Suriano, Francesco, 135 n. 1.
Syrians (Suryān) *see:* Christians.

taḥrīr, 3–18. and passim.
taḥrir heyetı, 3.
Taḳāʿina, community of (in Gaza), 121, 123, 125, 126, 128.
Taḳūʿ, 32, 121 n. 18.
Talmudists, 30.
ṭālyān, 67, 168.
tamğa-i çoḳa, 60, 168.
tannery, 63.
tapu, 3 n. 2, 4, 170.
Tapu defterleri, 3, 4, 27, 170.
tapu senedi, 3 n. 2.
ṭarh (forced purchases), 23, 28.
Tarikh-i Osmani Encumeni mecmuası ılavesi, 99 n. 67.
tecdīd, 6.
Temple Mount *see*. Dome of the Rock.
Tiberias, 67, 167.
Tibnin, 168.
Tietze, A. 67 n. 70.
tīmār, 34, 42, 44, 54, 64, 74.

tìmār, serbest, (free tīmār), 74, 153.
Togan, Z. V., 34.
trade, trade routes, 23, 27, 46–59, 68.
Tripoli, 48.
Tripoli, vilayet of, 24.
Tritton, A. S., 83 n. 14.
Tunçer, H. 5 n. 16, 7 n. 26, n 29.
Ṭurābāy, *iḳṭāᶜ* of, 9.
Turābāy tribes, 17, 37, 110 n. 15, n. 16.
Turcomans, 14, 34, 35, 119, 152 n. 22.
Turkuman (quarter in Gaza), 119, 120, 123, 124, 126, 127.
Turkuman (quarter in Ramle), 137, 138, 139, 140.
Tyre (Raʾs Sūr), 12, 57, 58, 67, 167 n. 54.

ᶜUbaydiyya, *mezraᶜa* of, 168.
ᶜushr, 65, 75 n. 91, 131, 142, 151, 165.
ᶜUyūn Tujjār, 57, 58, 166.
Uzunçarşılı, H., 3 n. 3, 7 n. 25.

Vefīk Bey, ᶜAbd al-Raḥmān, *Tekālif kavāʿidi*, 47 n. 14.
vegetables, 51 n. 22, 52, 54, 95, 141.
vegetable gardens (*ḥākūra*), 42, 64, 65, 114, 151, 172.
vineyards (*bāğ* or *karm*), 42, 52, 64, 65, 104, 112, 131, 142, 151 n. 20, 152, 165, 172.

Wādah, community of (in Gaza), 119, 121, 123.
Wādī Dılbāy ("Wādī of the mills"), 61, 163.
Wādī Mūsā, Christians of (in Gaza), 125, 126, 128.
Wansbrough, J., 60 n. 45.
al-Waṭā (quarter in Safed), 155, 157, 159, 161.
waqf, 42, 64, 68, 72, 82, 97, 142, 153, 165, 171, 172.
Wilson, C. W , 81 n. 4, 82 n. 7, n. 11, 85 n. 23.
wine-shops (*khammāra*), 68, 152, 169.
Wittek, P., 15 n. 51.
Wright, W. L., 5 n. 11.
wool, 54, 60, 61.
Wusṭā (quarter in Jerusalem) *see:* Maslakh.
al-Wuṣṭā (quarter in Hebron), 108, 109, 110, 111.

Yaᶜarī, A., 83 n. 15, 109 n. 12, 113 n. 25, 145 n. 1, 156 n. 10, n. 11, 166 n. 44.
al-Yahūdā or: Yahūdiyyān (quarter in Hebron), 108, 110, 111.
Yamanī (quarters in Hebron), 17, 36, 107 n. 3, 108 n. 9.
Yāsmīn (quarter in Nabulus), 147, 148, 149.
Yūnis, timār of (in Hebron), 114, 115.
Yūsuf, ᶜAbd al-Wadūd, 54 n. 29, 61 n. 49.
Yūsuf, timār of (in Hebron), 114.

Zarāᶜina (quarter in Jerusalem), 81, 83, 85, 89, 91, 92.
zāwiya, 15, 73 n. 89.
Zaytūn (quarter in Gaza), 37, 117, 119 n. 9, 120, 122, 124, 125, 127.
Zenāta tribe, 119 n. 6.
zeytūn-ı Islāmī, 151 n. 20.
zeytūn-i Rumānī or: *kāfirī*, 151 n. 20.
ziᶜāmet, 42, 60, 153.
Zuallart, J. *Le très dévot voyage de Jerusalem*, 95 n. 54.

1

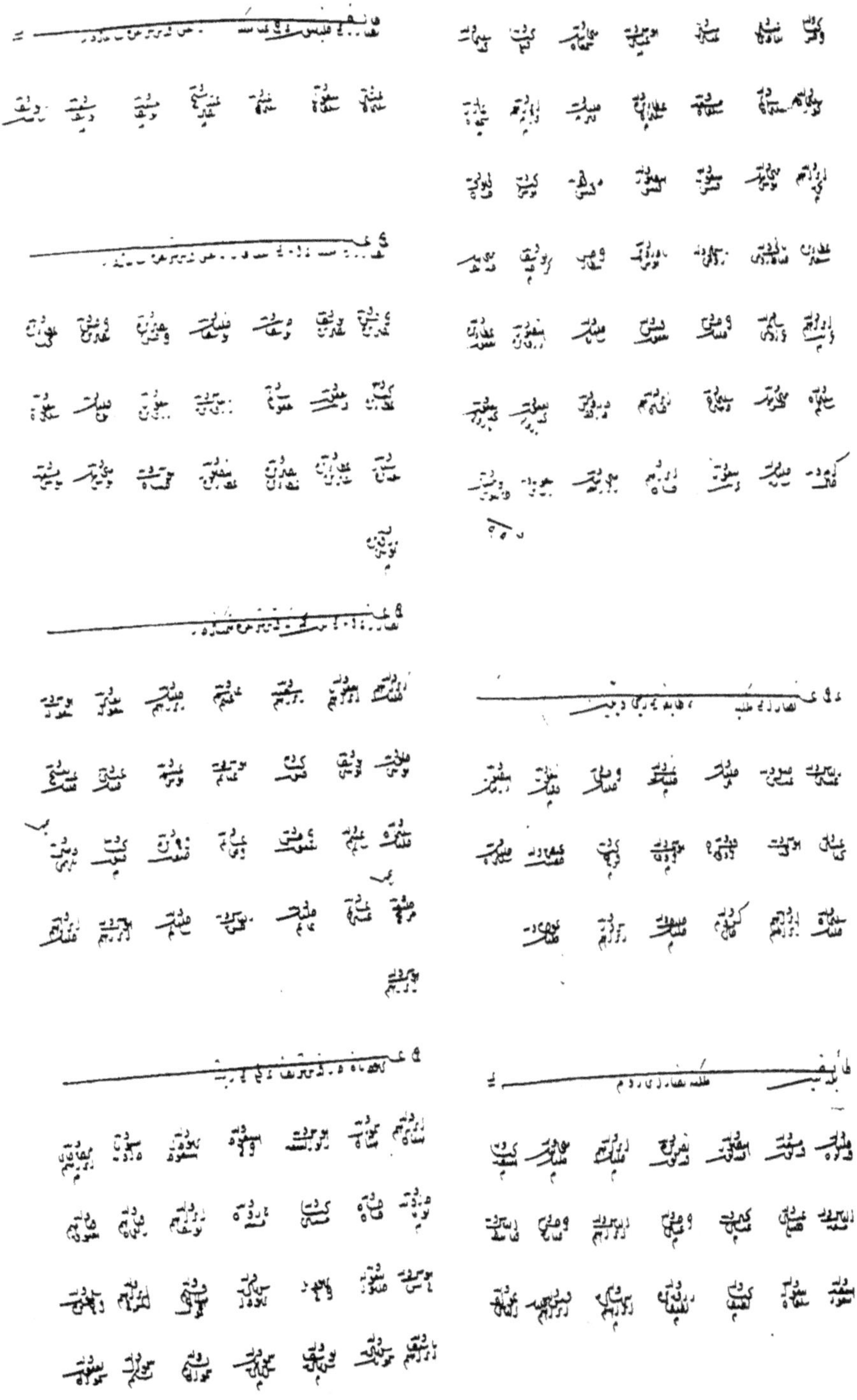

Plates 1-4 Jerusalem. Register 516, fols. 14-17, showing Christian and Jewish quarters, and part of the enumeration of revenue.

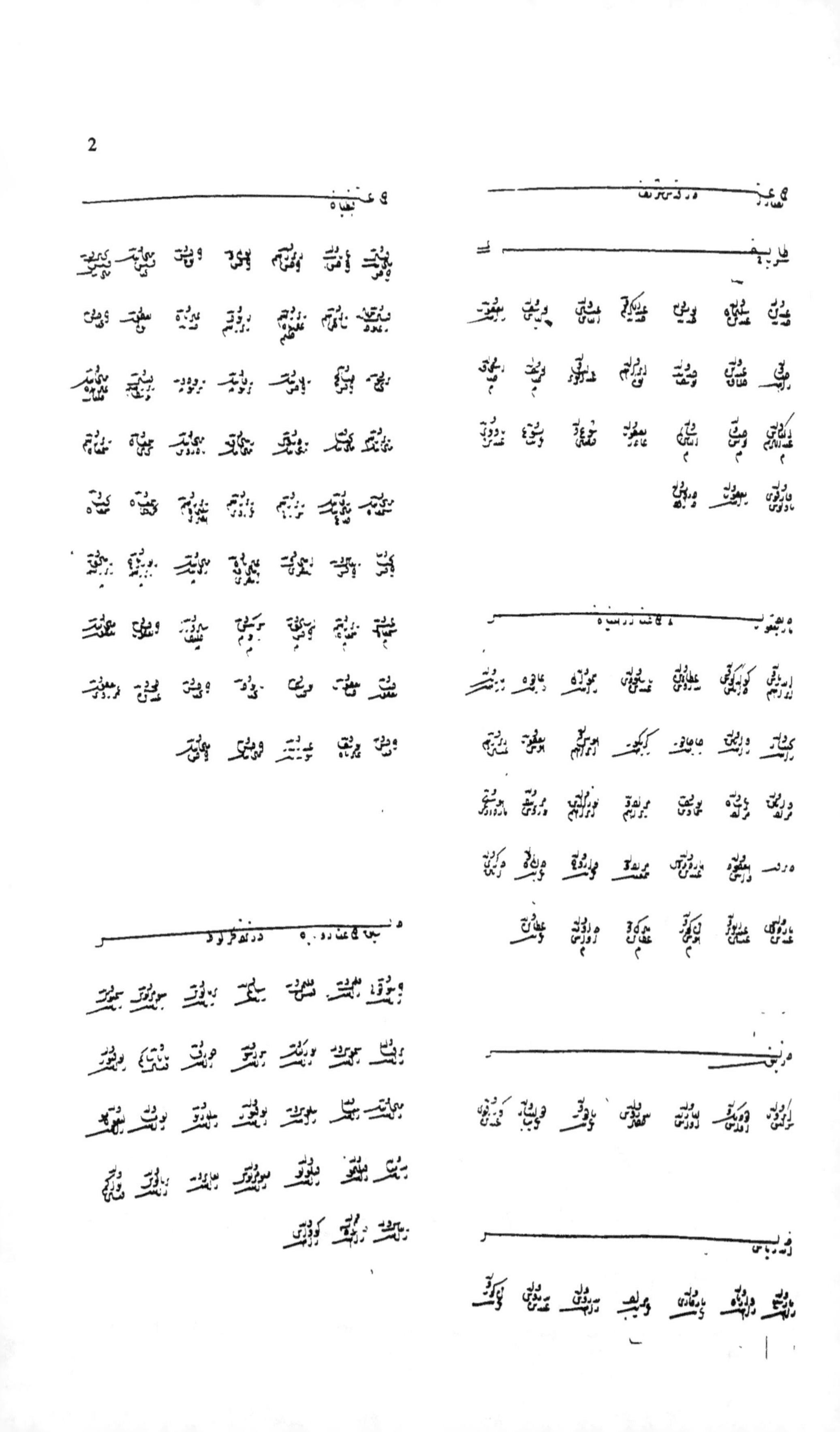

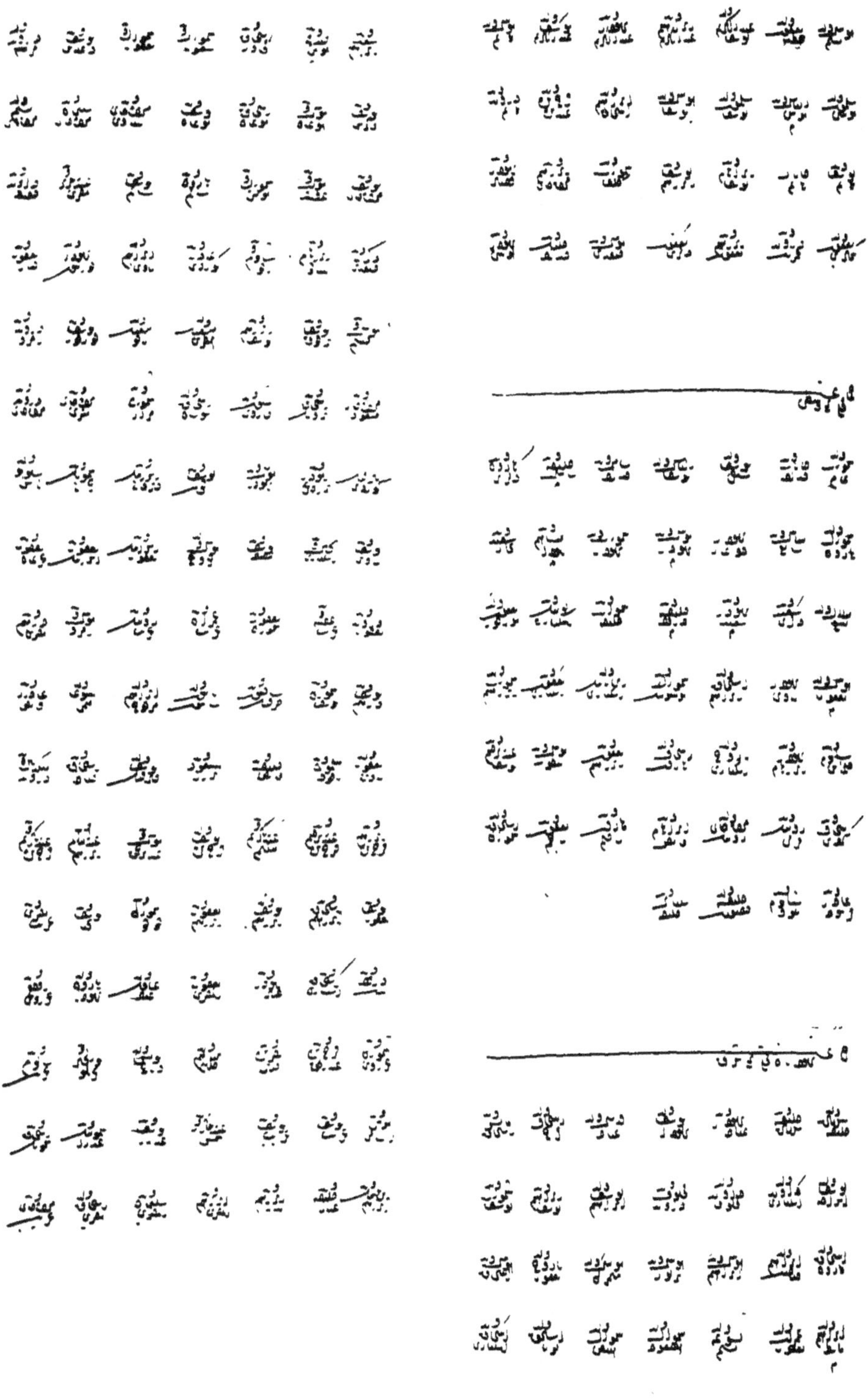

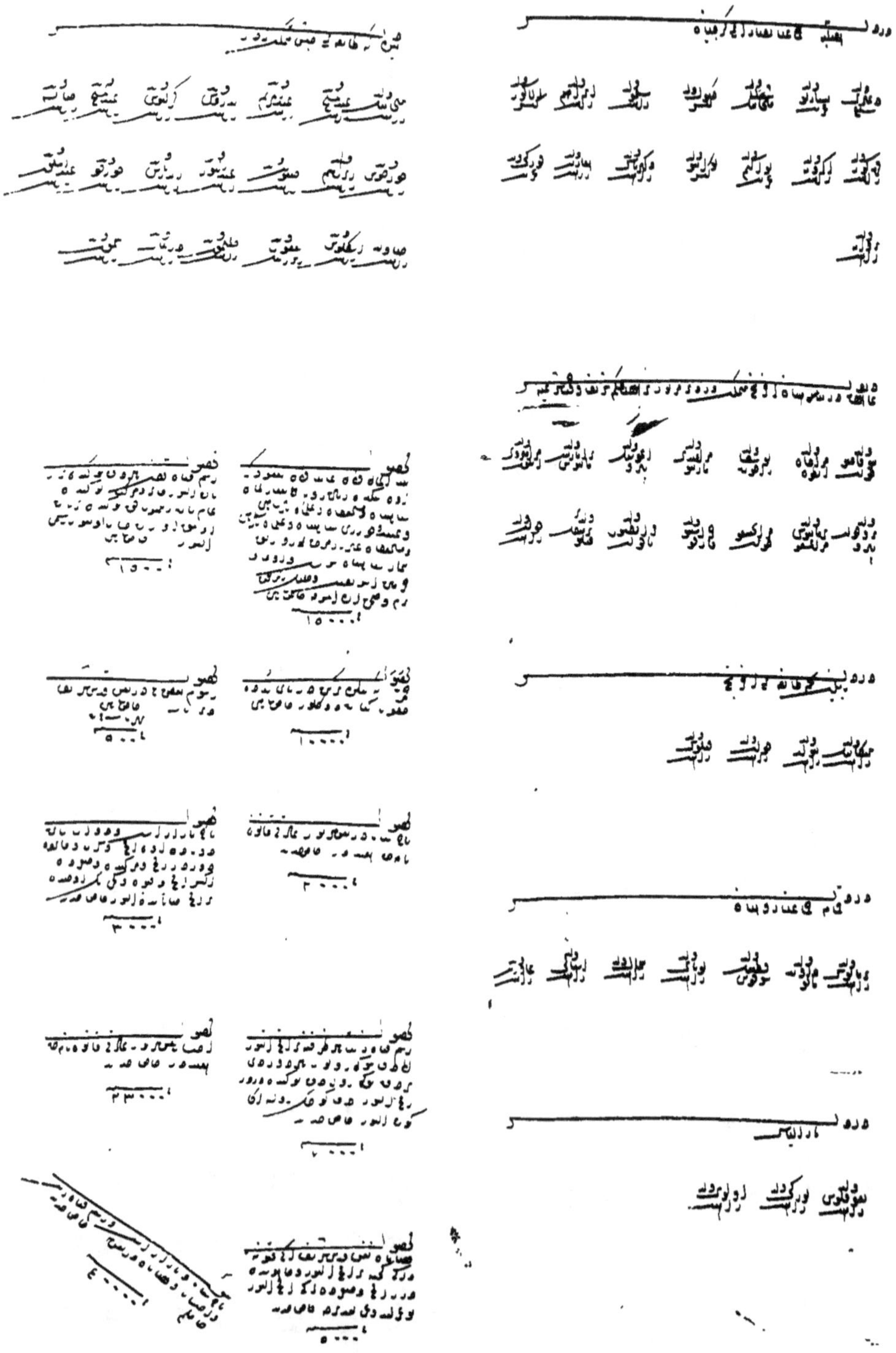

5

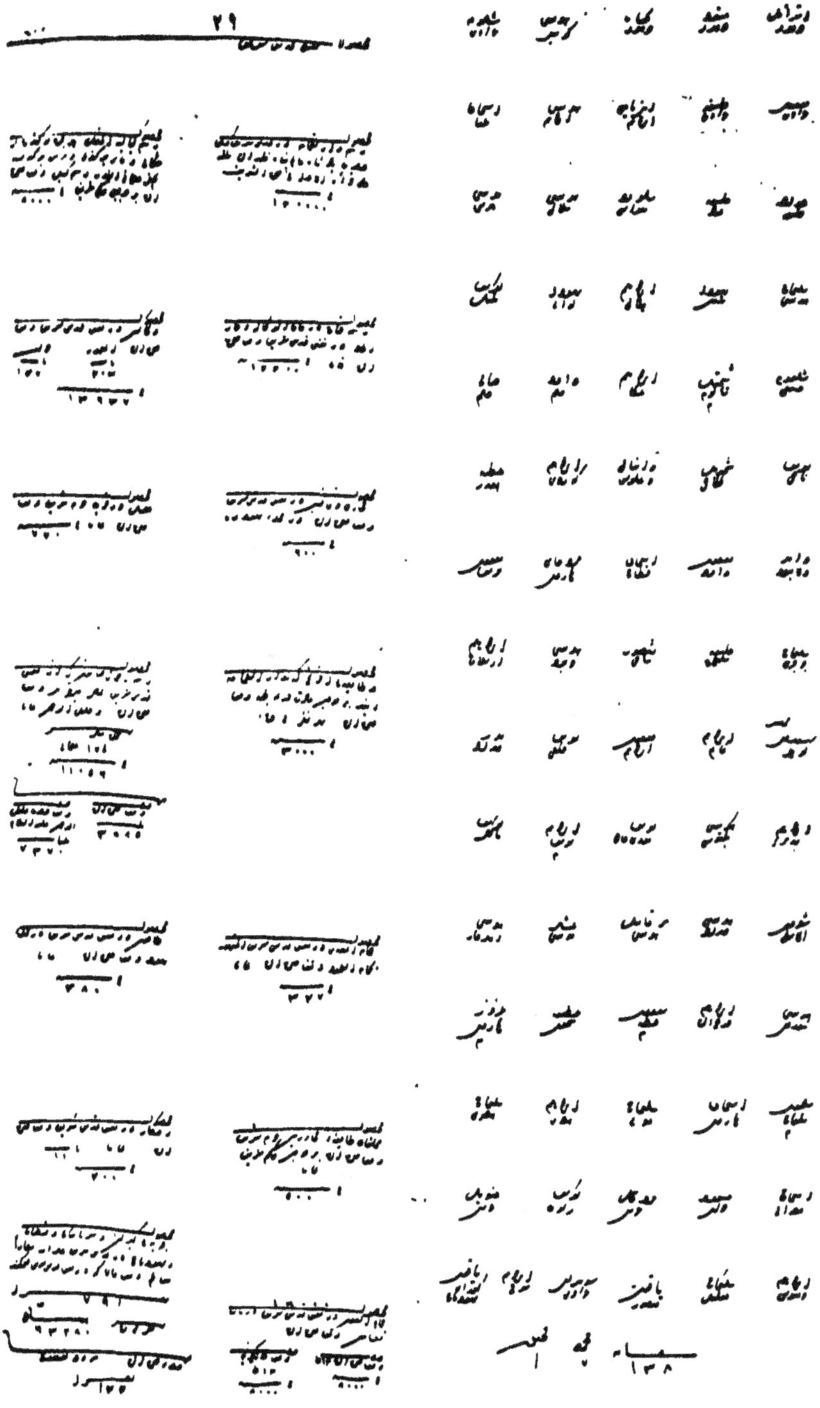

Plates 5-6 Jerusalem. Register 289, pp. 44-46, showing the enumeration of revenues.

6

7

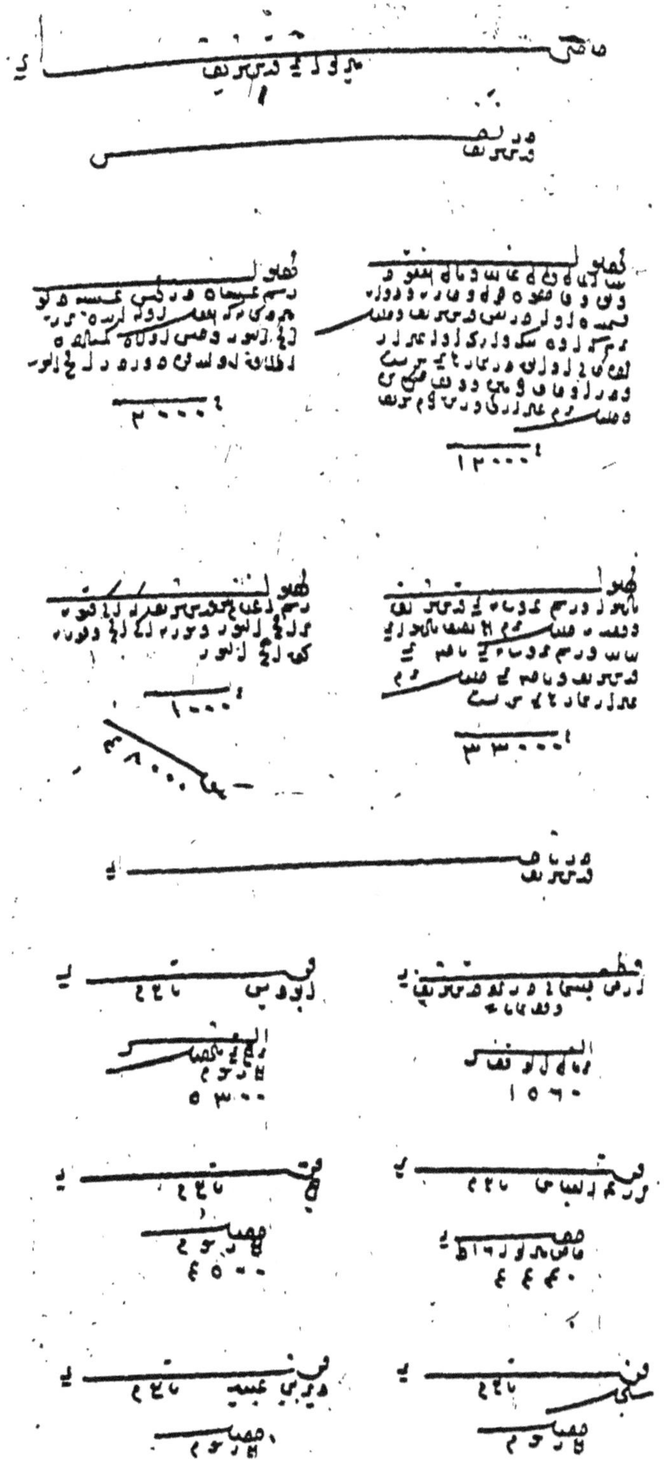

Plates 7-9 Jerusalem. Register 346 showing *Ḫāṣṣ* of governor and new *Ḫāṣṣ*.

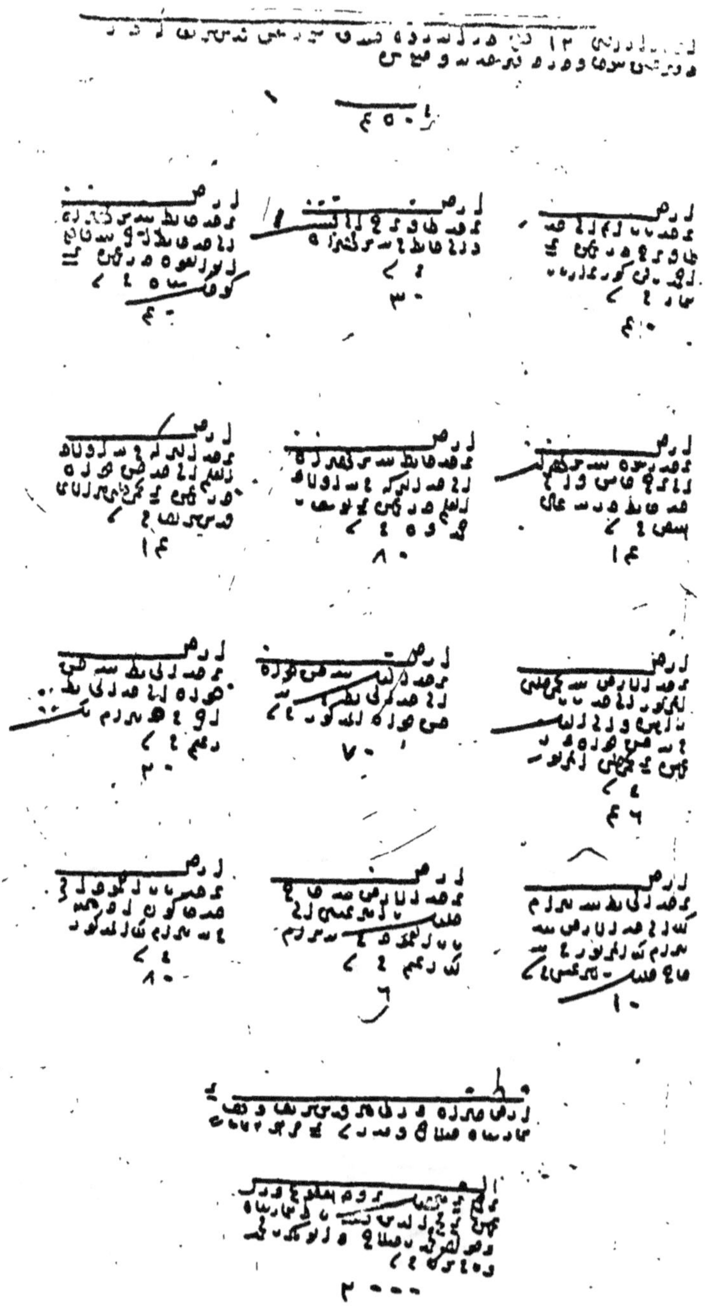

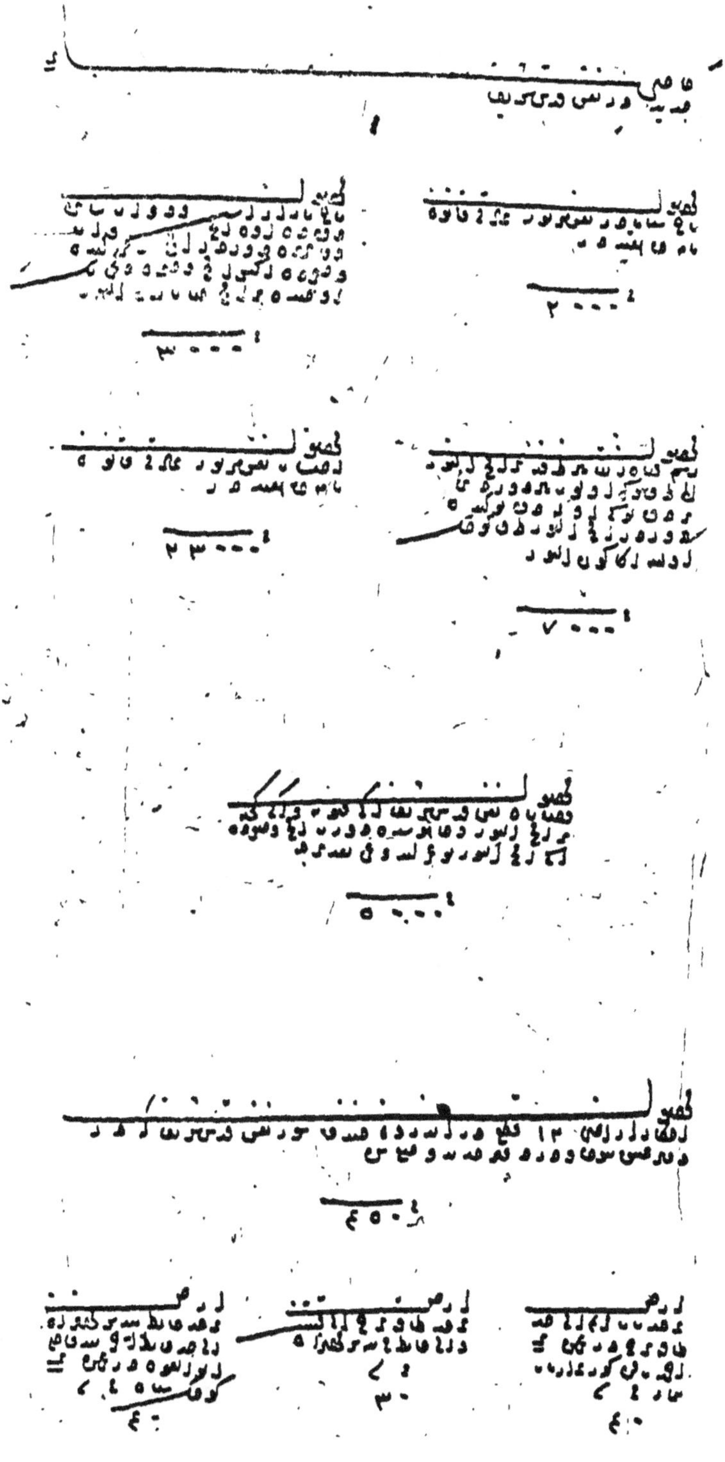

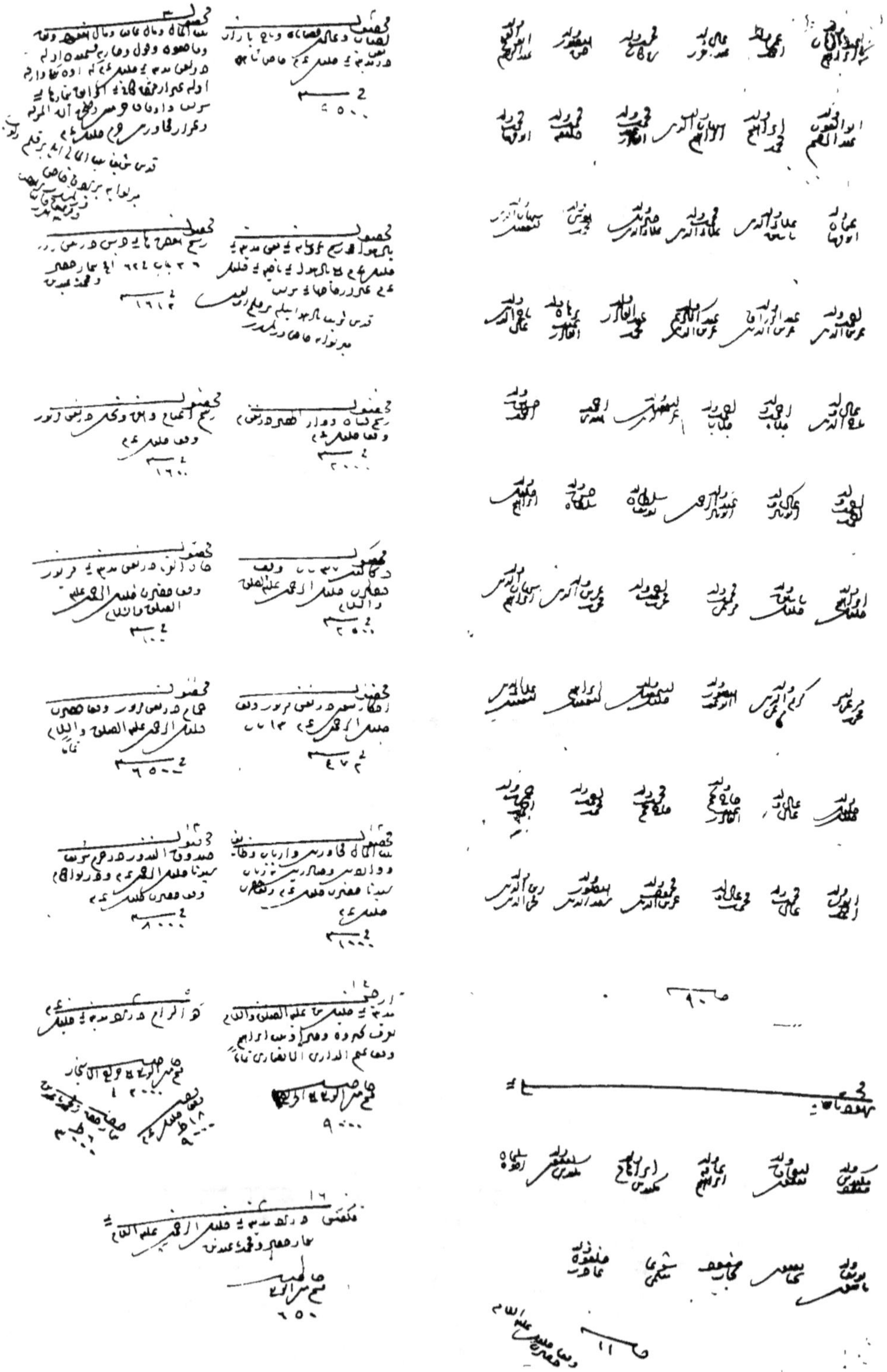

Plate 10 Hebron. Register 515 (end of quarters—enumeration of revenues).

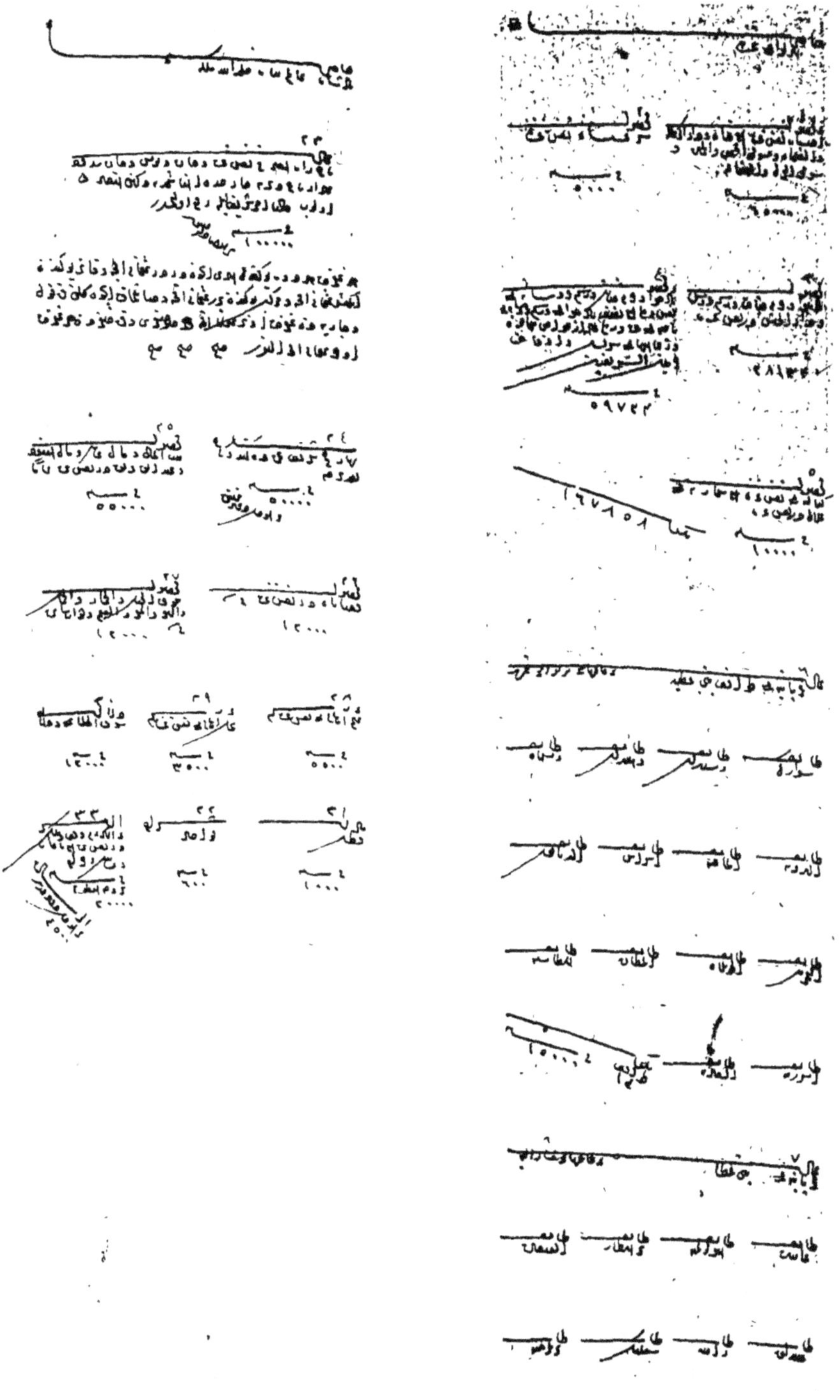

Plate 11 Gaza. Register 546, fols. 10a and 48b. Beginning of enumeration of *Ḫāṣṣ* of sultan and of governor.

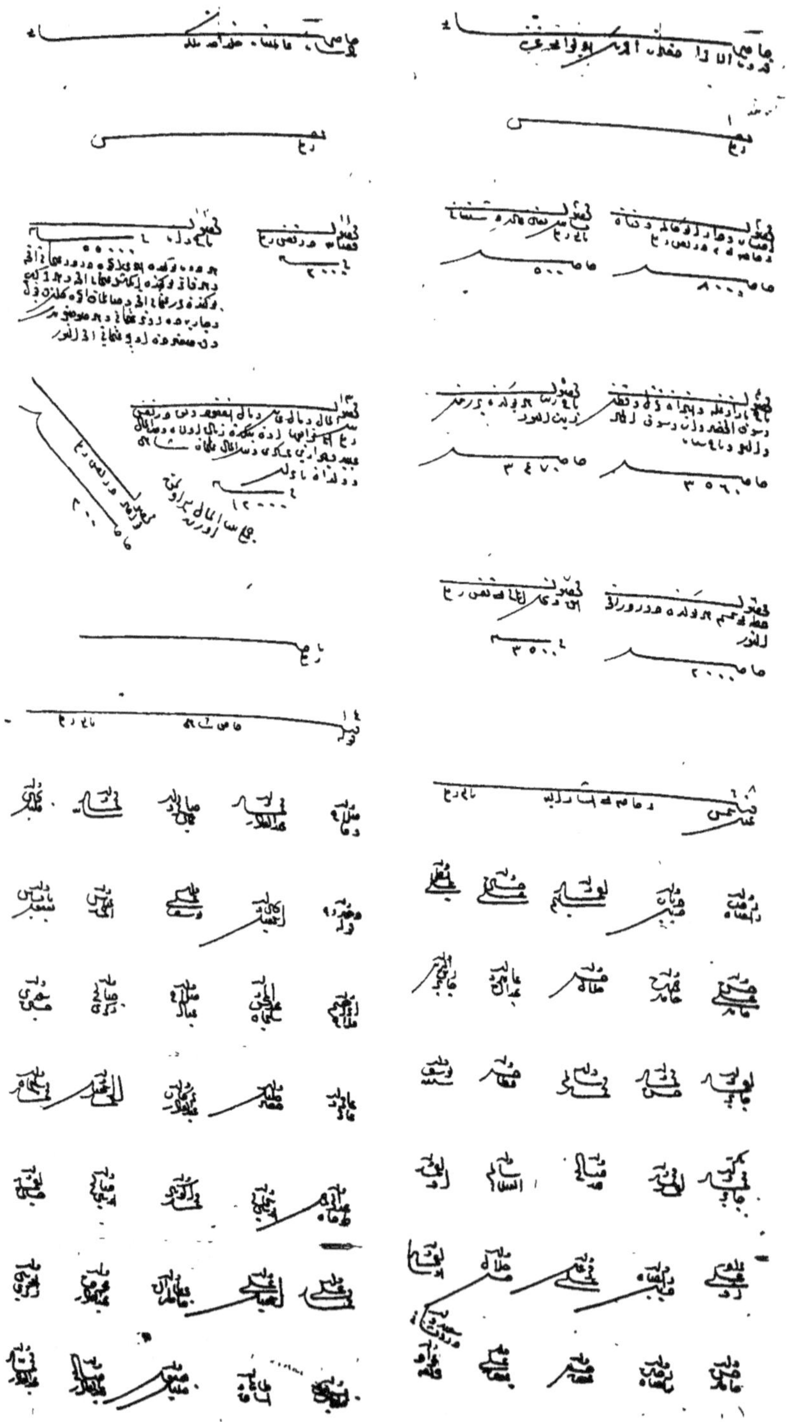

Plate 12 Ramle. Register 546, fols. 121b and 128b showing *Ḫāṣṣ* of sultan and of governor.

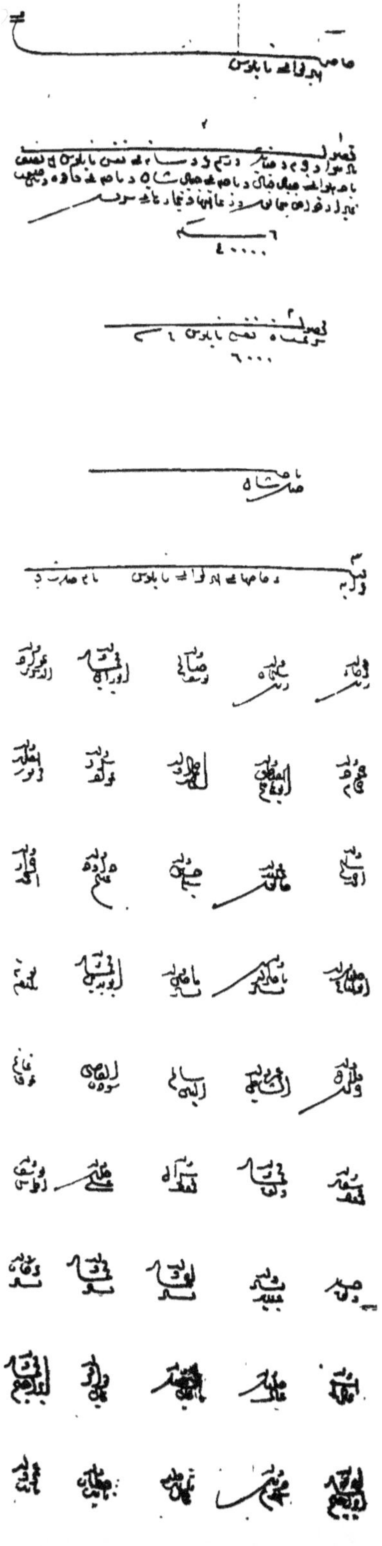

Plate 13 Nabulus. Register 549, fols. 9b and 67b, showing *Ḫāṣṣ* of sultan and of governor.

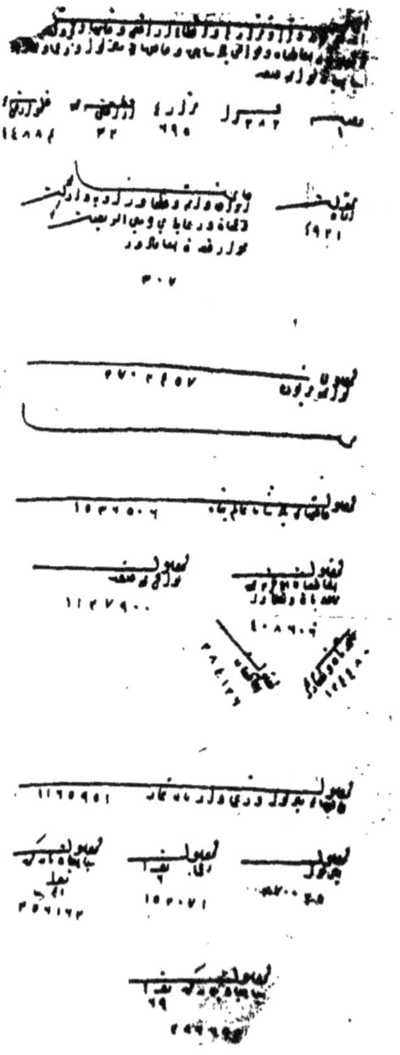

Plate 14 Safed. Register 300, synoptic survey of the sanjak.

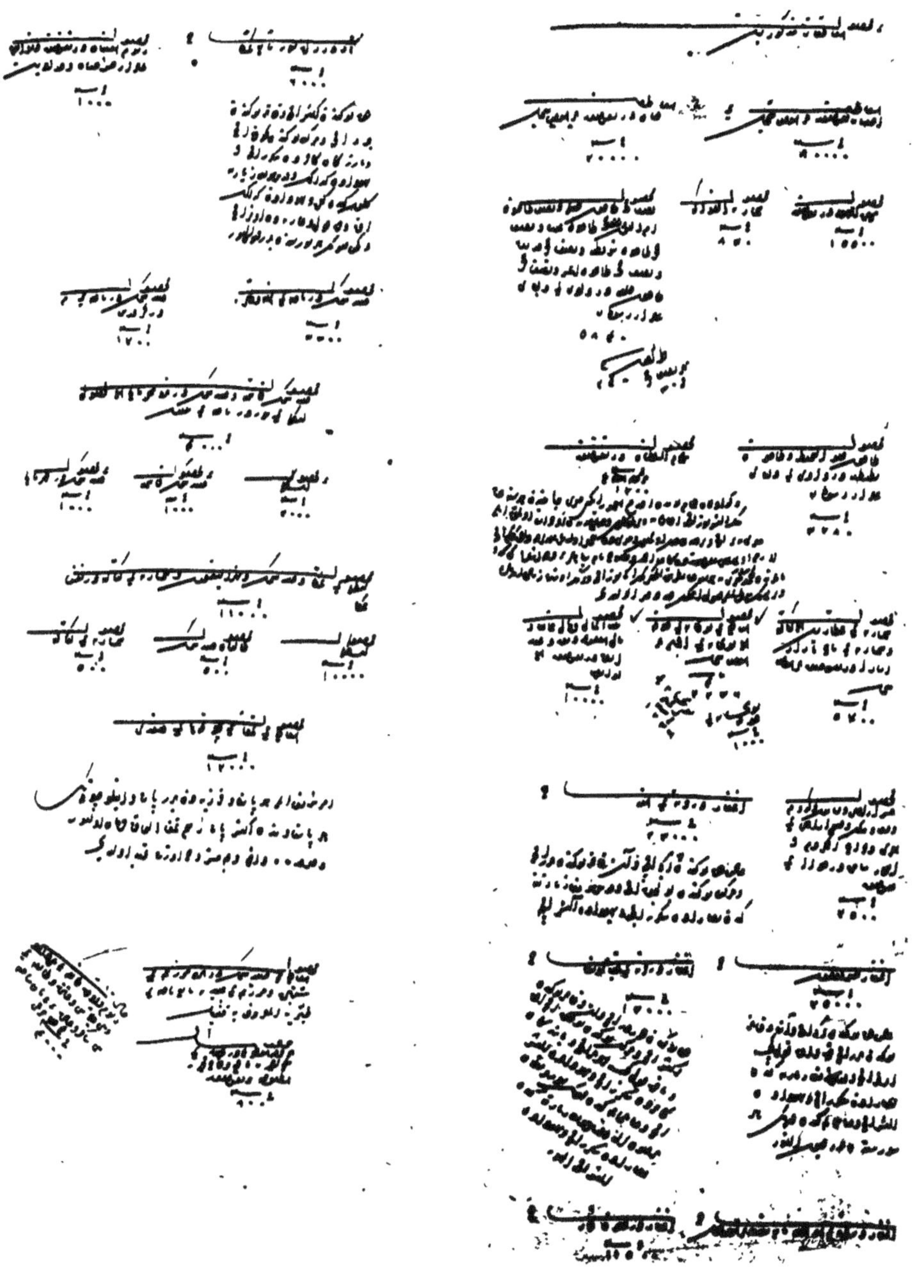

Plate 15 Safed. Register 300, pp. 41-42. Enumeration of revenues.

LIBRARY OF CONGRESS CATALOGING IN PUBLICATION DATA

Cohen, Amnon, 1936-
Population and revenue in the towns of Palestine in the sixteenth century.

Bibliography: p.
Includes index.
1. Palestine—History, Local. 2. Palestine—Population. 3. Taxation—Palestine—History. I. Lewis, Bernard, joint author. II. Title.
DS124.C64 956.94′03 78-51160
ISBN 0-691-09375-X

GPSR Authorized Representative: Easy Access System Europe - Mustamäe tee 50, 10621 Tallinn, Estonia, gpsr.requests@easproject.com

www.ingramcontent.com/pod-product-compliance
Lightning Source LLC
Chambersburg PA
CBHW052039300426
44117CB00012B/1891
9780691602837